WAR NO MORE

WAR NO MORE

THE ANTIWAR IMPULSE
IN AMERICAN LITERATURE
1861–1914

CYNTHIA WACHTELL

Louisiana State University Press
Baton Rouge

Published by Louisiana State University Press
Copyright © 2010 by Louisiana State University Press
All rights reserved
Manufactured in the United States of America
First printing

DESIGNER: Michelle A. Neustrom
TYPEFACES: Arno Pro, text; Circus Ornate, display
PRINTER: McNaughton & Gunn, Inc.
BINDER: John H. Dekker & Sons

LIBRARY OF CONGRESS CATALOGING-IN-PUBLICATION DATA

Wachtell, Cynthia, 1967–
War no more : the antiwar impulse in American literature, 1861–1914 / Cynthia
Wachtell.
    p. cm.
Includes bibliographical references and index.
ISBN 978-0-8071-3562-4 (cloth : alk. paper) 1. War in literature. 2. American
literature—History and criticism. 3. American literature—19th century—History
and criticism. 4. American literature—20th century—History and criticism. 5. War
and literature—United States—History. 6. United States—History—Civil War,
1861–1865—Literature and the war. I. Title.
PS169.W27W33 2010
810.9'358—dc22

                                                                    2009030239

Portions of chapter 4 appeared in "'Battle No More Shall Be':
Heman Melville's War Writings," in Literatures of War, ed. Richard Pine
and Eve Patten (Cambridge Scholars Publishing, 2008). Published
with the permission of Cambridge Scholars Publishing.

The paper in this book meets the guidelines for permanence and durability
of the Committee on Production Guidelines for Book Longevity
of the Council on Library Resources. ∞

This book is dedicated to my sons, Julian and Gabriel.
May they live in peaceful times.

They shall beat their swords into plowshares, and their spears into pruning hooks: nation shall not lift up sword against nation, neither shall they learn war any more.

—Isaiah 2:4

The dream of a time when the nations shall war no more is a pleasant dream, and an ancient. Countless generations have indulged it, and to countless others, doubtless, it will prove a solace and a benefaction.

—Ambrose Bierce, "Modern Warfare," 1899

CONTENTS

ACKNOWLEDGMENTS

In the great academic paradise in the sky, all scholarly works are completed in less than a week and are so flawless that their authors have no need for the help of advisers, colleagues, editors, or indulgent spouses. Such is not the case on earth. This study has been many years in the works and has left me indebted to many people who generously shared with me their knowledge, enthusiasm, and time. Three advisers, in particular, played key roles early in the process: Alan Heimert, William Gienapp, and Lawrence Buell. Likewise, Jessica Dorman, Rachelle Friedman, Bryan Daves, and Jim Gilchrist all offered me the benefit of their expertise and their experience at critical junctures as the work took form.

I have been extremely fortunate to have John Easterly as my editor, and I am very grateful to James H. Justus, Anne R. Gibbons, and everyone at Louisiana State University Press who helped with the crafting of this book. My thanks also go to my family members, one and all, and to Yeshiva University, where I have been privileged to call Stern College my academic home. Lastly, I am deeply indebted to my husband, Jeffrey Neuman, who has carried my books and in so many other ways helped to bear the weight of this project.

WAR NO MORE

n the pages of *Walden,* Henry David Thoreau describes a ferocious battle waged on the shores of Walden Pond in Concord, Massachusetts, in 1845. In a chapter titled "Brute Neighbors," he explains, "It was the only battle which I have ever witnessed, the only battle-field I ever trod while the battle was raging." Although Thoreau enjoyed a perfect view of the combat and of the combatants, the "dead and dying," and of the attacks and counterattacks, the meaning of their fight completely eluded him. He witnessed the "ferocity and carnage," yet he admits, "I never learned which party was victorious, nor the cause of the war."[1]

The deadly battle that Thoreau observed is chronicled in no history textbook or military report. It was, after all, a battle waged between insects: legions of black and red ants. Thoreau records:

> On every side they were engaged in deadly combat . . . and human soldiers never fought so resolutely. I watched a couple that were fast locked in each other's embraces. . . . The smaller red champion had fastened himself like a vice to his adversary's front, and through all the tumblings on that field never for an instant ceased to gnaw at one of his feelers near the root, having already caused the other to go by the board; while the stronger black one dashed him from side to side, and, as I saw on looking nearer, had already divested him of several of his members. . . . Neither manifested the least disposition to retreat. It was evident that their battle-cry was Conquer or die.

Having watched the fighting between the "two races of ants," Thoreau can only speculate on its meaning. He wryly observes, "I have no doubt that it was a principle they fought for." If the battle that Thoreau witnessed must forever escape satisfactory explanation, even more stupendously baffling are the wars of men.[2]

Nonetheless, writers long have striven to put words to war. Whether to express their support or condemnation, their ambivalence or their enthusiasm, poets, novelists, memoirists, journalists, and others have written voluminously on the subject of battle. They have written about conflicts past and present. They have written about wars actual and wars imagined. They have written celebratory accounts of battle and scathing accounts of barbarism. But how close have they come to capturing war?

The task of writing about war demands an act of interpretation. What transpires on the battlefield, in the military camp, and within the field hospital must be translated onto paper, and there are no neutral terms. There are, though, many overused words: "butchery," "heroism," "bravery," "horror," "glory," "murder," and the list stretches on. Each term connotes a subjective view of events. Truth, the old adage goes, is the first casualty of war. But the saying does not do justice to the complexity of warfare. It implies that an objective truth exists.

In the case of war, no universal truth exists to be lost. War is monumental, and war is multitudinous. Truth depends on perspective, allegiance, and time. However, if it is impossible to uncover the truth of war, it is possible to examine how war has been interpreted. At different places and at different times, war has been assigned radically different meanings. So too at the same place and at the same time, war has been assigned astoundingly different meanings.

This book examines the moral meaning assigned to war by a particular group of writers in a particular place during a particular period of time. Specifically, it charts the rise of antiwar literature in America from the Civil War to the eve of World War I. In so doing, it takes as its definition of antiwar writers those individuals who, whether in public or private works, questioned the fundamental morality of warfare.

The antiwar authors studied in this book shared a common impulse to rewrite and redefine war. They challenged the conventional understanding of war as morally righteous and instead presented it as inherently immoral and horrific. Whether focusing on the carnage of the battlefield and the disfigurement of bodies left exposed to sun, rain, and fire, or describing the hellish scenes of amputation and anguish played out in field hospitals, they boldly defied the literary status quo.

Antiwar writing was spurned during the Civil War era, when a highly romantic and idealized conception of warfare prevailed. Popular American

writers recorded the events of the war in a manner that was at once rhapsodic, optimistic, euphemistic, and anachronistic. War was ennobling. And
if it was not, most writers and artists of the Civil War era were not prepared
to admit it.[3] Dissension in the era of the Civil War equaled failure in the literary marketplace. Yet antiwar literature, including revisionist works about
the Civil War, steadily gained favor during the late nineteenth and early
twentieth centuries as realism gained traction and the implications of modern warfare became increasingly evident. Indeed, pacifist ideology reached
an unprecedented level of acceptance on the very cusp of World War I.

As America finds itself, once again, engaged in combat, a careful examination of the antiwar writings of some of our nation's most highly revered
authors—Nathaniel Hawthorne, Herman Melville, Walt Whitman, Mark
Twain, Stephen Crane, and others—serves as a timely reminder that the
debate about the morality of warfare, modern weaponry, and American imperialism is not new.

War has long been a reality of American life and a staple of American literature. The colonists had been in America for less than two decades when
they became engaged in the Pequot War, their first major conflict with the
Native Americans of New England. That war was to be the first of many. To
study America's history is to acquaint oneself with several hundred years
of war making: the colonial wars, the Revolutionary War, the War of 1812,
the Mexican-American War, the Civil War, the Spanish-American War, the
Philippine-American War, World War I, World War II, the Korean War,
the Vietnam War, the Persian Gulf War, and, most recently, the war in Iraq.
Additionally, the nineteenth century witnessed a series of wars against Native American tribes, notable among which were the Creek War, the Semi-
nole Wars, the Black Hawk War, the Comanche Wars, the Sioux Wars, the
Navajo Wars, the Apache Wars, and the Sioux Ghost Dance War.[4]

The existence of nearly four hundred years worth of American war
literature—sermons, letters, diaries, memoirs, narratives, poems, short
stories, novels, essays, and other texts—testifies to America's painful and
prolonged experience with battle. The nation's sizable legacy of war literature also points to the important and long-recognized power of the written
word in shaping public opinion. Since 1638, when Captain John Underhill
published his chronicle of the Pequot War, *Newes from America . . . Containing, a True Relation of their War-like Proceedings These Two Yeares Last*

Past, writers have played a key role in determining how America's wars have been understood and remembered. With varying degrees of cocksureness, these men and women have striven to impose on readers their own understandings of war. They have attempted to fit and fix war on paper. Tellingly, Underhill prefaces his narrative with the self-effacing disclaimer that he has "indevoured according to [his] weake ability, to set forth the full relation of the Warre from the first rise to the end of the victory."[5]

Obviously, violence is inherent in war, so too is it inherent in war writing. The disjunction between war's violence and language has received considerable attention in the field. The experience of the battlefield, as a variety of critics have contended, does not readily lend itself to literary transcription. In *The Body in Pain* (1985) Elaine Scarry focuses on pain's inexpressibility to argue that the true violence of war transcends the power of language. Similarly, John Limon asserts in *Writing after War* (1994), "To get from war to literature . . . requires a mistranslation," and he attempts "to expose, describe, diagnose, and taxonomize . . . all such transfigurations." James Dawes also explores the relationship of language and violence—in literary, legal, and philosophical contexts—in the *Language of War* (2002). Nevertheless, even if language can only imperfectly capture violence—and even if, as Walt Whitman famously observed, "the real war will never get in the books"—it is still immensely important to consider what versions of war, and of violence, have made it into the books and when.[6]

What is key, in literature as in life, is the interpretation assigned to war's violence. The meaning of war is in the eye of the beholder, in the words selected by the writer. There is no more fundamental or important lesson to be learned in the study of American war writing. Describing the colonists' destruction of a Pequot fort at Mystic in May 1637, Captain Underhill records a horrific scene in which entire families were burnt alive.

> Captaine Mason entering into a Wigwam, brought out a fire-brand, after hee had wounded many in the house; then hee set fire to the West-side . . . my selfe set fire on the South end with a traine of Powder, the fires of both meeting in the center of the Fort blazed most terribly, and burnt all in the space of halfe an houre; many couragious fellowes were unwilling to come out, and fought most desperately . . . so as they were scorched and burnt . . . and so perished valiantly. . . . Many were burnt in the Fort, both men, women, and children.

Yet by drawing on his faith in divine providence, Underhill is able to view his role in the murder of the men, women, and children who died in the wigwam as a holy service, an act for which he can expect to be rewarded with heavenly recompense. Explaining the religious meaning of the war, Underhill writes, "The Lord is pleased to exercise his people with trouble and afflictions, that hee might appeare to them in mercy, and reveale more cleerely his free grace unto their soules." What to another writer might provide ample evidence of war's wickedness is read by Underhill as offering the promise of his own eternal salvation.[7]

Writing more than 125 years after Underhill, Benjamin Franklin perceived violence against the Native Americans quite differently. In an essay titled "A Narrative of the Late Massacres," Franklin describes two raids made by colonists in Pennsylvania against Conestoga Indians living in Lancaster Country during the winter of 1764. Of the first of the attacks, Franklin writes, "These poor defenceless creatures were immediately fired upon, stabbed and hatcheted to death! . . . All of them were scalped and otherwise horribly mangled. Then their huts were set on fire, and most of them burnt down." Of the second attack, Franklin writes, "They divided into their little families, the children clinging to the parents; they fell on their knees, protested their innocence, . . . and in this posture they all received the hatchet! Men, women, and little children were every one inhumanely murdered in cold blood!" Whereas Underhill saw the hand of God at work helping the early New England colonists, Franklin was appalled by the actions of a later generation of Pennsylvania colonists. Indignantly, he labeled the attackers, "Christian white savages."[8]

Everything in war literature depends on an individual's point of view. A single battle can serve as the basis for a multitude of divergent readings. What to one chronicler indicates a heroic sacrifice, to another suggests an appalling waste of life. The nation's entire wealth of war literature rests entirely on such distinctions. These differences are what divide the dedicated war supporter from the outraged war detractor.

Throughout America's history, thousands of writers have offered various and vying justifications for war and, concomitantly, for violence. They have explained war as divinely sanctioned, legitimate as a defensive measure, and excusable in the name of democracy, freedom, and patriotic service. Depending on the historical moment and the inclination of the writer, violence has been rationalized, romanticized, and minimized. But in the hands of war critics, violence has often been highlighted and used as the basis for a vigorous and vehement protest against armed battle.

American antiwar writers did not invent the horrors of war. They did not view scenes others had not witnessed. They did not have to. Instead, these men and women stripped war violence of its conventionally assigned meanings. And deprived of all exculpatory ideological frameworks, what could be more shocking than civilians and soldiers shot, maimed, or burned alive?

American writers who voiced their opposition to war in the fifty years preceding World War I did not write, as did Captain Underhill, in order "that God's name might have the glory, and his people see his power, and magnifie his honour for his great goodnesse."[9] They wrote in order to contest prevailing views of warfare and to offer a dissenting interpretation of war's violence. By attacking the viewpoints of war supporters and the accepted practices of warfare, these opponents attempted to force the nation's readers to reconsider the morality of armed conflict during a period when combat itself was quickly changing. Whether they wrote about the Civil War, the Spanish American War, or the war in the Philippines, about fantastical battles of the Middle Ages or futuristic showdowns, these authors challenged the standard readings and representations of battle.

Although their specific literary tactics varied, these American antiwar writers attempted to discredit the view of warfare that held that the battlefield was a testing ground, a "field of glory," on which brave and virtuous soldiers could prove their mettle. Whereas other writers tried to turn away from the disturbing realities of modern warfare, war critics eagerly exploited them. Sharpening their irony and outrage, they did their best to strip military training, combat, and death of all romantic rhetoric. They presented an unglamourous image of battle and routinely accentuated the dehumanizing and alienating aspects of combat. Modern war, these authors insisted, presented a test of endurance not of valor.

The first half of this work, "Writing the Civil War," focuses on the literary response to the Civil War. Following a discussion of popular wartime literature and the enduring influence of Sir Walter Scott, the section focuses at length on the works of three authors—Herman Melville, John William De Forest, and Walt Whitman—who in different ways challenged the standard, highly idealistic representation of the conflict.

As their published and unpublished war writings reveal, these three authors, all northerners, felt conflicted about the morality of the war. They flinched at the devastation wrought by the war's great battles, questioned the cost of fighting, and weighed the possible long-term benefits against the enormous loss of life. Yet their ambivalence, horror, and dissent rarely reached the reading public. These writers did not often dare to tell what they considered to be the whole truth about the war, and when they did, the public did not care to read it.

In the drafts of their war writings—in corrections, deletions, and substitutions—rest the telltale signs of their inner turmoil. Melville had staked out a strong antiwar position in his early novels. Nonetheless, he toned down his moral critique of war in his published poetry about the Civil War. He also intentionally omitted certain grim details of the war years, such as those concerning the deadly draft riots in New York. Whitman expressed his dismay at the butchery of battle in his journals and letters but presented a far more uplifting image of the war in his published war poems. De Forest was the most willing to speak his mind in both his private and public works of the 1860s. Years later, though, he admitted that he had not dared, for fear of being labeled a coward, tell the whole truth about battle and about the dread fear felt by soldiers.

Following individual chapters on these three writers, the first half of the study concludes with a broad examination of the ways in which the Civil War was rewritten by more outspoken war critics during the late nineteenth century.

The second half of the study, "The Changing Ways of Fighting and Writing War," examines the connection between the rise in the mechanization and modernization of warfare and the rise of war criticism in the late nineteenth and very early twentieth centuries. In particular, it analyzes the manner in which prominent figures—including Nathaniel Hawthorne, Mark Twain, Stephen Crane, Theodore Roosevelt, and William James—reacted to the impact of industrialization on warfare. During this critical period, when the weaponry of warfare became ever more deadly and alienating for the common soldier, antiwar works steadily gained ground in the literary marketplace and in the appraisal of readers and critics. Even war romanticists were hard pressed to reconcile modern war with their ideals.

The purpose of this study is not to weigh the literary merit of conventional war writing versus antiwar writing or to validate one body of literature over the other. The purpose is to arrive at a better understanding of American writers' complex, contested, and frequently self-conflicted understanding of war. It is a fundamental and fascinating paradox of American war literature that the genre embraces radically antithetical attitudes about war. Highly idealized tributes to fallen soldiers coexist with grisly accounts of bloated corpses. Celebrations of heroism sit uneasily beside works mourning the senseless deaths of the young. Optimistic forecasts of world peace share shelf space with dire predictions of destruction.

Typically, American antiwar literature is understood as an outgrowth of World War I (Ernest Hemingway, John Dos Passos, Dalton Trumbo), World War II (Norman Mailer, Joseph Heller, Kurt Vonnegut), and the Vietnam War (Michael Herr, Philip Caputo, Tim O'Brien). *War No More* provides an important corrective by offering a careful analysis of antiwar literature, and the changing ways of warfare, from the period of the Civil War to the eve of World War I.

An extensive study of American war writing—particularly antiwar writing—in the era preceding the First World War is long overdue. Much has been written about the literature of the Civil War. Major studies in the field include Richard A. Lively's *Fiction Fights the Civil War* (1957); Edmund Wilson's *Patriotic Gore* (1962); Thomas J. Pressly's *Americans Interpret Their Civil War* (1962); Daniel Aaron's *The Unwritten War* (1973); Timothy Sweet's *Traces of War* (1990); and Alice Fahs's *The Imagined Civil War* (2001). Much, too, has been written about the war literature of World War I. Classic works in the field include Stanley Cooperman's *World War I and the American Novel* (1967); Charles V. Genthe's *American War Narratives, 1917–1918* (1969); and Paul Fussell's *The Great War and Modern Memory* (1975). As yet, there is no full-length study of American war literature—much less American antiwar literature—in the decades stretching from the Civil War to World War I.[10]

Scholars long have noted that the antiwar genre became the dominant mode in both British and American war writing in the post–World War I era. However, they have failed to recognize the extent to which American antiwar literature achieved public acceptance and popularity in the period preceding World War I, the very decades that encompassed the advent of modern warfare.[11] Paul Fussell famously argues in *The Great War and Modern Memory* that the First World War was a watershed event that marked the divide between a literature of optimistic innocence and a literature of world-weary despair. For those who manned the trenches, Fussell contends, the long war of attrition was hugely disillusioning, and the disparity between preconceived notions of heroic battle and the reality of icy winter nights, vermin, exposed corpses, and unremitting suffering prompted a remarkable literary response.

But the distinction that Fussell and other cultural and literary historians —particularly those who focus primarily on Britain and continental Europe, including Samuel Hynes and Bernard Bergonzi—make between postwar and prewar sensibilities does not hold true for American authors.[12] Fussell claims, "The Great War took place in what was, compared to ours, a static world, where the values appeared stable and where the meanings of abstractions seemed permanent and reliable. Everyone knew what Glory was, and what Honor meant."[13] Yet during the decades leading up to World War I, a good many American authors, including some very popular ones, forthrightly questioned the morality of warfare and the possibility of achieving glory and honor on the modern battlefield. Moreover, Fussell's claim that the World War I generation "believed in Progress and Art and in no way doubted the benignity even of technology" is contradicted by the American literary record, which demonstrates that war writers were deeply concerned about the increasing mechanization, modernization, and dehumanization of combat from the time of the Civil War to World War I.[14]

If American writers were disillusioned in the postwar period, their literary "break" from the past was not as spectacular or as sudden as previous scholars have claimed. American antiwar literature made tremendous gains in popularity in the wake of World War I and would continue to gain popularity throughout the twentieth century, especially in the decades immediately following the Vietnam War. However, as this study demonstrates, American antiwar literature was already solidly established—if far from universally accepted—in the decades preceding World War I.

Nonetheless, certain voices were not heard among the war protesters during the period stretching from the start of the Civil War to the eve of World War I. Although several works, such as Faith Barrett and Cristanne Miller's *"Words for the Hour": A New Anthology of American Civil War Poems* (2005) and Jennifer C. James's *A Freedom Bought with Blood: African American War Literature from the Civil War to World War II* (2007), have pointed to the contributions of women and African Americans to war writing, white men wrote almost all of the antiwar works of the era.

Acknowledging the reluctance of African American writers to criticize the Civil War, James observes, "Judging from the descriptions of that war in [African American] literature, it appears that the outcome of that conflict gave rise to an initial reluctance to offer unsettling depictions of war and its damage, lest these images be construed as antiwar statements that might retroactively call into question the very means that facilitated black emancipation." And in her discussion of African American writers' response to the wars at the turn of the twentieth century, James focuses almost exclusively on two texts that were supportive of "the Spanish-Cuban-American War and the American wars in the Philippines." As James suggests, by "embracing imperialism, rather than rejecting it," African American writers found an alternative to being themselves the victims of racism.[15]

The relative silence of women is not as easily explained. Women wrote a tremendous number of romantic war poems, stories, and novels during the late nineteenth and very early twentieth centuries but almost no antiwar works. Whether because of social conditioning, a lack of firsthand battle experience, a disinclination for realist war writing, or other factors, women very rarely stepped forward to criticize war.

Julia Ward Howe is an interesting exception. Eight years after writing her immensely popular "Battle Hymn of the Republic," a Civil War anthem in which she celebrated the divine righteousness of the Union cause and praised the work of God's "terrible swift sword," she wrote an ardently pacifist work.[16] Howe's "Appeal to Womanhood throughout the World" is a concise manifesto that calls on women worldwide to arise and demand universal disarmament. "The sword of murder is not the balance of justice." Howe proclaims, "Blood does not wipe out dishonor, nor violence indicate possession." Howe's conversion to pacifism was fervent and sincere. Nonetheless, her dedicated efforts in the early 1870s to organize a Woman's Peace Congress met with failure. As she would recall in her 1899 autobiography, *Reminiscences,* "The ladies who spoke in public in those days mostly confined their labors to the advocacy of woman suffrage, and were not much interested in my scheme of a world-wide protest of women against the cruelties of war."[17] Not until the outbreak of World War I would literary ladies publicly join in protesting war.[18]

Although the focus of this study is American war literature, the writings of American authors are inextricably linked to those of writers in other countries. War literature is an ancient genre, and the effort to define war as moral or immoral is age old. It stretches at least as far back as the days in which Homer wrote *The Iliad* to memorialize the deeds of powerful Agamemnon, bold Hector, and the other mighty men of the Trojan War. The classical world also created a countertradition of war criticism. Euripides' *Trojan Women* stands as one of the most famous indictments of war ever written. Likewise, the comedy *Lysistrata* by Aristophanes presents a powerful, pacifist message.

Indisputably, these ancient works, as well as later war texts, have affected the literary tastes and styles of American writers. Thucydides' *History of the Peloponnesian War*, for example, was once standard fare for all well-educated Americans. In 1777 John Adams, the future president, wrote to his son John Quincy advising the boy, who was then just ten years old, to read Thucydides in order to prepare for the "Part which may be allotted you to act on the Stage of Life."[19] Similarly, Homer's *Iliad* enjoyed enduring popularity in America, and the eminent nature poet William Cullen Bryant completed a translation of the ancient war epic just five years after the conclusion of the Civil War.[20]

Although it is impossible to determine the precise extent to which American war literature has been affected by the works of writers of other nations and other ages, certain broad observations can be made. In addition to being influenced by works of antiquity, American war writers—especially antiwar writers—have been notably influenced by the writings of their counterparts in England, France, Canada, Germany, Austria, and Russia. So too American war writers have had a notable effect on their fellow writers abroad, as the following examples demonstrate. In the mid-1850s Leo Tolstoy wrote a shocking series of short stories about the Crimean War, *The Sevastopol Sketches*. Several decades later, young Stephen Crane, who had yet to experience war at firsthand, set to work on a novel about the Civil War, *The Red Badge of Courage*, and took Tolstoy as his guide. Roughly twenty years later, the French writer Henri Barbusse was influenced by Crane's book when he wrote his momentous antiwar novel *Under Fire* about World War I. In turn, the British World War I poets Siegfried Sassoon and Wilfred Owen read Barbusse's work and composed their own war-bitter verses under the French author's influence. And more than fifty years later, Philip Caputo, an American marine who served as an officer in Vietnam, made clear his debt to both Sassoon and Owen by placing excerpts from their poetry at the start of several chapters of his explosive memoir *A Rumor of War*.[21]

War writers, especially antiwar writers, have always been aware of one another. They have felt the impact of writers whose mother tongues, allegiances, and war experiences were far different from their own. Thus Caputo, a disenchanted U.S. veteran of the Vietnam War, drew both directly and indirectly on the antiwar works of American, British, French, and Russian writers who preceded him. He relied on a literary exchange that stretched as far back as the Crimean War, if not to the days of the Peloponnesian War.

This book does not attempt to cover the entire world history of antiwar literature. To do so would be virtually impossible. Rather, it illuminates the works of a group of American writers who, between the start of the Civil War and the start of World War I, questioned the morality and methods of modern warfare. Their words remain surprisingly relevant today.

WRITING THE CIVIL WAR

Nov. 30th To an absent Wife

Wish I was sitting by thy side,
    My dear beloved wife,
Far from the cannon's awful roar
    Far from this awful strife

My thoughts are of thee through the day,
    I dream of thee at night;
I long to kiss thy lips once more,
    And see thy face so bright

O God! When will this strife be o'er?
    When will we learn to war no more?

—**Obadiah Ethelbert Baker,**
    2nd Iowa Cavalry Volunteers, 1862

WRITING A BATTLE:
THREE VERSIONS OF CHICKAMAUGA

Chickamauga! Chickamauga!
O'er thy dark and turbid wave
Rolls the death-cry of the daring,
Rings the war-shout of the brave;
Round thy shore the red fires flashing,
Startling shot and screaming shell—
Chickamauga, stream of battle,
Who thy fearful tale shall tell?
—"Chickamauga, 'The Stream of Death!'" ca. 1863

n September 19, 1863—two years, five months, and one week into the slog of the Civil War—the Army of the Cumberland, under the command of the Union general William S. Rosecrans, inadvertently engaged the Army of Tennessee, under the command of the Confederate general Braxton Bragg, along the densely wooded and thoroughly inhospitable banks of the Chickamauga Creek in northwest Georgia. What ensued, the Battle of Chickamauga, was one of the bloodiest encounters of the Civil War.[1] Neither general had intended to fight amid the thick forests, and both armies were frustrated by the terrain. Battle lines were impossible to maintain. The density of the trees and smoke limited visibility and often rendered cannons and rifles nearly useless.

As military historians have noted, confusion prevailed on the battlefield.[2] "The main battle began," Byron Farwell explains in *The Encyclopedia of Nineteenth-Century Land Warfare*, "when the two sides, mostly floundering about in thick woods, neither knowing the other's position, lumbered up against each other." And the leadership displayed by the opposing generals was unremarkable. Farwell concludes his summary of the battle with the succinct observation, "Neither commanding general exhibited any brilliance."[3]

Three accounts of the battle—a single conflict fought over the course of two days during a devastating and debilitating four-year struggle—demonstrate how the events of war can lend themselves to a wide range of literary representations. A handwritten entry in the personal diary of a participant, a highly romanticized poem by a civilian, and a revisionist and realist short story written by a veteran each present the Battle of Chickamauga. Yet the three works attach very different meanings to the conflict. To understand the war writing of the Civil War, and more broadly the biases inherent to all war writing, is to understand how the same battle can yield such divergent readings.

The unpublished journal of Captain Allen L. Fahnestock of the 86th Illinois Volunteer Infantry offers a fascinating, firsthand glimpse of the battle.[4] The thirty-five-year-old officer, a grocer in civilian life, was not a professional writer. But details in Fahnestock's work surpass any formal history or polished literary work in capturing and conveying the participants' hour-to-hour experience of the battle.

Fahnestock's record plainly reveals the confused haphazardness of the fray. Describing the fighting at the start of the second day, Fahnestock writes, "We passed the field hospital. The woods [were] on fire. The smoke from the fire and of battle was so dense we could not see twenty paces ahead. So we came near marching into a Rebel battery." Later that same morning, after Fahnestock had positioned his battery in a precarious position on the side of a ridge, his men were temporarily spared harm due to the enemy's poorly aimed artillery fire. Fahnestock notes, "The Rebels [were] shelling us all the while, [but] the smoke prevented them getting a good range, and their shells passed over us doing no damage."[5]

Fahnestock also offers glimpses of various deadly and disturbing aspects of the battle. He describes the death of the first man killed in his company. "Ezra Sellick was killed in line of battle. He was shot in the face, the ball coming out the back of his neck." He records the experience of coming under friendly fire. "[A Union general] mistook our brigade for rebels and fired two shots from his battery at us, the balls passing about ten feet in front of our lines." He notes the misconduct of a Union officer. "Major Fountain got drunk and disgraced himself." And he writes that a Confederate soldier called him a "yankee Son of a B." (Fahnestock promptly shot the man.)[6]

Moreover, Fahnestock records some of the emotions felt by soldiers and their officers. Of the end of the second day of battle, he writes, "The sun was getting low and looked as red as blood, and there is no doubt but what both armies prayed for the sun to set and let darkness end the battle." Of the mood of the defeated Union soldiers later that night, Fahnestock concisely states, "Our army badly demoralized."[7]

Fahnestock even attempts to frame the battle more broadly within the context of the larger war. Before giving a tally of each side's reported losses, he notes, "More men lost in this battle than any general battle according to the number of men engaged of any battle in this war." And he reflects on the conduct of the men in command. In particular, he commends General Thomas, who would soon be tapped to replace General Rosecrans, as deserving the "Honor and Glory of this Battle."[8] In sum, Fahnestock's handwritten account of the Battle of Chickamauga—which concludes with his notation that at the end of the second day of battle he marched eight miles—offers a detailed, highly personal, and distinctly private chronicling of a particular battle of the Civil War.

Fahnestock did not initially intend for his diary to serve as a public record. Indeed, not until nearly a half century after the Battle of Chickamauga did he give the book, at the prompting of his surviving comrades, to the public library in his home county of Peoria, Illinois. In presenting the journal to the board of directors of the library in 1910, Fahnestock explained—in a letter printed on the stationery of his dry goods store—his motivations: "This book giving a daily account of all that transpired while in the service is of great value to the members of this Regiment, and a true history that will be of interest to our children should there ever be another war." As an old man, Fahnestock wanted to see his "true history" preserved for posterity. He recognized its importance as a historical record and its potential to serve as an object lesson in the ways of war for future readers.[9]

Unlike Fahnestock, other authors intentionally set out to write about the Battle of Chickamauga for a public audience. In the months and years that followed the two deadly days in September, an assortment of men and women, northerners and southerners, crafted poems, short stories, and other literary works about the battle. Whereas Fahnestock clearly strove to keep a detailed and accurate log of his experiences during the battle, other writers took liberties with the facts. These authors' texts are not so much conscientious chronicles of combat as they are works of imagination and interpretation.

Two such literary versions of Chickamauga, written roughly a quarter of a century apart, offer dramatically different interpretations not only of the battle but also of the entire Civil War. The actual events that took place at Chickamauga are only dimly recognizable.

Among the many poignant poems written while the events of the September days were still fresh in memory was an unabashed tribute to southern heroism written by a precocious Texas teenager named Mollie E. Moore.[10] In 1860 Moore's verses had begun to appear in the *Tyler Reporter*, her local paper, and during the Civil War years, her war poetry appeared in the *Reporter*, the *Houston Telegraph*, the *Southern Literary Messenger*, and other southern newspapers.

In thirteen tidy stanzas Moore paints the opposing armies as they met early on the battle's second day. The second stanza of her poem "Chickamauga" reads:

> Morn dawned upon the field, the bugle's blast
> Wound out its shrilly summons, and the word
> Leaped down the lines, and fiery hearts beat fast:
> Two gallant armies bared the murderous sword,
> And fearless breasted battle's bitter waves,
> And eager thousands sought their nameless graves
> By the River of Death!

Moore's is a highly idealized field of battle on which all soldiers march bravely, even eagerly, into the deadly fray. In her florid rendition of the second day's events, there is no mention of the blinding smoke, general disarray, or incompetence that shape Fahnestock's account. Instead, the focus is on a single soldier. He is a man whose "stalwart Texan's heart" beats "high amid the deepening strife." This Texan bravely fights for his boyhood home, his wife, mother, infant son, and his sisters until, in the course of the day's battle, he is mortally wounded.[11]

With euphemism and romantic flourish, Moore lays the young Texan to rest. His heart slowly ceases "its own faint earth-born melody," and while thinking of his young wife and their dark-eyed little boy, the soldier dies. Later that night, his comrades bury him "upon their field of glory" among the "noble slain." Then, gathered at their campfire, they recall "how well he fought."[12]

Moore's "Chickamauga" offers a good example of popular poetry written during the Civil War years. Her presentation of battle and death is highly conventionalized, and there is no moral ambiguity. The poem pays tribute to a soldier who fought honorably for an honorable cause, and the unnamed soldier serves as a sort of southern everyman. His bravery and self-sacrifice are meant to represent the same qualities possessed by all of his comrades on the battlefield. Full of patriotism, optimism, and flushing romanticism, the poem is indistinguishable in sentiment and tone from hundreds of others written during the war.

The poem stands out from so many others of the era only because it was written by so young a poet. Moore was only a teenager during the early Civil War years. Yet despite Moore's relative youth, her verses won the approval of her readers. A volume of her poetry, including "Chickamauga," was published as *Minding the Gap and Other Poems* in 1867. Two years later a second volume was published, and that same year a literary critic admiringly noted in *The Living Writers of the South,* "With a genius vigorous and free, stimulated into activity by the stern life of war, Miss Moore is just taking her position among Southern authors." Indeed, the critic congratulated Moore on avoiding "that [insipid] sentimentality that too often marks the verses of young ladies" and admired the "earnestness and directness of utterance in her best poems."[13]

More than a quarter of a century after the dead of Chickamauga were laid to rest, the Civil War battle inspired a very different sort of literary reckoning. In 1889 the short-story writer and journalist Ambrose Bierce, a Union veteran who had fought at Chickamauga and elsewhere during four years of military service, published a short story in the *San Francisco Examiner* that bore the same title as Moore's poem, "Chickamauga." The title, however, is virtually all that the two works have in common.

Bierce's "Chickamauga"—which was included in his 1891 short story collection *Tales of Soldiers and Civilians*—does not focus, as does Moore's poem, on a brave soldier. Instead, Bierce's story focuses on a fearful civilian. In Bierce's tale a mute and deaf six-year-old boy strays from his mother's side one fine fall morning in Georgia. Wooden sword in hand, the child wanders off to play in a nearby forest, where he wages imaginary battle against "invisible foes."[14] Then, scared by a rabbit, the child runs away, becomes lost among the trees, and sobs himself to sleep.

Although the boy played at war with his puny sword and invisible adversaries, he does not recognize war, the real thing, when it arrives in his Georgia woods. He wakens in the "gloom of twilight" to find men creeping all around him "upon their hands and knees." Throughout the forest they come "by dozens and by hundreds." The men are the wounded and dying soldiers of Chickamauga, but the boy does not understand that. He finds the sight of these new and mysterious visitors to his Georgia woods "a merry spectacle." The boy imagines the men are involved in a game and tries to climb on the back of a horribly injured soldier for a ride. The lower half of this man's face has been completely mangled, "from the upper teeth to the throat was a great red gap fringed with hanging shreds of flesh and splinters of bone." The soldier fiercely flings the child to the ground.[15]

Confused but not entirely discouraged, the boy heads toward a "strange red light" that shines through the trees. He crosses a creek—where some of the wounded soldiers have drowned—and rushes toward the "pillar of fire." When he arrives at the blaze, he is stunned by what he sees.

> His little world swung half around; the points of the compass were reversed. He recognized the blazing building as his own home!
>
> For a moment he stood stupefied by the power of the revelation, then ran with stumbling feet, making a half-circuit of the ruin. There, conspicuous in the light of the conflagration, lay the dead body of a woman— the white face turned upward, the hands thrown out and clutched full of grass, the clothing deranged, the long dark hair in tangles and full of clotted blood.

The boy has found his mother. Her forehead has been torn away by a shell, and her brain protrudes from the jagged hole, "a frothy mass of gray, crowned with clusters of crimson bubbles."[16]

It is hard to imagine a more shocking or grotesque war story. Bierce's account of the Battle of Chickamauga tells not only of the devastation war visits on soldiers but also of the destruction that war visits on the most innocent of civilians, a mother and a hapless, handicapped child. Bierce's "Chickamauga" is horrific and utterly unredemptive, and that is just how Bierce intended it to be.

Why did a battle of 120,000 men, fought over the course of two days in the tangled woods of northwest Georgia along Chickamauga Creek, evoke such strikingly different published responses? Moore wrote about "battle's bitter waves." Bierce, who had won for himself the nickname "Bitter Bierce," wrote about mangled soldiers drowning in a blood-stained creek. Moore's poem throbs with a highly sentimental pulse. Bierce's story, as one scholar notes, "probes the very depths of material horror."[17] Each author veers toward a different extreme. Moore sanitizes the battle. Bierce invents new outrages.

It would be easy simply to ascribe the differences in these two works to a matter of personal experience. Unlike Mollie Moore, Ambrose Bierce had participated in the Civil War. He enlisted at the age of eighteen in the Ninth Indiana Volunteers and weathered the war from 1861 to 1865 against daunting odds. He fought, among other places, at Shiloh, Chickamauga, and Kennesaw Mountain, where he was severely wounded when a lead ball lodged in his skull. Or the two writers' different outlooks on the battle might be ascribed to a difference in temperament. Moore was described by the editor of the *Houston Telegraph* as a "sweet young poetess."[18] Bierce was a cynic extraordinaire. (In his famous *Devil's Dictionary*, an A to Z compendium of some of his most barbed wit, Bierce defines "fidelity" as "a virtue peculiar to those who are about to be betrayed.")[19] But although Moore may have been a sweet southerner and Bierce certainly was a sour northerner, the difference in their writing reflects more than just a difference in personality, age, gender, allegiance, and wartime experience. More fundamental than any of these factors is that the two writers held radically different views concerning the morality of the Civil War. And unlike Fahnestock, who wrote his detailed account of the conflict without a public audience in mind, Moore and Bierce hoped to shape their readers' understanding of the war.

Written at a distance of a quarter of a century from each other, Moore's and Bierce's versions of the battle point toward the struggle waged by professional writers of the late nineteenth century to define the moral meaning of the Civil War for contemporary readers. Both renderings of "Chickamauga" are highly mediated and emotionally manipulative. Both try to sway readers toward a particular understanding of the war. Moore imputes heroic meaning to the Texan's death. Bierce stubbornly refuses to allow any uplifting, transcendent, or redemptive message into his war story. In Moore's poem, the dead man's comrades gather to tell "how well he fought." In Bierce's story, the deaf, mute boy stands alone over the ravaged body of his dead mother and utters a "series of inarticulate and indescribable cries."[20]

The two works reflect a broad shift in literary taste in the late nineteenth

century, as romanticism gradually yielded to realism. They also reflect the
changing attitude toward antiwar literature in the postwar decades. In the
quarter century separating the publication of the poem and the short story,
American war literature began to incorporate a harshly critical consciousness. This emergent antiwar strain is both reflected in, and furthered by,
Bierce's writings.

If no one in the 1860s published anything as graphic or unsettling as
Bierce's story of a helpless boy wandering among the wounded soldiers and
the corpses at Chickamauga, it was not because writers were completely
unaware of the brutality and gore of the Civil War battles. Fahnestock's
matter-of-fact description of a soldier shot squarely in the face forcefully
dispels that notion. But during the war years there was a shared understanding between most writers, editors, publishers, and readers that anything
other than uplifting, patriotic, sentimental, and reverential works was not
in good taste. These literary norms did not change quickly in the postwar
era, but change they eventually did. Mollie Moore described the "blood-
stained" Confederate flag. Roughly twenty-five years later, Bierce described
a Confederate woman's hair "full of clotted blood." From the brave soldiers
"who fell like brothers" to the deaf child crying over the gruesome corpse of
his mother, Civil War literature traveled a long way in the closing decades of
the nineteenth century.[21] The following chapters track that difficult journey.

THE CIVIL WAR IN POPULAR POETRY:
"GOD AND RIGHT"

And a Nation springs once more to the fight,
With the deathless war-cry of "God and Right!"
—Henry Howard Brownell, "Only a Word,"
Lyrics of a Day, 1864

o the ears of modern readers, the high-toned lines written by men and women who were moved by the spectacle of a war that for four years transfixed the attention of all citizens can often sound sappy, naive, and embarrassingly idealistic. As early as 1918 one literary critic tactfully noted, "Much of this verse [of the Civil War] has naturally lost its appeal, but its national and historical significance cannot be overlooked."[1]

Edmund Wilson, writing in the early 1960s, was less diplomatic. In his mammoth study of the literature of the Civil War, *Patriotic Gore* (the title of which he borrowed from a line in James Ryder Randall's well-known poem "My Maryland"), Wilson observes, "The period of the Civil War was not at all a favorable one for poetry. An immense amount of verse was written in connection with the war itself, but today it makes barren reading."[2] It is a measure of how much war literature changed during the intervening decades that even readers of the early and mid-twentieth century found the tenor and tone of Civil War era poetry so notably outdated.

However, the harsh judgments of later critics in no way lessen the importance that the intensely partisan poetry held for the war generation. There is great wisdom in the words of the poet and literary critic E. C. Stedman, who during the Civil War went to the front as a correspondent for the *New York World*. He cautioned, "One who underrates the significance of our literature, prose or verse, as both the expression and the stimulant of national feeling, as of import in the past and to the future of America . . . shuts his eyes to the fact that at times, notably throughout the years resulting in the

Civil War, this literature has been a 'force.'"[3] The literature of the Civil War era was a consoling and inspiring "force" that bolstered the morale of civilians and combatants during the long years of loss and deprivation. And poetry, among other literary forms, enjoyed a degree of near universal popularity that is hard for more modern readers to understand.

All of the celebrated poets of the era, those who viewed the war as a fight against northern tyranny and those who conceived of it as a battle against southern treason, were unified in an effort to impart to the war a coherent meaning and to preserve a semblance of war's order and dignity. They did not draw attention to the unseemly aspects of the war or question the way in which the war was being conducted. They did not cast doubt on the merit of the war's aims or question the war's morality. In turn, Americans trusted their writers to reveal the true and lofty significance of the war and to impart to battlefield injuries and deaths a transcendent meaning.

Poetry allowed writers to respond to the war and was well suited to capturing the mood of the hour. In the flush of victory, as in times of despondency, writers used the quick release of poetry to pour out their emotions, and their verses were often quickly set into print. Examples abound of famous Civil War works written and published in a notably expeditious fashion.

Richard Henry Stoddard's rallying cry "To the Men of the North and West" was composed on April 17, 1861, the day Virginia seceded from the Union, and made it into print the following day in New York's *Evening Post*. In Stoddard's distinctly partisan assessment, the Rebels had "trampled the laws," "stifled the freedom they hate," and struck "at the life of the State." And with bold directives Stoddard commanded his fellow Unionists:

> Men of the North and West,
> Wake in your might,
> Prepare, as the Rebels have done,
> For the fight;
> You cannot shrink from the test,
> Rise! Men of the North and West![4]

Stoddard's poem is a call to arms, literally, and well captures the strong passions of April 1861.

Similarly, Lucy Larcom's "The Nineteenth of April," published in the *Boston Transcript* on April 25, 1861, reflects a northerner's proud and angry emotions during those charged days. The poem compares the first deaths of the Civil War to the first deaths of the Revolutionary War. Specifically, it commemorates the deaths of three soldiers from the Sixth Massachusetts Regiment who were killed in a confrontation with a mob of southern sympathizers in Baltimore. Without stinting on exclamation marks, Larcom writes:

> To war,—and with our brethren, then,—if only this can be!
> Life hangs as nothing in the scale against dear Liberty!
> Though hearts be torn asunder, for Freedom we will fight:
> Our blood may seal the victory, but God will shield the Right![5]

Both poems were written in the heat of the moment. Both poems presuppose that the northern cause is absolutely morally "right." Both poems demonstrate the way in which poetry was used to respond quickly to the war's unfolding events.

Unlike a novel or a longer work of writing, poetry can be written in a single feverish flash of inspiration. Julia Ward Howe drafted the rousing verses of her "Battle Hymn of the Republic" at early dawn with, as she later recalled, "an old stump of a pen." The poem, first published in the *Atlantic Monthly* in February 1862, would become the unofficial northern war anthem. Describing the exhilarated state in which she composed the work, Howe once explained, "I scrawled the verses almost without looking at the paper."[6]

Howe's poem, so speedily completed and so popular in the North during the war years, demonstrates the sensibilities of wartime readers and writers. The Union's cause is presented as unambiguously just, and Union soldiers are presented as members of God's army, fighting a righteous battle. The poem's opening lines proclaim:

> Mine eyes have seen the glory of the coming of the Lord:
> He is trampling out the vintage where the grapes of wrath are stored;
> He hath loosed the fateful lightning of His terrible swift sword:
> > His truth is marching on.

The cause of the Union, according to Howe, is divinely blessed. God fights, figuratively if not literally, beside the soldiers in blue. The final three verses all end with the words, "God is marching on."[7]

Southerners, too, experienced flashes of poetic and patriotic inspiration. In late April 1861, James Ryder Randall wrote the stirring verses of

"My Maryland," a rallying song of the Confederacy, in a single sitting. Randall, a Maryland native, was teaching at a college in Louisiana when he heard of the deadly encounter that had recently taken place in his home state between soldiers from a Massachusetts regiment and citizens of Baltimore (the same event addressed in Larcom's "The Nineteenth of April").[8] As Randall later explained, "About midnight I arose, lit a candle, and went to my desk. Some powerful spirit appeared to possess me, and almost involuntarily I proceeded to write the song of *My Maryland*."[9] Within days Randall's poem was published in the *New Orleans Delta,* and before long the poem had been widely reprinted and set to music. (The most popular adaptation had Confederates singing Randall's verses to the tune of the Christmas carol "O Tannenbaum.")[10]

The words that Randall dashed off at the desk in his room at Poydras College would become the most famous of all Confederate poems. Maryland, Randall proclaimed, had borne the affront of the "despot's heel" on her "shore." To redress this outrage, Randall asserted, it was incumbent upon Maryland to "burst the tyrant's chain," "avenge the patriotic gore of Baltimore," and spurn "the Northern scum." The second stanza of "My Maryland" reads:

> Hark to an exiled son's appeal,
> > Maryland!
> My mother State, to thee I kneel,
> > Maryland!
> For life or death, for woe and weal,
> Thy peerless chivalry reveal,
> And gird thy beauteous limbs with steel,
> > Maryland! My Maryland!

The poem continues in a similar vein for seven more stanzas. Mother Maryland, Randall asserts, need only reveal her "peerless chivalry" and the incipient war would be won. But that southern victory was not to be.[11]

The way in which the Civil War appeared in poetry was often antiquated, anachronistic, and defiantly antimodern. But poetry had a cultural function, and the liberty it took with historical facts only heightened its appeal. For example, soon after Lee surrendered to Grant at Appomattox, the South's defeat was recorded in a poem titled "The Conquered Banner." Written by

Father Abram Ryan, who had served for four years as a chaplain in the Confederate army, the poignant lines of the work (which reportedly had been drafted in its entirety in less than an hour) would become extremely popular and invite a variety of poetic responses.

Throughout the war, numerous poems by southerners paid tribute to the Confederate flag, routinely referred to as "the stars and bars" or the "Southern Cross." Ryan's poem focuses on how that flag should be treated following the Confederacy's defeat.

> Furl that Banner! furl it sadly!
> Once ten thousands hailed it gladly,
> And ten thousands wildly, madly,
>   Swore it should forever wave;
> Swore that foeman's sword should never
> Hearts like theirs entwined dissever,
> Till that flag should float forever
>   O'er their freedom or their grave!

Ryan draws on an outdated vocabulary: "foeman," "entwined," "dissever." Even more notably, he draws on an outdated version of war.[12]

The war that Ryan witnessed was fought primarily with rifles and artillery, but the war he describes is one contested with swords.[13] The poem's first stanza begins:

> Furl that Banner, for 'tis weary;
> Round its staff 'tis drooping dreary;
>   Furl it, fold it, it is best;
> For there's not a man to wave it,
> And there's not a sword to save it . . .

Although Ryan's extensive wartime experience had qualified him to give an accurate description of the weaponry of the Civil War, he drew on the literary conventions of his day rather than on his own observations. And these literary conventions were, by the war's end, already well worn with use.[14]

The Civil War, to judge from many of the most popular works of poetry, was fought with weaponry straight out of the Middle Ages. Julia Ward Howe warned of God's "terrible swift sword" in the rousing lines of her very popular "Battle Hymn of the Republic." James Ryder Randall praised Maryland's "beaming sword" and her "bright and strong" shield in his famous

Confederate anthem "My Maryland."[15] Father Ryan titled another postwar poem "The Sword of Robert Lee" and began it with the following stanza:

> Forth from its scabbard, pure and bright,
>   Flashed the sword of Lee!
> Far in the front of the deadly fight,
> High o'er the brave in the cause of Right
> Its stainless sheen, like a beacon light,
>   Led us to Victory![16]

However outdated and outmoded swords and shields had become by the mid-nineteenth century, they continued to figure prominently in popular war literature. They appealed to readers' romantic imagination. Ryan even went so far as to anthropomorphize Lee's sword. In the final stanza, he writes:

> 'Tis shrouded now in its sheath again,
> It sleeps the sleep of our noble slain,
> Defeated, yet without a stain,
>   Proudly and peacefully!

The sword is the stand-in for the conquered Confederacy. It symbolizes all that made the war noble for the South. Nowhere in Civil War poetry is there a poem that pays such loving tribute to a rifle. Nowhere is there a verse that eulogizes an artillery gun. Of no other weapon than a sword would a Civil War writer claim, as does Ryan, "It slumbered peacefully."[17]

The romanticism of Civil War literature was based on a myth, and the myth was distinctly antimodern. The cavalier—the gallant, sword-bearing warrior—was the representative fighter who figured in popular song and verse. And if he more accurately belonged to the days and ways of the English Civil War than to the era of the American Civil War, it mattered little.

The Civil War, as painted by Stoddard, Larcom, Howe, Randall, Ryan, and so many others, was an idealized war. If the war that emerged in the lines of their poems did not correspond with how the Civil War actually was waged, it reflected how the nation's readers and writers thought the Civil War should have been waged. America's leading poets, North and South, were writing the perfect war, even if the war the divided nation was fighting was less than perfect.

* * *

Not every poem was written as quickly, and few attracted as much attention as the works of Julia Ward Howe and James Ryder Randall. Nonetheless, war poetry flourished in America during the long years of war. Men and women of all degrees of talent wrote poems commemorating specific battles, poems praising favorite generals, poems expressing fiery scorn for the wrongheaded foe, and poems lamenting the loss of individual soldiers. As Alice Fahs notes in her study of popular literature from the war years, *The Imagined Civil War,* the patriotic poetry published in newspapers North and South was widely regarded by ordinary citizens as an appropriate and meaningful response to the long, painful war.[18]

By one count, the tragic death of Stonewall Jackson, a beloved Confederate general who was accidentally shot by his own troops during the Battle of Chancellorsville, resulted in no fewer than forty-eight published poems.[19] And a full seventeen of these works eventually were gathered together in *The Southern Amaranth,* a collection of southern war poetry published in 1869 as a tribute "to the memories of the *brave men* who perished in the late ineffectual effort for Southern Independence."[20] One of the most famous of these poetic tributes, "Monody on the Death of General Stonewall Jackson," which appeared in the wartime collection *Rebel Rhymes and Rhapsodies* as well as in *The Southern Amaranth,* begins:

> He fell as the hero should fall;
>   'Mid the thunder of war he died.
> While the rifle cracked and the cannon roared,
> And the blood of the friend and foeman poured,
> He dropped from his nerveless grasp the sword
>   That erst was the nation's pride.[21]

Signed "By the Exile," the poem delicately omits the fact that Jackson was shot by a picket in his own army.

In the South, newspapers such as the *Charleston Mercury,* the *Richmond Examiner,* the *Louisville Courier,* and the *New Orleans Delta,* and magazines such as the *Southern Literary Messenger,* the *Southern Field and Fireside,* and the *Southern Illustrated News* all published an abundance of war poems written by contributors from every Confederate state.[22] Indeed, southerners bombarded newspapers with such a quantity of unsolicited poetry on war-related topics that one publication apparently threatened to charge aspiring poets the same rate to print their verses as it charged to print obituaries.[23] In the North the situation was much the same. But whereas in the South there were a dearth of book publishing houses during the war, the North was rich with publishers and printing presses. Indeed, the wartime anthology *Rebel Rhymes and Rhapsodies* was published in New York as a companion piece to two volumes of northern war poetry.

If the North and South could agree on little else during the war years, they were in easy agreement about their literary preferences. Whether their allegiance was to the Confederacy or the Union, readers wanted to be reassured that their sons, brothers, and fathers were playing parts in a noble endeavor that was favored by God. Popular wartime writers drew on a shared vocabulary of highly sentimentalized expressions of pain, sorrow, and sacrifice. Less rosy and idealized interpretations of the war were unwelcome.

"The poetic muse still lingers in the Southern land." So began an assessment of Confederate wartime poetry that ran in *Harper's Weekly* during the summer of 1864. "The Latest Rebel Poetry" continues, "We have come into possession of late files of Southern newspapers, containing numerous specimens of fresh poetical contributions. These rhymes are of all sorts, and written in every kind of meter. The elegiac, lyric, sentimental, amatory, and patriotic are all represented; and although their order of merit is not of the highest, their value as literary curiosities is not of the lowest." If the literary critic for *Harper's Weekly* saw fit to mock the outpouring of verse in the South, it was not because the northern taste rejected the "elegiac, lyric, sentimental, amatory, and patriotic" styles in which so much southern war poetry was written. Rather, it was flagrant northern chauvinism.[24]

A few months earlier, the magazine's sister publication, *Harper's New Monthly Magazine*, had published a notably florid battle report written by Captain Daniel McCook, an assistant adjutant general in the Union army. Describing the aftermath of the battle at Shiloh, McCook recorded:

> As we passed through the orchard, lying with his shoulders propped against a peach-tree, I saw the mangled form of one of my best-loved classmates dressed in rebel uniform. The mist gathered in his silken beard showed he had died the day before. The pitiless rain had fallen on his upturned face all night. A smile beautified his features, while his eyes seemed gazing far to the southward, as if there an anxious mother were waiting for words of hope from that war-swept field. A cannon-ball

had partly severed a branch of the tree. Flower-laden, it fell in scarlet festoons about his head—a fitting pall for his gallant, pure- hearted, yet erring nature.

Though ostensibly a factual account of the actions of the Second Division at Shiloh, McCook's report—which begins with the words, "The highest romance in military life centres in a succoring army"—clearly borrows heavily from the highly idealized and sanitized conventions of Civil War poetry. Even one's enemy is granted a tranquil death in a scenic orchard.[25]

As McCook's account demonstrates, it was possible to infuse all sorts of war writing with a romantic tinge. By and large, though, poetry allowed far greater flexibility—and more license with the facts—than journalistic reporting. Moreover, poetry proved particularly well suited to the high-pitched emotions and quick-paced action of the war years. Poetry's adaptability as an antiwar tool, however, was rarely on display.

3

SIR WALTER SCOTT'S LEGACY AND THE ROMANCE OF THE CIVIL WAR

[Sir Walter Scott] was of his own nature chivalrous and martial, and he revelled in the pictures which his imagination drew of the daring, and the physical prowess of the old knights, and the gallantry of the cavaliers.

—S.L.C., "Thoughts upon English Poetry," *Southern Literary Messenger,* 1850

In order fully to understand the literary proclivities of the war generation, it is necessary to understand the impact of the writings of a certain Scotsman who died nearly three decades before the Civil War began. The novelist and poet Sir Walter Scott played no small part in shaping the romantic taste of the Civil War era. Indeed, his works, more than those of any other author, probably had the greatest influence on popular Civil War writing.

In the half century leading up to the Civil War, American readers and writers had caught a lingering case of what Mark Twain later would diagnose as "the Sir Walter disease." As Twain ruefully observed in the early 1880s, "If one take up a Northern or Southern literary periodical of forty or fifty years ago, he will find it filled with wordy, windy, flowery 'eloquence,' romanticism, sentimentality—all imitated from Sir Walter." In the prewar decades, Americans became infatuated with Scott's works and the works of his countless imitators. The lasting influence of Sir Walter Scott, into the 1860s, significantly shaped the literary representation of the Civil War and, very likely, the way in which some war participants and observers conceived of the war itself.[1]

How did one man, not even an American, come to influence so strongly the literary taste of the era? It began quite simply. In 1814 the Scottish author published his first full-length work of fiction, the novel *Waverley.* Set in Scotland against the background of the Jacobite rebellion of 1745, the work was an immediate and immense success both in Great Britain and in

America. Other volumes soon followed in what came to be known as the Waverley series.

In the United States, northerners and southerners alike were smitten. They devoured Scott's historical romances, and Scott dug further and further into British history to mine his material. The more far-fetched the plot and remote the setting, the more pleased Scott's distant readers seemed to be. Among Scott's most famous works was *Ivanhoe,* published in 1819. Like Scott's other romances, *Ivanhoe* tells a tale of intrigue, love, and valor. Set in the Middle Ages, the story traces the fortunes of the novel's protagonist, young Wilfred of Ivanhoe, the only son of Cedric the Saxon, from the time he is disinherited by his father, in part for loving his father's ward the beautiful Lady Rowena, to the time that he takes Rowena as his bride. In the several hundred pages that intervene and serve to separate the young adventurer from his lady love, both King Richard I and Robin Hood appear, and Ivanhoe performs many a remarkable feat. He travels to Palestine, gains fame in the Crusades, returns home in disguise, bravely distinguishes himself in a two-day jousting tournament, and last but surely not least, singlehandedly rescues a beautiful, raven-haired Jewess named Rebecca who has been abducted and is in grave peril.

Not only the elaborate plots but also the florid language of Scott's works appealed to American readers. A yeoman addresses Ivanhoe after the jousting tournament, "Noble knight, . . . if you disdain not to grace by your acceptance a bugle which an English yeoman has once worn, this I will pray you to keep as a memorial of your gallant bearing."[2] At once archaic and romantic, the yeoman's tribute to Ivanhoe offers a fair sampling of Scott's carefully crafted, faux-medieval writing style.

Americans were enamored. In less than a decade, from 1814 to 1823, more than half a million volumes of Scott's novels and poems were sold in the United States. American publishers vied with one another to be the first to print pirated editions of his works. Indeed, at times the printers and presses of an entire city were kept busy racing to meet the demand for new Scott fare. The New England publisher Samuel Griswold Goodrich records in his autobiography, published in 1856:

> I suspect that never, in any age, have the productions of any author created in the world so wide and deep an enthusiasm. . . . The appearance of a new tale from [Scott's] pen, caused a greater sensation in the United

States than did some of the battles of Napoleon, which decided the fate
of thrones and empires. Everybody read these works; everybody—the
refined and the simple—shared in the delightful trances which seemed
to transport them to remote ages and distant climes. . . . I can testify to
my own share in this intoxication.

If quaffing Scott's literary outpourings resulted in inebriation, it is no exag-
geration to say that the Civil War generation was drunk on Scott.[3]

Throughout the decades following Scott's death in 1832, his books remained extremely popular. They were enthusiastically read and reread by
generations of Americans in both the North and the South. Henry Adams,
the great-grandson of President John Adams and grandson of President
John Quincy Adams, recalls in his autobiography, *The Education of Henry
Adams,* that the "happiest hours" of his boyhood in the late 1840s and early
1850s "were passed in summer lying on a musty heap of Congressional
Documents in [his grandfather's] farmhouse at Quincy [Massachusetts],
reading 'Quentin Durward,' 'Ivanhoe,' and the 'The Talisman,'" three historic romances by Scott.[4] In the decades preceding the Civil War, Scott's romances were no less popular on the other side of the Mason-Dixon line. A
young plantation mistress named Ella Gertrude Clanton Thomas confided
in her journal in 1855 that she intended to read through the Waverley novels
during the coming long winter nights. "I have read them before," she wrote,
"when I was much younger and hardly able to appreciate their beauties so
well as I would now."[5]

Some of Scott's American readers took pleasure in masquerading as his
well-known heroes and heroines. For a "fancy party" held on Christmas
Eve in 1858, Thomas came dressed as Diana Vernon from Scott's medieval
romance *Rob Roy.* Her costume included a "cap trimmed with feathers—
Gauntlets, linen collar and undersleeves and a riding whip."[6] Some southern
families even went so far as to name their estates and children after places
and characters in Scott's stories.[7]

Scott's tales of exalted heroism helped shape the literary taste of prewar
America. As John Hay, who would serve as President Lincoln's assistant
secretary during the Civil War, would remark decades later, "The books a
boy reads are those most ardently admired and longest remembered. . . .
Through all [the] important formative days of the Republic, Scott was the
favourite author of Americans. . . . [The influence of his books] was enor-

mous upon the taste and the sentiments of a people peculiarly sensitive to such influences."[8] Numerous authors imitated Scott's style. As a critic named G. Harrison Orians long ago noted in an essay titled "The Romance Ferment after *Waverley*," Scott's historical novels "set a whole generation of Englishmen and Americans dreaming and prating about the chivalries of a by-gone age" and "were held up everywhere as the standard of historical fiction by which American materials were judged." Orians concludes, "In this way the ingredients of Scott's novels became the marks of romantic excellence which novelists and critics sought to match in American history."[9]

At the same time as the tensions that would culminate in the Civil War were brewing, Scott's works kept American readers' attention focused on a bygone age. In 1850, a year commonly recalled for the fierce sectional debate that culminated in the Compromise of 1850 (which included the passage of the Fugitive Slave Act), one admirer of Scott's works wrote in the *Southern Literary Messenger*, "Scott's purpose was not to give an analytic account of man in general, but to present a bold and glowing picture of the men of a particular age, and the age selected by him was that when knighthood was the profession of every gentleman, and war the principal occupation of almost every monarch."[10] As northern Free Soilers faced off against southern slaveholding interests, the past, at least as Scott portrayed it, seemed more appealing than the present. And the present was becoming ever bleaker.

Even the outbreak of fighting—and the nation's rude initiation into the pain and suffering of an extended fratricidal war—did not diminish the popularity of Scott's works. Especially in the South, Scott's works remained extremely popular throughout the war years. In fact, the Waverley novels ranked high on Confederate soldiers' lists of favorite reading matter. As one soldier, a former student at Washington and Jefferson College, wrote home from his military camp, "I have read all of Sir Walter Scott's novels within the last month."[11] And the historian—and now Harvard University president—Drew Gilpin Faust observes, "Scott's immensely popular Waverley novels celebrated Scottish struggles against English domination and oppression in a manner southerners found increasingly resonant with their own situation, and these volumes became soldiers' acknowledged favorites in camp libraries."[12]

The generation of soldiers that headed off to fight the Civil War had been raised on Scott's lofty legends of heroism, and they were comforted and encouraged by Scott's works as they fought their own war. Civilians,

too, escaped to the enchanted land of Scott during the war years. The diary of Mary Chesnut, the wife of a prominent South Carolina politician,
reflects Scott's enduring influence. In November 1861 Chesnut wrote in her
journal the terse sentence, "Read Scott." Nearly four years later, after the
"War of Northern Aggression" had been lost, Chesnut again mentioned
Scott in her diary. She noted, "Sir Walter Scott says, 'Never let me hear that
brave blood has been shed in vain. It sends a roaring voice down through
all time.'" Then, improvising a few words of her own in Scott's pseudo-
antiquated vocabulary, she mused, "*In vain,* alas, ye gallant few!"[13]

Even the lived reality of the Civil War—a war unprecedented in American history in its scale of death and devastation—did not change Chesnut's
and other contemporary readers' predilection for romantic tales of derring-
do. In the wake of the Civil War, Scott still had his staunch devotees. In 1866
a contributor to *DeBow's Review,* published in New Orleans, avowed: "The
modern novel was born in the brain of Walter Scott. The publication of the
Waverley Novels marked the advent of a new era. . . . Without question,
[Scott] opened new paths of thought and feeling. He was a benefactor to his
race, for he lit up the common life of man with the beautiful lights of a vivid
imagination; and with the radiancy of a fine humor he flashed an honest
glow into the hearts of thousands."[14] The Confederacy might have died, but
the cult of Scott remained robust.[15]

Only half jokingly, Mark Twain years later would assert, "Sir Walter had
so large a hand in making Southern character, as it existed before the war,
that he is in great measure responsible for the war."[16] Twain might well have
added that Scott was also in great measure responsible for the literature of
the Civil War. Sir Walter Scott's romances, and America's romance with Sir
Walter Scott, profoundly influenced the broad public attitude toward war.

During the actual war years, Scott's works provided an example of bravery
and manliness, an idealized image of men at war, that legions of American
authors, both in the North and in the South, eagerly emulated. As the literary scholar Bernard Bergonzi has noted, Scott "exploited a nostalgia for the
clear-cut heroics of a past age of chivalry," and legions of writers of the Civil
War tapped into that nostalgic vein.[17] In countless works of poetry and fiction
from the Civil War era, authors portray the soldiers who engage in battle as
stouthearted warriors who live, fight, and die according to near chivalric stan-
dards. Often the signs of Scott's influence on Civil War authors are obvious.

The popular poem "The Virginians of the Valley" provides one such example. The work was written during the war by Francis Orray Ticknor, a physician and acclaimed poet who ran the war hospitals in the area of Columbus, Georgia. Ticknor's wife hailed from a prominent Virginia family, and the poem unabashedly celebrates the preeminence of the men and women of Virginia. The work begins by describing Virginians as

> The knightliest of the knightly race,
> Who, since the days of old,
> Have kept the lamp of chivalry
> Alight in hearts of gold . . .

After recounting the great accomplishments of Virginians of the past, the poem pays tribute to the sons of Virginia of the present. These "Golden Horse-shoe knights," as they are called, do not slumber as danger looms. Instead, they band together and prove themselves worthy of their "noble sires." Although not all Civil War poetry is so blatantly indebted to Scott, Americans' fixation on the ways and days of chivalry clearly influenced the general literary representation of the Civil War.[18]

"Ashby," a wartime poem by the popular southern poet John Reuben Thompson, offers another example of Scott's enduring influence. General Turner Ashby, a Virginia gentleman and Confederate cavalry officer, was hit in the chest with a musket ball while fighting a rear-guard action under General Stonewall Jackson's command in early June 1862. He died at the age of thirty-three. Ashby had been regarded by his peers as the "Knight of the Confederacy."[19]

Thompson, who served as editor of the *Southern Literary Messenger* from 1847 to 1860 and of the *Richmond Record* and the *Southern Illustrated News* during the war, well understood his readers' preferences. Exercising his poetic license, Thompson strove to create the most pleasing portrait he could craft of Ashby, both in life and in death. In the first stanza of "Ashby," Thompson beseeches the reader, as well as various celestial bodies, to pay due reverence to the memory of the slain general.

> To the brave all homage render,
> Weep, ye skies of June!
> With a radiance pure and tender,
> Shine, oh saddened moon!

> "Dead upon the field of glory,"
> Hero fit for song and story,
> Lies our bold dragoon.

Elevating Ashby to "hero" status, Thompson offers an exemplary tale of human loss. Ashby's death is so consequential, Thompson suggests, that even the cosmos mourns in sympathy. Moon and sky, in Thompson's vision, are expected to grieve, along with mortals, the death of a brave man. And earth, summer showers, birds, bees, and flowers are commanded to make "the gloom" of Ashby's grave "seem gay." [20]

In memorializing and dignifying Ashby's death, Thompson presents a vision of war correlated with his readers' fantasies and hopes. And in so doing, he makes explicit reference to Sir Walter Scott's *Ivanhoe*. In the poem's second stanza, Thompson reverentially observes:

> Well they learned, whose hands have slain him,
> Braver, knightlier foe
> Never fought with Moor nor [Pagan],
>   Rode at Templestowe,
> With a mien how high and joyous,
> 'Gainst the hordes that would destroy us
> Went he forth we know.

Later in the poem, Thompson refers to Ashby's "sabre," "crest," and "manly breast." General Ashby is assigned all the trappings and attributes of a knight. In Thompson's adoring portrait, Ashby seems better outfitted for a medieval joust than for mid-nineteenth-century armed combat. If Ashby did not literally wear a crest or die precisely upon a field of glory, Thompson trusted that his readers would appreciate these imaginative flourishes. Moreover, Thompson trusted that his readers would recognize his reference to Templestowe, the mythical place from which Ivanhoe rescues Rebecca in Sir Walter Scott's famous novel. And it is surely worth noting that a critical jousting tournament in *Ivanhoe* occurs against the backdrop of a place that happens to be called Ashby Castle. [21]

If Thompson did not present war as it was, he presented war as it should be. In so doing, he helped fortify the resolve of the Confederate nation for which Ashby fought. Denying the anonymity of battlefield confrontations —in which men died by the dozens, hundreds, and thousands—Thompson insists on a vision of war in which each death is consequential, each man dies a hero, and nature shares in human sorrow. Throughout its verses "Ashby" is filled with lofty language, lofty sentiments, and lofty deeds.

Numerous other southern poets also memorialized General Ashby. Among them was Margaret Junkin Preston, wife of Confederate lieutenant colonel John T. L. Preston and sister-in-law of General Stonewall Jackson. Preston's "Dirge for Ashby" provides another example of the ways in which poets of the era drew inspiration from a distant, half mythical, past.

Throughout her poem, Preston lavishes praise on the fallen Ashby, but her points of reference seem oddly outdated. She describes Ashby as

> Bold as the Lion-heart,
> Dauntless and brave;
> Knightly as knightliest
> Bayard could crave . . .[22]

The men to whom Preston compares Ashby are heroes of bygone eras. King Richard the Lionheart lived in the twelfth century, and Seigneur de Bayard (a French soldier born as Pierre Terrail) was knighted in the late fifteenth century.[23] Nonetheless, Preston clearly assumed that the names of these warriors of the Middle Ages still held currency in nineteenth-century America. Preston also assumed that her readers would welcome her decidedly antiquated—not to say anachronistic—representation of a beloved Confederate general. Ashby was shot in the chest in an infantry engagement that took place more than a year into an unremitting, full-scale war in a still-rustic America. However, in Preston's verses he appears as a hero straight out of Europe in the Middle Ages.

Describing Ashby's death, Preston asks, "Did not our hero fall / Gallantly slain?" It is a strictly rhetorical question. Ashby is portrayed both by Preston and by Thompson as an ideal, if not an outright idolized, soldier. He epitomizes the very qualities most highly valued in a Civil War fighter. He is "bold" (a word used by both poets), "dauntless," and "knightly." Yet, according to Preston, he is also "sweet" and "tender." The news of his death, she claims, causes veterans to "sob 'mid the fight they win."[24]

These two poems about General Ashby reflect the extent to which writers of the Civil War era were enamored with the distant past. Southerners, in particular, revered the gallantry and heraldry associated with warriors who fought in the ages of old. To call a Confederate soldier a "bold dragoon," as Thompson called Ashby, was to pay the modern fighter a high compliment. It put him in league with the great European warriors of olden days. (Not until decades later would the barb-witted Ambrose Bierce, in his acerbic *Devil's Dictionary,* define a dragoon as, "a soldier who combines dash and steadiness in so equal measure that he makes his advances on foot and his retreats on horseback.")[25] The age of medieval knights and the feudal codes of chivalry had a powerful hold on the literary imagination of the generation of wartime writers, especially poets. Knightly credentials were the bona fides of manliness.

It is telling that in eulogizing Ashby neither Thompson nor Preston refers to any warrior of recent history. General Turner Ashby was the son of Colonel Turner Ashby, who fought in the War of 1812, and the grandson of Captain Jack Ashby, who fought in the Revolutionary War. Rather than compare Ashby to the accomplished military men from whom he was actually descended, Preston and Thompson create for Ashby an alternative lineage. They make Ashby into the figurative son of Richard the Lionheart, Bayard, and the knights of the Round Table. Preston and Thompson's emphasis on Ashby's "knightly" qualities and, of course, Ashby's nickname, "the Knight of the Confederacy," point to the literary inclination of the Civil War generation. And that literary inclination was very much influenced by the long-dead Sir Walter Scott. Yet there were dissenters who challenged the romanticized norm.

4

HERMAN MELVILLE:
"BATTLE NO MORE SHALL BE"

> Dismantle the fort,
> Cut down the fleet—
> Battle no more shall be!
>
> —Herman Melville,
> "The Conflict of Convictions," 1866

 espite tremendous resistance from readers, editors, and critics, some authors did stray from the accepted conventions in their depictions of the Civil War. Among the war's early chroniclers in the 1860s were writers, although few in number, who painted a more graphic and morally complex picture of the war than was typical. Not surprisingly, these writers found themselves out of step with the literary tastes of their era. Herman Melville, John William De Forest, and Walt Whitman all were unwilling to subscribe to a conventionally romantic view of the deadly contest. Yet they were uncertain about how to interpret—for themselves and for their potential readers—the conflict that engaged their torn nation.

Throughout the war years and in the years that followed, these three authors, all northerners, struggled to sort out their opinions and emotions about the deadly contest. To borrow a phrase from Herman Melville, they felt a "conflict of convictions."[1] Although they were all Unionists, they wavered in their stance on the war. They wanted to support the North but were unable to reconcile themselves to the brutality of the battlefield and the moral compromises involved in waging war. Consequently, they could neither fully reject nor fully embrace the popular literary norms of the war era.

In their texts, both published and unpublished, these three established writers revisited certain standard topics of war literature—battles, deaths, graves, nature—but did not turn out standard descriptions. Each of them, in his own way, challenged the lofty and sentimental vision of war that was so popular in the era of the Civil War. Yet each writer was reluctant to share publicly the full range of his views on the morality and the horror of the war.

Herman Melville was long past his writing prime by the time of the Civil War. Or so, at least, it was generally believed. When he published a volume of seventy-two war poems titled *Battle-Pieces and Aspects of the War* in the summer of 1866, the collection received scant praise. A reviewer for the prestigious *Atlantic Monthly* judged, "Mr. Melville's work possesses the negative virtues of originality in such degree that it not only reminds you of no poetry you have read, but of no life you have known."[2] Only slightly more generous was a reviewer who wrote for the *Ladies' Repository*—a women's monthly magazine devoted to literature, arts, and religion—who described Melville's volume as "another book of poems, war-inspired, not exhibiting a very high order of poetry, but interesting as detailing in measured form many of the stirring incidents and events of our country's great strife." By contrast, the assessment of a new Latin primer that appeared on the same page of the *Ladies' Repository* was far more positive. Describing *An Introductory Latin Book*—an elementary drill book on the inflections and principles of the language—the magazine's reviewer giddily enthused, "Beyond question, the many excellencies of this book will secure for it a very general acceptance."[3]

Herman Melville's volume of war poems failed to win "general acceptance" in the 1860s. The book was neither a popular nor critical success. But was it general acceptance that Melville was after? Herman Melville's Civil War poetry is best viewed against the backdrop of his failed literary career. With *Battle-Pieces*, Melville was at once courting the audience that had deserted him during the 1850s and challenging his critics to take his true measure and appreciate his genius. He was both conceding to popular dictates and boldly challenging the conventional representation of the Civil War.

In his volume of war poems, Melville offered support for the northern cause but moved far beyond the flowery romantic tropes favored during the war years. But he did not go quite as far as he might have. He invited popular recognition and risked it at the same time. He retreated from the strong antiwar stance that he had marked out for himself in the 1840s, but he retreated only so far.

The morality of war was a subject that had long occupied Melville's thoughts, and confronted by the Civil War, he found himself troubled by his own conflict of convictions and inhibited by the preferences of his readers.

Melville's literary route to the Civil War was one of steep descent. Melville's early works *Typee* and *Omoo*—exotic and exciting tales based on his exploits among the savages and sirens in Polynesia and the South Seas—had won for him immediate and immense success when they were published in the 1840s. These adventure tales had been followed in quick succession by other well-received novels—*Mardi, Redburn,* and *White-Jacket*—and for a number of years young Melville had ridden high on a wave of literary celebrity. But in the early 1850s, his boat began to sink. He spent fifteen months writing a mammoth work about an elusive whale.

No matter that *Moby-Dick* has been hailed by modern critics as a leading contender for the "great American novel," most readers in Melville's own day viewed the lengthy work as a prodigious flop. "*Moby-Dick* proved a very tiresome yarn indeed," wrote a critic for the *Southern Literary Messenger.* "The book before us is a new disappointment," reported *To-Day: A Boston Literary Journal.* Although some critics, such as a writer for *Bentley's Miscellany,* detected in the thick tome evidence of "the truest and most original genius," the publication of *Moby-Dick* in 1851 was a commercial and critical failure. It marked the beginning of Melville's precipitous fall from the heights of fame and fortune.[4]

Rather than returning to the literary formula that had spelled out success in his early career, Melville continued in the 1850s to experiment, which further alienated his readership. In 1852 he churned out a dark, metaphysical novel, *Pierre: or, The Ambiguities.* There were no ambiguities in the public response. Its sins in the eyes of Melville's mid-nineteenth-century readers were manifold. The *American Whig Review* bluntly denounced the work as "A bad book! Affected in dialect, unnatural in conception, repulsive in plot, and inartistic in construction." Other contemporary reviewers concurred. They not only faulted the novel but also questioned the sanity of the author. A review in the *Southern Quarterly Review* proclaimed, "That Herman Melville has gone 'clean daft,' is very much to be feared; certainly he has given us a very mad book. . . . The sooner this author is put in [a] ward the better." Readers objected both to the work's content and its style. As one twentieth-century critic explains, the novel was "almost universally scorned by contemporary reviewers for its stylistic eccentricities, its strained and digressive narrative, and its violation of genteel sexual taboos." In the words of Robert Penn Warren, it was "a work which seemed consciously designed in arrogant perversity to compound the failure of *Moby-Dick*."[5]

Pierre was followed in the 1850s by two more novels and a number of shorter works, but none recovered for Melville any measure of his early success. Indeed, his works seemed only to fulfill the harsh assessment of a writer for the *Democratic Review* who, after the publication of *Moby-Dick*, had pronounced, "The truth is, Mr. Melville has survived his reputation." As this critic judged, Melville had destroyed not only "his chances of immortality" but also his chance of "a good name with his own generation."[6]

Discouraged, Melville gave up on writing. Poor and desperate, he attempted to make a living on the lecture circuit. He toured various states holding forth on such subjects as "Statues in Rome," "The South Seas," and "Traveling: Its Pleasures, Pains, and Profits." Even so, it took the help of his illustrious father-in-law, Judge Lemuel Shaw, to keep the Melville family—Herman, his wife, Elizabeth, and their four children—financially afloat. At the time the Civil War began, Melville had not published anything since 1857.

From his farmhouse in the Berkshires and later from New York City, Melville monitored the war. He was not drafted. He did not volunteer. He was in his early forties but seemed older. His health, both physical and mental, was poor. In late 1862 he was thrown from a wagon by a skittish horse and seriously injured his shoulder and back. In addition, he suffered from chronic sciatica and acute attacks of neuralgia. As for his psychological state, there were hushed rumors in his wife's family that he had come unhinged.[7]

In April of 1864 Herman Melville made his sole trip to the battlefront. With the help of Senator Charles Sumner of Massachusetts, he received a pass to travel to Virginia and visit his cousin Henry Gansevoort, who was then serving as a lieutenant colonel and commander of the Thirteenth New York Volunteer Cavalry. During his stay of less than a week, Melville toured assorted battlefields and went on a scouting expedition led by Colonel Charles Russell Lowell (who would be killed before the year was out). The three-day long "scout," in which five hundred men of the infantry and cavalry participated, was not successful in its effort to capture the Confederate renegade John Singleton Mosby and his rangers, but it gave Melville a taste of army life. He ate cold rations, took part in a charge (albeit a thoroughly uneventful one), and passed two near sleepless nights on the hard and unwelcoming ground.[8]

Melville's brief visit to Vienna, Virginia, and its environs—not long before the Battle of the Wilderness, the Battle of Spotsylvania, and the Battle of Cold Harbor—constituted the extent of his firsthand experience of the fighting arena of the Civil War. Whatever else he knew of battles, generals, prisons, and forts, he garnered from newspaper and magazine accounts, compilations such as the *Rebellion Record* (a multivolume compendium of maps, articles, and other materials that began to be published early in the war), and the tales of returning soldiers. Other details that would appear in his poetry were supplied by his own imagination. And his imagination was vivid.

In his mind's eye, Melville had long pondered the spectacle of war. Years before his trip to Virginia, years before the Confederates ever took aim at Fort Sumter, Melville had formulated his views on the morality of warfare. Although he was not a sworn pacifist, he held very strong antiwar convictions, and in his early novels he had unambiguously denounced war as barbaric. Often employing bitter irony to hammer home his point, he had addressed the mechanics, ethics, and butchery of battle.

In the works that won him fame in the 1840s—two novels based on his experiences among the cannibals and heathen beauties of the South Seas —Melville repeatedly presents war as inglorious and evil. In the very first of these adventure novels, *Typee*—the publication of which, in 1846, coincided with the start of the Mexican War—Melville forthrightly states, "The fiend-like skill we display in the invention of all manner of death-dealing engines, the vindictiveness with which we carry on our wars, and the misery and desolation that follow in their train, are enough of themselves to distinguish the white civilized man as the most ferocious animal on the face of the earth."[9] With clear conviction, Melville asserts that war is a stain on all of humanity. The fact that "white civilized man" uses his superior cunning to perfect deadly engines of destruction is proof of man's innate barbarism. Civilized man, according to Melville, is more bestial than the beasts. It is, Melville senses, a vast cosmic joke. But it was a cruel joke that in 1846 gained an undeniable immediacy. Commenting on the Mexican War in late May of that year, Melville was warily dismissive. "People here are all in a state of delirium about the Mexican War. A military ardor pervades all ranks. . . . Nothing is talked of but the 'Halls of the Montezumas.'" The war, he worried, would lead to a larger conflagration, a conflict with England or another great power.[10]

In *Mardi*, published in 1849, Melville returns to the subject of war. In the allegorical romance he both parodies idealized tales of battle and comments, if obliquely, on the recently concluded Mexican War.[11] He imagines a fantastical place called Diranda, the bellicose isle, where battles follow the whims of two maniacal kings. On this unenchanted island, Melville explains, there is no lofty cause for which warriors fight. Instead, men slaughter and are slaughtered for sport and, conveniently, to keep overpopulation in check. Openly ridiculing those who romanticize battle, Melville writes:

> 'Tis glory that calls
> To each hero that falls,
> Hack away, merry men, hack away![12]

Lofty language, Melville contends, has no place in warfare. To write of glory and fallen heroes is misleading. When stripped of grand and false embellishments, war is revealed as plain murder.

Melville's disgust with war romantics is unmistakable. Whereas Sir Walter Scott and his legions of admirers lionized the legendary outlaw Robin Hood and his Merry Men, the "merry men" that Melville depicts are contemptible. They do not champion the cause of the poor. They do not help the oppressed. They are nothing but ignoble and ignorant hackers. Repeatedly in the pages of *Mardi*, Melville uses irony to convey his contempt for the high-flown vocabulary typically used to describe war. He openly ridicules, for example, the notion that battlefields are "hallowed grounds" that have been made sacred by "glorious sacrifice." Describing the valley where the war games of Diranda are played, he writes, "Beneath the heaped turf of this down, lay thousands of glorious corpses of anonymous heroes, who here had died glorious deaths. Whence, in the florid language of Diranda, they called this field 'The Field of Glory.'" Melville masterfully turns the language of chivalry, "the florid language of Diranda," against itself. The fighters are not valorous, and the turf they meet on is not mystically sacrosanct. The "Field of Glory," under which the supposed heroes of Diranda lie, is really a field of disgrace.[13]

However, Melville was not optimist enough to think that war could be brought to a permanent halt. His perception of human nature led him to believe otherwise. And he pointed, implicitly, to the Mexican War as providing supporting evidence. Writing in *Mardi* he asserts, "There are many, who erewhile believed that the age of pikes and javelins was passed. . . . But it has not so proved. Mardi's peaces are but truces. Long absent, at last the red comets have returned. And return they must, though their periods be ages. And should Mardi endure till mountain melt into mountain, and all the isles form one table-land; yet, would it but expand the old battle-plain."[14] Fighting would remain, Melville believed, for all eternity. Peace would be only an interregnum of war.

In both *Typee* and *Mardi* Melville freely vented his contempt for those who glamorize war, and in his novel *White-Jacket* he extended his critique of militarism and warfare. After he had jumped ship in the South Pacific from a whaling voyage in the early 1840s and sampled Polynesian life, Melville served for fourteen months aboard the man-of-war *United States. White-Jacket,* published in 1850, draws on Melville's experiences on the warship and can be read as a full-length attack on war. As one scholar considering the subject of pacifism in Melville's novels observes, "*White-Jacket's* indictment of war and accompanying evils is strong and sustained, and at times Melville's passion for peace reaches an apocalyptic intensity."[15] Forgoing irony, Melville writes in a style both angry and direct. War, he contends, is dehumanizing. It robs men of their autonomy. They lose control over their lives and their deaths. "There is little or no skill and bravery about it. Two parties, armed with lead and old iron, envelop themselves in a cloud of smoke, and pitch their lead and old iron about in all directions. If you happen to be in the way, you are hit; possibly, killed; if not, you escape." A soldier's or sailor's chance at survival, Melville asserts, also depends to a large extent on the character of the officer in charge. And Melville paints military commanders in an extremely unflattering light.[16]

In particular, Melville rails against vainglorious officers who seek promotions at the cost of the lives of the men they command. He fumes, "If some brainless bravo be captain of a frigate in action, he may fight her against invincible odds, and seek to crown himself with the glory of the shambles, by permitting his hopeless crew to be butchered before his eyes." In such a situation, the unlucky crew members "must consent to be slaughtered by the foe." If they attempt to rebel, they will face a court-martial and be "murdered by the law." For the sailors it is a no-win situation.[17]

Melville's depictions of battle in *White-Jacket* are notably graphic and horrific. In one passage an old sailor named Tawney recalls what it was like to be on a boat called the *Macedonian* when it was under attack. With sickening detail he describes the boat's "slaughter-house," the section of the ship at which the enemy directed its shot in an attempt to topple the mast:

> Here the men fell, five and six at a time. . . . The beams and carlines over-head in the Macedonian *slaughter-house* were spattered with blood and brains. About the hatchways it looked like a butcher's stall; bits of human flesh sticking in the ring-bolts. A pig that ran about the decks escaped unharmed, but his hide was so clotted with blood, from rooting among the pools of gore, that when the ship struck the sailors hove the ani-mal overboard, swearing that it would be rank cannibalism to eat him.[18]

It is hard to find a passage from the mid-nineteenth century that is less in keeping with the era's highly sanitized literary norms.

One of the closest matches from the period appears in a work about the Mexican War written by H. Judge Moore, who had served in the Palmetto Regiment under General Winfield Scott. In his war memoir, *Scott's Campaign in Mexico* (1849), the former soldier describes with disturbing explic-itness the "horrors of war" that were on display at Cerro Gordo three days after the battle there had ended. Moore recalls the "putrid carcasses of men torn and mangled by cannon balls, and left, half devoured by the beasts and birds of prey." But Moore's is no antiwar work.[19]

Although Moore ventured to give an unusual degree of descriptive detail about the mauled and massed battle-dead, he shared none of Melville's cyn-icism. On the same page on which he notes the presence of hungry vultures "hovering near, and perching upon every tree and shrub, ready to whet their barbarous beaks upon the bones of the gallant dead," Moore writes, in all apparent sincerity, of "the pomp and pride of glorious war," "distinguished gallantry," and "daring and brilliant exploits." And on the following page, Moore hails the battle of Cerro Gordo as a "decisive and brilliant victory." At least for Moore, the "horrors of war" did not negate war's glory.[20]

Melville's horrific description of the "slaughter-house" in *White-Jacket* shares more in common with antiwar writing published in the late nine-teenth and twentieth centuries than with war writing of his own day. In-deed, in a famous French novel about the First World War there is a scene that parallels the one of butchery that Melville describes. In *Under Fire* (1917), written by Henri Barbusse, an underground first aid station is bom-barded and wounded soldiers are "blown to bits." Their "pendant entrails [are] twisted among the beams of the shattered woodwork." When a Red

Cross sergeant tries to disentangle the "strips of viscera and rags of flesh," he looks like "a butcher at some fiendish task."[21]

Yet even *Under Fire* did not include the added horror, found in *White-Jacket*, of a flesh-devouring pig. Much later in the twentieth century, the Vietnam War veteran Philip Caputo would record in *A Rumor of War* his memory of watching "pigs rooting around forms which resemble black logs, but which are charred corpses." And as early as 1889, Ambrose Bierce would include in his story "The Coup de Grâce" a scene in which a herd of swine with "crimson muzzles" commits "monstrous mutilations" on injured, but still living, soldiers.[22]

Melville, writing long before the Civil War began, sought to demystify and demythologize war. He stripped it of its fancy language and fancy imagery. War, Melville let it be known, is anything but pretty. Far from painting images of majestic battle and daring heroes, he used his early novels to present men who are the playthings of tyrannical and egotistical warmakers. Powerless to determine their own fates, these sailors and soldiers must bow helplessly to the will of their superiors. Nearly three hundred pages into *White-Jacket*, Melville offers a clear summation of his views on martial matters: "But as the whole matter of war is a thing that smites common sense and Christianity in the face; so everything connected with it is utterly foolish, unchristian, barbarous, brutal, and savoring of the Feejee islands, cannibalism, saltpetre, and the devil."[23] In his early condemnation of war, Melville appears absolute. So too he dismisses with disgust the very sort of romantic war writing that would flood the literary marketplace during and after the Civil War.

But how did Melville, the outspoken war critic of the 1840s and 1850s, react to the major war of his lifetime? Was he as scathing in describing the Civil War as when he was deriding the wars on the fantastical island of Diranda?

Despite his published denunciation of "the whole matter of war," Melville did not condemn the Civil War. Indeed, he did not publicly oppose the Civil War at all. Melville despised war in the abstract, yet he believed that the Civil War, from the Union perspective, was a just war. The author of *White-Jacket* and *Mardi*, who had pledged his hatred of all wars, made an exception in his formulation for what he called "The War for the Maintenance of the Union."[24] In *Battle-Pieces and Aspects of the War*, his volume of poetry published less than a year and half after Lee's surrender at Appomattox, Melville offered the clearest articulation of his rationale. The South, according to Melville's reckoning, was deeply at fault. And as the poems make clear, he held the Confederates, "zealots of the Wrong," guilty for the bloodbath of the war.[25]

For Melville, the Civil War was about big concepts worthy of capitalization: Right and Wrong, the Cause and Treason. In "Inscription for Graves at Pea Ridge, Arkansas" Melville contends that the Union soldiers fought for "the Cause / Hallowed by hearts and by the laws." They "warred for Man and Right." Although he found individual Confederate soldiers and officers worthy of praise, Melville believed that the Union cause was morally, legally, even divinely sanctioned. As he explained in this poem dedicated to the memory of fallen Union soldiers, "The choice of warring never laid with us. / There we were ruled by the traitor's choice."[26]

In *Mardi* Melville had presented the battle games on Diranda as pointless exercises in bloodlust, but the battles of the Civil War were imbued by Melville with much more complex meaning. He strongly believed in the Union, and he pleaded with God, "In this strife of brothers . . . / Let not the just one fall."[27] Melville even went so far as to suggest that the North's victory would bring about the triumph of heaven over hell. Using one of the most original—and surely one of the oddest—invectives to be penned during the entire war, Melville referred to the southern enemy as "the helmed dilated Lucifer."[28]

In Melville's interpretation, the Civil War was not just a contest being waged between mortal armies for political and material aims. It was part of the age-old cosmic struggle between the forces of good and evil, "the war of Wrong and Right."[29] Celebrating the war's conclusion and the Union's triumph in a poem titled "The Fall of Richmond," he wrote, "God is in Heaven, and [General] Grant in the Town, / And Right through might is Law."[30]

Nevertheless, Melville was greatly troubled by the war. Despite his repeated claims that the North was engaged in a "fight for the Right" and that the Confederate forces were in league with the devil, Melville could not wholeheartedly endorse the war.[31] Although he acknowledged the weighty issues at stake, Melville still believed that the Civil War, at a certain level, was profoundly immoral. His state of inner turbulence registers clearly in the titles of the three poems he placed at the start of the *Battle-Pieces* collection: "Misgivings," "The Conflict of Convictions," and "Apathy and Enthusiasm." And in the postwar poem that ends the collection, "A Meditation," Melville refers to the war as "the sanctioned sin of blood."[32]

According to Melville's moral reckoning, the Civil War was, at once, a sacred and a sinful undertaking. The war had been won, but its cost had been terribly, perhaps too terribly, high. Slavery had been ended and the nation reunited, but at what price? In "A Meditation" Melville rhetorically asks, "Can Africa pay back this blood / Spilt on Potomac's shore?"[33] There could be no adequate recompense for the lost years or the lost lives. America's sin of slavery had been redressed by the sanctioned sin of war.

Throughout the Civil War and in the months and years that followed, Melville struggled to reconcile his faith in the Union with his abhorrence of war. His poetry of the mid-1860s is the literary record of that struggle. In *Battle-Pieces* Melville distances himself from his youthful critique of the wickedness of war. He offers no broad condemnation of warfare. He offers no verse as graphic or disturbing as his description of the "slaughter-house" in *White-Jacket*. Yet Melville's war poetry little resembles the popular war poetry of the Civil War.

The history of one particular poem demonstrates Melville's ambivalence. Most of his Civil War poems were written after the northern victory. As he explained in a brief preface to *Battle-Pieces*, "With few exceptions, the Pieces in this volume originated in an impulse imparted by the fall of Richmond [in April 1865]."[34] However, the earliest of his published war poems, "Inscription for the Slain at Fredericksburgh," appeared during the war, and the events leading up to its publication offer a fascinating glimpse of Melville self-editing his writing.

Early in 1864 Melville was among various northern writers solicited to contribute works for a planned volume, *Autograph Leaves of Our Country's Authors*, that was to be published to benefit the Northern Sanitary Commission. Obligingly, Melville sent in a poem, but he soon regretted his action. As he explained in a letter to the volume's compiler, "In the hurry of despatching my Contribution the other day, I now find that I enclosed to you an uncorrected draught—in fact, the *wrong sheet*." In his letter, Melville included a new "*right*" version of the poem and requested that it be published instead of the draft he had sent earlier. "Or, if that be too late," he wrote, "may I beg of you, by all means, to *suppress* the one you have."[35]

Whether Melville actually had sent a rough draft in error or simply had second thoughts about his poem and invented an excuse to submit a revised version, he clearly was worried. If the poem could not be published in its *"right"* form, then he preferred that it not be published at all. Yet the changes between the "uncorrected draught" and the second version involve only a couple of words and a few details of punctuation. Why did Melville attach such importance to these changes?

The brief poem pays tribute to the soldiers who were killed during the Battle of Fredericksburg in December 1862. Only six lines long, the work is compact and stands as a single stanza. It reads in its *"right"* version:

Inscription for the Dead at Fredericksburgh

A dreadful glory lights an earnest end;
In jubilee the patriot ghosts ascend;
Transfigured at the rapturous height
 Of their passionate feat of arms,
Death to the brave's a starry night,—
 Strewn their vale of death with palms.

Despite its brevity, though, the poem conveys a great deal about Melville's outlook on the war. There is a sumptuous, mournful beauty to the lines. Melville pays homage to the dead with rich imagery. In both versions, the soldiers die "at the rapturous height / Of their passionate feat of arms." In both versions, their "patriot ghosts" ascend to heaven. Envisioning death as if it were a long slumber, Melville writes, in both versions, "Death to the brave's a starry night."[36]

The alterations that Melville made to this graciously elegiac poem are slight but revealing. Apart from changes in punctuation, two small differences distinguish the drafts. The first of these variations appears in the title. The "uncorrected" version of the poem bears the title, "Inscription for the Slain at Fredericksburgh." In the version that Melville resubmitted, the word "Slain" is replaced with "Dead." This word substitution is interesting. It ever so subtly changes the poem's tone and meaning. "Slain" is borrowed from the flowery lexicon of popular Civil War writers. It belongs to the language of chivalry along with "heroism," "gallantry," and "bravery." It also depends for its meaning on an enemy. In order for a soldier to be slain, there must be a slayer. "Dead," by contrast, is stark and factual. What prompted Melville to change "slain" soldiers into "dead" soldiers? It is tempting to try to imagine Melville as he sat hunched over his work, his poor eyes troubling him, and replaced one word with the other. Why did he finally opt for the undisguised starkness of "dead" over the positive associations of "slain"? Why did he choose cold fact over poetic euphemism?[37]

The second notable alteration Melville made to his poem is deceptively simple. He added a single word. The change appears in the work's first line. "A glory lights an earnest end" reads the "uncorrected" draft of the work. In the poem's revised version, the line becomes, "A dreadful glory lights an earnest end." Melville's insertion of "dreadful" to modify "glory," like the substitution in the poem's title of "dead" for "slain," subtly alters and challenges the otherwise reverential tone of the work. In the vocabulary of popular Civil War writers, glory ranks with honor and valor among the loftiest and noblest concepts of war. The word seems to have stuck in Melville's craw.[38]

The man who had written mockingly of "the florid language of Diranda," the man who had ridiculed the notion that a field of battle could be called a "Field of Glory," could not bring himself to assert that the deeds of the Civil War soldiers were purely glorious. A "dreadful glory"—like the "sanctioned sin" in the poem "A Meditation"—hints of Melville's own conflicted convictions. When it came to writing about the Civil War, he was driven to make use of oxymorons. His matching of mismatched words—his pairing of glory and dread, of sin and sanction—point to his own difficulty in interpreting the war's moral meaning.

The two versions of the poem show Melville caught in the act of editing his work. More precisely, these drafts reveal the writer caught in the process of editing his reaction to the war. With his small revisions, Melville struggled to balance two different literary modes of understanding and representing the soldiers' battlefield deaths. He weighed the glossy vocabulary of romanticism against the starker vocabulary of nascent realism. And in the end he compromised. The final and "correct" version of the poem retains some lofty language —"patriot ghosts," "rapturous height," "feats of arms," and a reference to the "brave"—but the word "glory" has been modified by the word "dreadful" and the "slain" soldiers have become simply "dead."

As the history behind the poem's publication makes clear, Melville attached great importance to using exactly the right words to express his views on the subject of war. Over time, though, his choice of words shifted away from the bold denunciations found in his early novels.

During the war years, Melville did his best to control which of his writings would meet the public's eye and which would not. When he contemplated the possibility that the wrong draft of the poem might appear in print, he felt a level of anxiety verging on panic and begged the compiler of the Civil War collection to use "all means" to "suppress" the "uncorrected" draft. Through other means, Melville ensured that certain of his works would never make it into print. Midway through the Civil War, Melville made a bonfire in which he burnt stacks of his manuscripts. The event is recorded in a poem he titled "Immolated."[39] Much of the poetry and prose that Melville fed to the flames likely belonged to his younger years, what he referred to as his "Tempe prime," but it is possible that Melville also burned some of his earliest attempts at writing about the Civil War.[40]

Whatever the pages that Melville fed to the flames, "Immolated" makes clear that during the war years Melville intentionally destroyed some of his own works. In the 1850s he had experienced the pain of having his books spurned by readers and critics, and with the bonfire he guaranteed that other writings of his would not be seen by unsympathetic eyes. Apologizing to his burnt texts in "Immolated," Melville implores, "Ah, spare / Reproach; spare, and upbraid me not." By feeding the works to the flames, he insists, he has saved them from the worse fate of being ignored or misunderstood by the "insincere / Elect of Mediocrity."[41]

Nonetheless, Melville was eager, after the Civil War ended, to have more of his war poetry published. Despite his wariness of unappreciative readers and his derisive claims that insincerity and mediocrity reigned in the literary marketplace, he proactively worked to have his war poems set in print. As Leon Howard records in his biography of Melville, in late 1865 the author approached his publishers, Harper and Brothers, with the proposition that they produce a collection of his war poetry, and he "received the suggestion that a few of the poems be tried on the public through the columns of *Harper's New Monthly Magazine*." Between January and July 1866, several of Melville's poems appeared in the magazine, but as if in quiet acknowledgment of the fact that Melville's name no longer could be counted on to impress readers, the poems were published anonymously.[42]

If the inclusion of these poems in the magazine was intended to measure public reaction to Melville's poetry, the venture was both successful and misguided. The readers of *Harper's* were not provided with a very representative sampling of what *Battle-Pieces and Aspects of the War*, which Melville completed during the spring of 1866, held in store. As Robert Penn Warren wryly observes, "It is probably a compliment to the editorial astuteness of the publishers (or of Melville) that these poems [included in *Harper's*] . . . have not the slightest hint of the qualities that make *Battle-Pieces* memorable; these pieces are, without exception, 'official' celebrations of Federal victories, with no undertone or overtone of irony of any sort, and without any embarrassing suggestion of poetic talent."[43] The poems that appeared in *Harper's New Monthly Magazine* were gauged to suit popular taste. The poems in the final collection were not. Although celebrations of victories and words of praise for outstanding soldiers and generals appear in *Battle-Pieces*, they are accompanied by poems that are strikingly unconventional.

Particularly notable among the poems that appeared in *Battle-Pieces*, but not in *Harper's*, is a long work titled "The Armies of the Wilderness." In it, Melville describes the wooded landscape of Virginia, where the contending armies fought repeatedly between 1862 and 1864. He guides his readers along a "path down the mountain" that leads to a glade where some of the dead are buried. But the graves are too shallow. In conventional Civil War poetry, dead soldiers lie safely buried beneath the soil as bees and birds frolic above them. Not so in Melville's depiction of this late battle site. Melville writes, "A hand reaches out of the thin-laid mould / As begging help which none can bestow."[44] The partially revealed corpse, the hand reaching out from the too shallow grave, has far more in common with Edgar Allan Poe's tales of gothic horror than with popular Civil War verse.

Elsewhere in "The Armies of the Wilderness," Melville presents even more disturbing depictions of death and decay. In one of the poem's most macabre sections, Union soldiers return to the Wilderness in the spring of 1864 and encounter the remains of men who died the previous year.

> In glades they meet skull after skull
>   Where pine-cones lay—the rusted gun,
> Green shoes full of bones, the mouldering coat
>   And cuddled-up skeleton;
> And scores of such.[45]

Rotted corpses, scores of them, are on full display. These dead soldiers have not been buried, not even in shallow graves. In *Battle-Pieces* Melville boldly ventures to address topics that other Civil War writers of his day studiously avoided.

In "The Armies of the Wilderness" and elsewhere, Melville refuses to allow his readers the easy comfort of imagining soldiers snugly entombed. He refuses to subscribe to the standard literary conventions of the war. He refuses to disguise war's horror. In a poem titled "Donelson," Melville describes "ice-glazed corpses, each a stone."[46] Not until the British World War I poet Wilfred Owen drafted the poem "Exposure"—containing the lines, "The burying party, picks and shovels in their shaking grasp, / Pause over half-known faces. All their eyes are ice"—would there appear an equally evocative image of soldiers frozen in death.[47]

The way in which Melville presents nature in his war poetry further proves him an iconoclast. In Civil War poems, nature typically figures as an empathetic and merciful witness to man's strife. Not so in Melville's war poetry. A lofty work titled "Dirge, For One Who Fell in Battle" serves as a good example of the popular norm. The poem was written by the northern poet Thomas William Parsons to commemorate the death of a socially prominent New Englander, Theodore Winthrop, who had died in the Battle of Big Bethel in June of 1861.[48] The work describes the ideal burying place for a soldier who has fallen in battle. The second of the five stanzas reads:

> Bear him to no dismal tomb under city churches;
> Take him to the fragrant fields, by the silver birches,
> Where the whip-poor-will shall mourn, where the oriole perches:
>   Make his mound with sunshine on it,
>   Where the bee will dine upon it,
>   Where the lamb hath lain upon it,
>   And the rain will rain upon it.[49]

Resting in a field of clover, the slain soldier will be kept company by birds and bees, lambs and trees. With his grave pillowed over with rosemary and ferns, he will find eternal tranquility. All of nature will be his solace. Sun, moon, and rain will make amends for a life violently cut short. In "Dirge" nature serves as the dead soldier's compassionate helper. But according to Melville, "Nature is nobody's ally."[50]

Most Civil War poetry describes nature as being in sympathy with man. Melville denied his readers this pleasant poetic and pathetic fallacy. In his poem "Malvern Hill" Melville imagines himself paying a springtime visit to the famous hill in Virginia that the Union had successfully defended at the end of the Seven Days' Battles in July 1862. He asks the trees on Malvern Hill if they remember the deadly battle. "Does the elm wood / Recall the haggard beards of blood? . . . Does Malvern Wood / Bethink itself, and muse and brood?" The elms reply that they remember everything but have no time to brood or mourn for the dead. "Sap the twig will fill: / Wag the world how it will, / Leaves must be green in Spring."[51] In Melville's poem, the towering elms on Malvern Hill, radiating vitality, stand as a rebuke to the war generation that destroyed life so recklessly. On Malvern Hill, spring brings rebirth to all living things. Sap rises. But the blood is forever drained from the Civil War dead. Nature is engaged in an endless and irresistible cycle of seasons. It is only man, Melville hints, who is full of enough fury and folly to defy the natural order of things.

In Melville's war poetry, nature pushes onward and does its best to conceal the wreckage of the war. Even the smallest inhabitants of the forest seem embarrassed by the wrath and destruction that the Civil War visited on their tranquil home. "The field-mouse small and busy ant / Heap their hillocks, to hide if they may the woe."[52] Defying the norms of Civil War poetry, Melville presents nature as self-absorbed, judgmental, intolerant, and even deadly.

"The Armies of the Wilderness" not only describes the decomposition of the unburied dead but also alludes to an even more disturbing reality of the Civil War. Heavily wooded battlefields sometimes caught fire, and when they did, corpses caught flame and soldiers who were trapped or injured were burned alive. In the lines of "The Armies of the Wilderness," Melville describes the wooded terrain where Rebel met Yank as, "Tramped like the cindery beach of the damned— / A site for the city of Cain." More pointedly, he notes that a "Pillar of Smoke" rose "ashy and red" from the battlefield, "brand-like with ghosts." And at the end of the poem, Melville concedes, "None can narrate that strife in the pines." His own "entangled rhyme," he acknowledges, "but hints at the maze of war." The "fires which creep and char" are a "riddle of death, of which the slain / Sole solvers are."[53]

Melville resisted the popular inclination to use poetry to disguise and prettify the harsh realities of war, and his graphic descriptions can be read as a studied response to the works of the popular poets of the era who offered florid verses filled with reassuring imagery. In a poem titled "In the Wilderness," for example, the northern poet George Henry Boker describes a "poor boy" wounded during the Battle of the Wilderness:

> But when the light came, and the morning dew
>   Glittered around him, like a golden lake,
> And every dripping flower with deepened hue
>   Looked through its tears for very pity's sake,
>   He moved his aching head
>   Upon his rugged bed,
> And smiled as a blue violet, virgin-meek,
> Laid her pure kiss upon his withered cheek.[54]

Melville, by contrast, presents nature and the elements inflicting additional suffering on soldiers. Describing the same Battle of the Wilderness, he offers images of the unburied dead and of soldiers burned alive. Melville explains in the lines of his poem:

> The fight for the city is fought
>   In Nature's old domain;
> Man goes out to the wilds,
>   And Orpheus' charm is vain.[55]

Orpheus, of Greek mythology, was a magical poet who could charm beasts and even rocks and trees. Yet not even powerful Orpheus, Melville claims, is a match for the devastating destruction wrought by war in "Nature's old domain."

Melville wrote about men caught in flames; he wrote about men frozen to death ("Our heedless boys / Were nipped like blossoms. Some dozen / Hapless wounded men were frozen"); he wrote about men left unburied.[56] However, even Melville did not stray beyond certain bounds. Apparently, there were certain topics that he consciously left off the page. In a footnote to a poem about the deadly draft riots that took place in New York City during the summer of 1863, Melville quotes an ancient French historian: "I dare not write the horrible and inconceivable atrocities committed."[57] Even Melville did not "dare" tell all.

As his poetry makes clear, for Melville the Civil War did not admit of easy answers. *Battle-Pieces* reflects Melville's complicated and often unconventional outlook on the war. The title of the poem "The Conflict of Convictions" well captures his state of inner turmoil as he struggled to reconcile his long-held condemnation of war with his support for the Union's "fight for the Right." His war poems were written, as Melville explains in a prefatory note to his volume of poetry, in "moods variable, and at times widely at variance."[58] Revealingly, he concludes "The Conflict of Convictions" with the following lines:

> Yea and Nay—
> Each hath his say;
> But God He keeps the middle way.
> None was by
> When He spread the sky;
> Wisdom is vain, and prophesy.[59]

There can be no definite answer to the grand moral question posed by the war: Yea or Nay? Although Melville employed the language of Right and Wrong, when faced with the complexity of the war—when trying to reconcile his pacifism with his belief in the North's cause—he can only feel "misgivings" and conclude, "Wisdom is vain."

But if Melville found it difficult to make up his mind about the Civil War, critics had a much easier time making up their minds about Melville's representation of the war. Perhaps, if *Battle-Pieces* had contained only celebrations of Union victories, such as the poems that first appeared in *Harper's*, it would have fared better. As it was, reviewers were put off both by Melville's treatment of his subject matter and by the unorthodox form of his poetry. Melville expressed unconventional sentiments, and he expressed them unconventionally. His war poems have unusual rhymes and rhythms. They include invented words—"steepy banks," "emulous hearts," "palely eye." They reflect Melville's eclectic vocabulary—"nathless," "glaive," "targed."[60] These qualities combine to give the poems collected in *Battle-Pieces* a heterodox ring.

Melville did not pander to popular taste, and among casual readers and literary critics, his volume found little appreciation or understanding. An unsigned article, "More Poetry of the War," published in the *Nation* in September 1866 was notably unflattering.

> Unless the poet is as great as his theme, he must submit to be crushed by it. . . . It is impossible, in view of what Mr. Melville has done and of his intention in his present book, not to read his "Battle Pieces" with a certain melancholy. Nature did not make him a poet. . . . [We] cannot refrain from expressing surprise that a man of Mr. Melville's literary experience and cultivation should have mistaken some of these compositions for poetry, or even for verse.[61]

Equally disparaging was a brief review of the work that ran in the *Massachusetts Teacher*, "Could not some kind friend have persuaded the clever author of Omoo and Typee, that nature never meant him for a poet, and thus saved the waste of so much good paper? The book is sad rubbish."[62] Even members of Melville's own family were less than flattering about his poetry. His cousin Catherine Gansevoort confessed in a letter to her brother, "I must say I cannot get interested in his style of Poetry. It is too deep for my comprehension."[63]

Melville's longtime publishers, Harper and Brothers, seem to have anticipated that the unusual book of war poetry would not reap great profits for their coffers. A promotional note in the *New York Herald*'s column "The Book World"—published on August 12, 1866, before *Battle-Pieces* had even reached the shelves of booksellers—reads, "Harper & Bros. announce 'Fetridge's Guide Book of European Travel,' 5th year; 'The Hidden Sin,' a novel; 'Bound to the Wheel,' a novel, by John Saunders; 'Battle Pieces and Aspects of the War,' by Herman Melville (for ten years the public has wondered what has become of Melville)."[64] Apparently, Melville's own publishers did not see fit to give *Battle-Pieces* top billing. Nor did they seem to have high hopes that the author, who had all but vanished into obscurity during the previous decade, would redeem himself in the eyes of his critics with an odd volume of war poems.

The dismal failure of *Battle-Pieces*, which sold in the vicinity of five hundred copies in its day, surprised only Melville.[65] He had dared to express both his beliefs and his doubts about the war and had hoped that he would find a receptive audience. As Daniel Aaron concludes in *The Unwritten War*, "Melville defied consensus and took one further step toward popular oblivion."[66]

Four months after the publication of *Battle-Pieces*, Melville gave up on a career as a professional writer and obtained a steady position in New York City as a customs inspector. It was a job that he would hold—working six days a week for fifty weeks a year—until his retirement nearly two decades later. As he began the routine work of a customs inspector, well might he have regretted that he had not lit a bonfire with the "draught" versions of the poems of *Battle-Pieces*. Instead, the poems felt the scorch of public criticism.

5

JOHN WILLIAM DE FOREST:
"THE WHOLE TRUTH ABOUT WAR AND BATTLE"

Two funerals yesterday, and as many today, but none of them mine.
—John William De Forest, Letter to His Wife, 1863

n an article for *Harper's New Monthly Magazine,* Captain John William De Forest described the period in 1863 during which he had helped lay siege to Port Hudson, Louisiana, as "forty days and nights in the wilderness of death." During the interval between the original assault in late May and the eventual Union victory in early July, De Forest explained, danger was "perpetually present." The northerners were shot at from afar by "invisible" marksmen, and "hardly a day passed that [he] did not hear the loud exclamations of the wounded, or see corpses borne to the rear."[1] It was also a time of dreadful physical discomfort and monotony. Some officers took to sharpshooting. The soldiers played cards. Neither pastime appealed to De Forest. With pointed wit, De Forest explained, "I could never bring myself to what seemed like taking human life in pure gayety, and I had not as yet learned to play euchre."[2]

While Melville watched the Civil War from afar, John William De Forest viewed the war at close range. Far removed from the battlefields, Melville depended on newspapers and other sources for battle news. When composing his war poetry, he relied on the *Rebellion Record.* When De Forest wrote about the conflict—in letters, essays, and a novel—he had no need for reference books. He had ample firsthand experience upon which to draw.

De Forest was a military officer who dutifully served through the tedium and the terror of the Civil War. On January 1, 1862, he was officially commissioned as a captain in Company I of the Twelfth Connecticut Volunteers. Years later he would tally his service in the military as follows, "Counting service in war and in peace, I was six and a half years under the colors. I was in three storming parties, six days of field engagement, and thirty-seven days of siege duty, making forty-six days under fire." And he took lasting pride in the role he had played in defeating the Confederacy. Decades after the war's conclusion, he wrote, "My chief regret . . . is that I could not take part in one of the greater battles, such as Gettysburg or Chickamauga. I am not only glad, but I am sincerely thankful that I did not miss Port Hudson and the final victories in the Shenandoah Valley."[3]

That John William De Forest joined the Union army at all was rather remarkable. Few would have thought the middle-aged writer had the makings of a military man. He seemed too physically unfit for military life. He had been a sickly teenager and as an adult suffered from chronic bronchitis, which he referred to as a "monotonous invalidism."[4] On the basis of his unsound constitution, he could have been exempted from military service entirely. But he volunteered to fight and was commissioned as an officer.

De Forest went into the army and remained in the army of his own volition. When his term of enlistment ended and he had the option of retiring from military service in December 1864, he took a couple of months off to recuperate, from ailments probably caused by dysentery, then reenlisted for three more years. In January 1865 he was pronounced "unfit for active field duty" but "fit for garrison duty," and in February he was commissioned as a captain in the Veteran Reserve Corps.[5]

De Forest brought to the war the practiced literary skills of a self-styled historian, travel writer, and novelist. At the start of the war, he was thirty-five years old, married, and already published, if not especially famous. Throughout the 1850s he had worked to build his literary credentials. He first composed a scholarly tome, *History of the Indians of Connecticut from the Earliest Known Period to 1850*. Next, drawing on his experiences during several years that he had spent living abroad, he wrote two travelogues, *Oriental Acquaintance* and *European Acquaintance*. Also, in the late 1850s, he completed two novels: *Witching Times*, a work about the Salem witchcraft trials, and *Seacliff; or, the Mystery of the Westervelts*, a convoluted melodrama. None of these works attracted much attention from the reading masses, yet taken together De Forest's efforts at historical, travel, and fiction writing served well to prepare him for the literary challenge of recording the Civil War. Moreover, following his marriage in 1856 to Harriet Silliman Shepard, De Forest had divided his time between New Haven, Connecticut, and Charleston, South Carolina. (According to family legend, he and his wife escaped on the last boat to depart from Charleston before Fort Sumter was fired upon.)[6] So he was well acquainted with the United States, both North and South.

Some literary critics have been inclined to describe De Forest, as he presented himself in the prewar years, rather unsympathetically. Edmund Wilson, for example, depicts De Forest as a "taut New Englander" and refers facetiously to his "indurated Protestantism."[7] But regardless of his inherent parochialism, De Forest boasted a far wider range of experience than the average young recruit. And as an officer in the U.S. Army, he would record his observations with precision, raw honesty, and a certain self-deprecating flair.

Out of his war experience, De Forest produced an impressive array of fictional and nonfictional texts. There were wartime letters to his wife and brothers, articles written in the late 1860s for *Harper's New Monthly Magazine* and the *Galaxy,* and a war novel, published in 1867, titled *Miss Ravenel's Conversion from Secession to Loyalty.*[8] De Forest was a remarkably disciplined and diligent writer. Even during times of intense suffering, such as the summer of 1863 when he was near starvation and the men under his command were dying of swamp fever, he did not fail to record his experiences.

De Forest was not only an unusually dedicated and observant chronicler of the war but also strikingly candid in his war writings. He regularly treated subjects that his literary peers avoided. In an era when it was the norm to shield women from unsavory details of army life and sanitize even private letters home, De Forest wrote his wife long, detailed letters about all manner of subjects: troops "desperate with malaria," the intoxication of the soldiers, the monotony of camp life in Louisiana, and the "incessant discomforts."[9] In a letter of early August 1862, De Forest admitted to her, "The truth is (although you must not publish it) that the division has run down terribly in numbers. There is a constant drain on troops in the field, much heavier than a civilian would suppose."[10]

In his letters to his wife, De Forest could write the unvarnished, unpublishable "truth." Though he could not be quite as open in his published works, even when he was writing for a broad audience, De Forest was markedly forthright. Certain information, such as the extent to which troops were being depleted by sickness and desertions, had to be kept secret during the war years. Publishing the stark truth about such a sensitive matter would have demoralized the North and bolstered the determination of the South. But De Forest shared other disturbing information.

In a distinctly unromantic postwar article printed in the *Galaxy,* De Forest devotes several pages to describing the agonies of marching on blistered, bloodied feet. "When you stand," he explains, "you seem to be on red-hot iron plates." Walking is even worse. "When you walk, you make grimaces at every step." Further detailing the pedestrian agonies endured by the men in the ranks, De Forest notes, "In the morning the whole regiment starts limping, and by noon the best soldiers become nearly mutinous with suffering. They snarl and swear at each other." De Forest's account focuses on suffering of the nonglamorous sort, agonies induced by blisters rather than bullets. His sore-footed, hot-tempered soldiers have little in common with the men presented in most Civil War literature.[11]

Unlike the soldiers of popular poetry and prose, who almost unfailingly are portrayed as supernally stoic, the marching men whom De Forest describes are not so obviously admirable. And the very title of De Forest's article, "Forced Marches," serves as a reminder that coercion often was required to keep the rank and file—not to mention officers—in line. De Forest recounts that he and the men under his command marched eighty-seven miles within seventy-six hours, and his article graphically reveals the extreme suffering entailed in the heroically unheroic jaunt.[12]

Whatever the audience for which he wrote, De Forest strove to achieve a level of truth-telling that was highly unusual in his day. He refused to mask the unpleasant aspects of the war. Answering the question of how he liked combat, he wrote in an essay published in *Harper's*, "With a courage which entitles me to honorable mention at the head-quarters of the veracities, I reply that I did not like it, except in some expansive moments when this or that stirring success filled me with excitement."[13]

As De Forest pointed out, sharing such "veracities" took courage. For at the very heart of the popular conception of fighting was the notion that soldiers marched into battle without regret or hesitation. De Forest offered the readers of *Harper's* a very different version of the emotions felt by men upon entering into combat, and he rebuked civilian writers who had never ventured onto a battlefield for misrepresenting the complexity of war. He bluntly judged such writers unqualified to describe the emotions actually felt by soldiers. Cautioning his readers against such uninformed and romantically inclined writers, he observed, "Certain military authors who never heard a bullet whistle have written copiously . . . to the general effect that fighting is delightful. It is not; it is just tolerable; you can put up with it; but you can't honestly praise it." Apart from "a few flashes of elation," De Forest declared with sharp-edged humor, "[Being in battle] is much like being in a rich cholera district in the height of the season."[14]

While popular "military authors" presented soldiers who fearlessly marched into the fray, De Forest offered a more complex definition of bravery. "Profoundly, infinitely true," he explained, "is the copybook maxim, 'Self-preservation is the first law of nature.'" The desire to seek safety, he insisted, is universal. "The man who does not dread to die or to be mutilated is a lunatic." Courage, according to De Forest, is not to be measured according to a fighter's degree of fearlessness; rather it is to be calculated in direct proportion to his dread. Fear and a desire to flee, De Forest argued, are the natural and sane reactions of any man entering into battle. "The man who, dreading these things, still faces them for the sake of duty and honor is a hero."[15]

Heroism, in De Forest's rule book, demands both more and less of a man than conventional Civil War writers indicated. Heroism demands tremendous self-discipline. It demands that a soldier resist the instinct "true of every species and of every individual" for self-preservation. But heroism does not require a conspicuously courageous act. Merely remaining on the battlefield is heroic enough.[16]

De Forest attempted to debunk the myth of the fearless fighter. Even more shockingly, he challenged the literary conventions surrounding the sensitive subject of death. To understand the extent to which De Forest's descriptions of dying soldiers deviate from mid-nineteenth-century norms, it is useful to consider the way in which death was routinely sentimentalized in the literature of the era.

A few examples, drawn from popular antebellum works, demonstrate the literary leanings that so powerfully affected the Civil War writers. With euphemisms and pleasant imagery, prewar writers presented death as a beautifully transcendent experience, at once poignant and inevitable. William Cullen Bryant, one of the most prominent poets of the early nineteenth century, gently reminds his readers in the elegant lines of his famous meditation on death, "Thanatopsis," that all living creatures are fated to die. "Yet not to thine eternal resting-place / Shalt thou retire alone," he promises. All people eventually "retire."

> The youth in life's fresh spring, and he who goes
> In the full strength of years, matron and maid,
> The speechless babe, and the gray-headed man. . . .

The universal experience of death, Bryant asserts, should not be feared. Envisioning death as a state of tranquil repose, Bryant suggests, "Approach thy grave / Like one who wraps the drapery of his couch / About him, and lies down to pleasant dreams."[17]

In particular, the bittersweet deaths of young men and women, what Bryant called "youth in life's fresh spring," appealed to the literary imagination of antebellum authors. Even Edgar Allan Poe, usually remembered for his works of gothic horror, idealized the death of the young. His poem "Lenore" begins:

> Ah, broken is the golden bowl!
>   The spirit flown forever!
> Let the bell toll!—A saintly soul
>   Glides down the Stygian river!
> And let the burial rite be read—
>   The funeral song be sung—
> A dirge for the most lovely dead
>   That ever died so young!

Elsewhere Poe would write about the not-quite-dead rising from their graves, but in poems such as "Lenore" and "Annabel Lee" he presents a highly sentimental vision of death.[18]

The most famous prewar depiction of a young person's death appeared not in a work of poetry but in a work of fiction—Harriet Beecher Stowe's *Uncle Tom's Cabin.* Near the end of the long, melodramatic novel, which was first published in 1852, an utterly angelic girl named Eva lies picturesquely presented on her deathbed. Her "crimson cheeks" contrast "painfully with the intense whiteness of her complexion." Her "large blue eyes" are full of tenderness for all. Both inwardly and outwardly, Eva is a child of perfect beauty. She is generous, kind, and thoroughly innocent. She has "long golden-brown curls."[19]

Eva's eventual death, as described on the pages of *Uncle Tom's Cabin,* is painless and tranquil. Stowe writes:

> For so bright and placid was the farewell voyage of the little spirit,—by such sweet and fragrant breezes was the small bark borne towards the heavenly shores,—that it was impossible to realize that it was death that was approaching. The child felt no pain,— only a tranquil, soft weakness, daily and almost insensibly increasing; and she was so beautiful, so loving, so trustful, so happy, that one could not resist the soothing influence of that air of innocence and peace which seemed to breathe around her.

Death, in Stowe's sentimental vision, is a slow and pleasant voyage to "heavenly shores," and little Eva sets sail on this final trip full of good cheer. She experiences no discomfort. Her beauty is marred by no unsightly signs of anguish or by any disfigurements. She dies at home, amid loved ones, spreading an "air of innocence and peace" around her. Her death is, at once, idealized and inspirational. But, of course, it is not a war death.[20]

The Civil War, with its distant battles and distant deaths, presented a tremendous challenge. In the course of four years, between six and seven hundred thousand Confederate and Union fighters perished. And these men did not die like those who died at home. How were wartime writers to portray the horrible suffering of men who died on battlefields? How were they to depict the protracted pain of men who died in military hospitals? The Civil War required both new rituals and new literary conventions for dealing with death.[21]

In *This Republic of Suffering: Death and the American Civil War* Drew Gilpin Faust makes clear the importance that the Civil War generation attached to dying properly. "The concept of the Good Death," she writes, "was central to mid-nineteenth-century America, as it had long been at the core of Christian practice." And central to a Good Death, as Faust explains, was that it take place within a domestic setting; that the soon-to-be departed express with words, and evince through behavior, his or her faith; and that the dying individual utter some "life-defining last words."[22]

If the realities of war made these intimately familial Good Deaths impossible, northerners and southerners did their best to approximate them under difficult conditions. As Faust notes, Americans "sought to manage battlefield deaths in a way that mitigated separation from kin and offered a substitute for the traditional stylized deathbed performance." She elaborates, "Soldiers, chaplains, military nurses, and doctors conspired to provide the dying man and his family with as many of the elements of the conventional Good Death as possible."[23]

Likewise, Civil War writers worked hard to erase, or at least minimize, certain raw realities of war deaths and transform them into Good Deaths. Borrowing heavily from the conventions of sentimental prewar literature, the writers tried to make the distant deaths of soldiers seem as domestic, and domesticated, as possible. Although writers could not ignore certain realities of war, they did their best to imaginatively overcome the chal-

lenges and difficulties that were involved in describing men who met brutal, and sometimes lingering, deaths far from home. In *The Imagined Civil
War*, a study of popular wartime literature, Alice Fahs describes the appeal
of highly sentimentalized "dying soldier" poems and songs. She explains,
"During the Civil War . . . many writers protested against the idea that
soldiers were alone or even anonymous when they died." Consequently,
"Hundreds of popular songs and poems during the war grappled with the
fact of mass, anonymous death by creating idealized deaths for soldiers."
By performing what Fahs describes as "the difficult cultural task of making those often anonymous deaths appropriately meaningful," popular literature helped ameliorate readers' anxieties and render distant deaths both
familiar and emotionally accessible.[24]

"Somebody's Darling," a popular Confederate poem written by Maria La
Coste and set to music, exemplifies the broad effort on the part of writers to
sanitize, sanctify, and sentimentalize war deaths. La Coste, a volunteer from
Georgia who worked in a military hospital in Savannah, presents a carefully crafted tale of a mortally wounded soldier. He is a handsome southern fighter who has been carried "into a ward of the whitewashed halls,
/ Where the dead and the dying lay." In this military hospital, the young
soldier's identity is unknown, but his beauty is plain to see. As life ebbs
from his body, his features are unmarred by bullet or artillery blast. And
the soldier—"so young and so brave"—elicits the admiration and unstinted
affection of those who care for him. Using the adoring vocabulary that a
mother or sweetheart might choose, La Coste describes the dying man's
appearance:

> Matted and damp are the curls of gold
> > Kissing the snow of that fair young brow;
> Pale are the lips of delicate mold . . .

This golden-haired youth, who could readily pass for Little Eva's brother,
has a saintly aura. He seemingly embodies male beauty and innocence. No
mention is made of where the young soldier with "blue eyes dim" and "smiling, child-like lips" is wounded. It is not even clear that he is wounded at
all. He lies dying of an unspecified injury or illness far from his home and
loved ones. Yet, he is surrounded by people who tenderly care for him and
who lovingly play the role of surrogate family members.[25]

Even in death, La Coste assures her readers, the soldier will receive the sort of attention and tender consideration that his loved ones would have shown him. The hospital staff members will play the designated role of mourners. La Coste writes:

> Cross his hands on his bosom now,—
> Somebody's darling is still and dead!
>
> Kiss him once for somebody's sake;
> Murmur a prayer, both soft and low.

The nurses and other workers at the military hospital are thus scripted to take on the duties and obligations of kith and kin. La Coste promises that even the burial of the anonymous soldier will be emotional:

> Tenderly bury the fair young dead,
> Pausing to drop on his grave a tear;
> Carve on the wooden slab o'er his head,
> *"Somebody's darling slumbers here!"*

Although the Civil War brought thousands upon thousands of such deaths, La Coste strives to assure her wartime readers that each soldier's death is special. The South's dead sons and brothers and husbands, she tacitly promises, will not be callously interred in unmarked graves and forgotten. Instead, they each will be mourned and missed.[26]

With her repeated reassurances that the soldier will be treated nearly the same as if he died among his loved ones, La Coste allowed her fellow southerners to read the boy's death divorced from its immediate context of violent war. In *Uncle Tom's Cabin* Little Eva distributes curls of her hair as keepsakes to the faithful slaves who visit her bedside. Similarly, "one bright curl" is snipped as a keepsake from the head of this soldier before his "pale sweet face" is to be "hid by the dust of the grave."[27] He is accorded the same tenderness and the same rites and rituals as someone who died at home in his own bed.

Northerners and southerners died all too frequently in the course of the Civil War and in all too many horrific ways, yet the literary treatment of their deaths typically adhered to a straightforward narrative. Rather than focusing on the specifics of the soldiers' wounds, writers focused on the fighters' noble sacrifices and their heavenly redemption. The deaths of young men, as presented in popular war poems, songs, and stories, were intended to evoke readers' sympathy. A brief introduction to "Somebody's Darling," published in the 1867 anthology *The Southern Poems of the War*, noted, "It will commend itself by its touching pathos to all readers."[28]

Striving to give coherent meaning to the war and war deaths, writers avoided ambiguity, pessimism, and doubt. They avoided grim details of guts and gore. In a poem titled "I'm Dying, Comrade" the northern poet Mary H. C. Booth included the following stanza:

> I do not think I'm wounded;
> I cannot feel a pain;
> And yet I've fallen, comrade,
> Never to rise again.
> The last that I remember,
> We charged upon the foe;
> I heard a sound of victory,
> And that is all I know.

Amazingly, the soldier is dying yet unable to explain the cause of his death. He is mortally wounded yet feels no pain. Instead, his attention is focused heavenward. He sees "a hundred thousand soldiers" standing "at the right of God." And he hears "the voice of God" calling him from life. Such tidy and inspiring, if improbable, descriptions of battlefield deaths reflect the taste of wartime writers and readers. By popular consensus, a level of silent decorum prevailed. But not all writers were inclined to exercise such tremendous tact.[29]

De Forest presented death scenes that ran directly counter to the sanitized images, so cherished by the war generation, of men passing tranquilly from shore to heavenly shore. In his fiction and in his battlefield accounts, he included graphic descriptions of dismembered and dying soldiers. Into seemingly harmonious war scenes, he introduced horror and havoc.

In *Miss Ravenel's Conversion from Secession to Loyalty*, De Forest's long Civil War novel, a soldier sits relaxing, reading a newspaper. He is engrossed in a reprint of a sermon by the famous northern preacher Henry Ward Beecher (one of Harriet Beecher Stowe's younger brothers). Suddenly, a stray shot from an unseen rifle connects with his head. The thud of the impact sounds like a bullet hitting wood. With something verging on the scientific precision of an anatomist, De Forest describes the path of the bul-

let through the soldier's body. "The ball had struck him under the chin, traversed the neck, and cut the spinal column where it joins the brain, making
a fearful hole through which the blood had already soaked his great-coat."[30]

In the account of the siege of Port Hudson that he wrote for *Harper's
New Monthly Magazine,* De Forest describes the death of another soldier.
There was, De Forest explains, a place in the trenches outside of Port Hudson known as "Dead Man's Corner" because it was so exposed to enemy
fire. During his first day in the trenches, De Forest recounts, "a still breathing corpse was brought down from this spot of sacrifice." He elaborates, "A
brave, handsome boy of our Company D, gay and smiling with the excitement of fighting, disdaining to cover himself, was reloading his rifle when a
ball traversed his head, leaving two ghastly orifices through which the blood
and brains exuded, mingling with his auburn curls. . . . In a few minutes he
was dead." In each of these descriptions of the death of a soldier—one ostensibly factual and the other ostensibly fictional—De Forest plays cruelly
with his readers' expectations. A young man enjoying a minute of pleasant
diversion is struck in the head. A "gay and smiling" boy fails to take cover
and is suddenly dead.[31]

De Forest manipulates the sentimental and romantic language of mainstream war writers to unexpected and horrific ends. The "boy" of Company
D is "brave," "handsome," and excited to be in battle. In all of these regards,
he seems like the soldiers of popular story and song, but the soldier's gruesome death entirely breaks with literary etiquette. He receives a bullet directly to the head.

Unusual, indeed, are works of literature published in the staid 1860s
that describe Civil War soldiers shot in the head. However, the occurrence
of such deaths was far from uncommon during the Civil War. As George
Worthington Adams reports in *Doctors in Blue,* a study of medicine and the
Union army, "Injuries of head, face, and neck represented 10.77 per cent of
all gunshot wounds," and these types of wounds accounted for a highly dis-
proportionate number of all battlefield deaths.[32] Captain Allen Fahnestock,
for example, recorded in his diary account of the Battle of Chickamauga the
death of a man in his company who was "shot in the face, the ball coming
out the back of his neck." Chaplain James B. Sheeran, of the Confederate
army, penned another graphic depiction of battlefield carnage in a journal
that remained unpublished at the time of his death in 1881. After the Battle
of Chancellorsville he recorded, "I have passed over many a battlefield but

this perhaps was the most revolting scene I had ever witnessed. . . . The dead bodies of the enemy [lay] in every direction, some with their heads shot off, some with their brains oozing out, some pierced through the head with musket balls, some with their noses shot away, some with their mouths smashed, some wounded in the neck, some with broken arms or legs, some shot through the breast and some cut in two with shells." But Fahnestock, Sheeran, and others like them kept their diaries private. What occurred so frequently on the battlefield did not make its way into popular literature.[33]

Mary Hunt McCaleb Odom's *Lenare: A Story of the Southern Revolution*, a lengthy verse narrative published in 1866, provides a rare description of a fatal head wound in a work intended for a general readership. Depicting a battlefield on which "thousands of the ghastly slain" lie, "their hearts' blood crimsoning the heath," Odom writes:

> A youthful Northman, too, is there,
> Deep dyed with blood his flaxen hair;
> The hissing lead had pierced his brain,
> He ne'er will meet the foe again;
> The silver cord of life is riven,
> He stands before the courts of Heaven.[34]

Yet, Odom addresses the soldier's death only fleetingly. It constitutes a passing detail in a romantic tale of glorious deeds and heavenly redemption in which flaxen-haired foes meet upon a heath and sacrifice crimson blood. De Forest, by contrast, describes the deaths of the two soldiers shot in their heads with a detached and almost ironic precision.

De Forest intentionally defies his readers' expectations, and one senses that doing so gave him a sort of grim satisfaction. He does not allow his readers the comfort of clichés. Like Little Eva and the Confederate soldier of "Somebody's Darling," the soldier from Company D whom De Forest depicts has the curls to play the part of innocent youth. But instead of being clipped as sentimental keepsakes, the boy's auburn locks end up wet with his own "blood and brains." When describing Eva on her death bed, Stowe assured her readers, "On the face of the child . . . there was no ghastly imprint,— only a high and almost sublime expression, . . . the dawning of immortal life in that childish soul."[35] By contrast, the boy soldier De Forest describes is referred to as a "corpse" even before he has stopped breathing, and his head bears "two ghastly" holes through which his "blood and brains" exude.

De Forest did not shy away from writing about even the most disturbing aspects of the war. Rejecting the euphemistic language usually used to describe Civil War deaths, he was blunt and irreverent. His grisly descriptions of the Civil War dead anticipate the angry, realistic works of future war writers. Indeed, the dead soldier of Company D, whose blood and brains coat his curls, seems to prefigure the dead mother—whose long dark hair is "full of clotted blood"—that Ambrose Bierce presents at the end of his story "Chickamauga."[36]

Likewise, De Forest's description of the dead soldier seems to anticipate a scene in *The Long March*, a brief novel about the Korean War written by William Styron. In Styron's work a young marine is killed in an accident while still in training. He is described as follows, "[The] boy's eyes lay gently closed, and his long dark lashes were washed in tears, as though he had cried himself to sleep. . . . Around his curly head grasshoppers darted among the weeds. Below, beneath the slumbering eyes, his face had been blasted out of sight."[37] In Styron's description, as in De Forest's, there appears the same interplay of imagery, the same disconcerting combination of innocence and horror, curls and gore. Both depictions of youthful death rely on a shocking inversion of romantic norms. But De Forest wrote for an audience unaccustomed to such gory candidness and unaccustomed to jaded cynicism in war writing. Styron, by contrast, wrote in the wake of World War I and World War II. His work was first published in 1952. Weary disillusionment and understated irony had long since come to fill the works of such American antiwar writers as Ernest Hemingway, John Dos Passos, Lawrence Stallings, Thomas Boyd, Dalton Trumbo, Norman Mailer, and others.

De Forest was a loose cannon on the literary battlefield. His descriptions of soldiers' deaths—half shocking, half clinical—bear no resemblance to the decorous norm. Even more graphic are his accounts of wounded soldiers and of the acute suffering men endured before dying. In the article published in *Harper's New Monthly Magazine* in which he describes the original assault on Port Hudson in Louisiana in late May 1863, De Forest recalls, "a woful [sic] procession of wounded streamed rearward under our eyes. One man was borne past us with both his feet shot off about midway, and the bare spikes of bone protruding white and sharp from the bloody flesh."[38] The same scene appears, slightly reworked, in De Forest's postwar novel, *Miss Ravenel's Conversion*. In the fictionalized account an officer writes

home, "When one of our men was borne by me with half his foot torn off
by a round shot, the splintered bones projecting clean and white from the
rags of raw flesh, I grew so sick that perhaps I might have fainted if a brother
officer had not given me a sip of whiskey."[39] Nor does De Forest stop at
detailing the repulsive injuries sustained by men on the battlefield. He follows wounded fighters into the field hospitals where, as he chronicles, their
suffering becomes even more acute.

In *Miss Ravenel's Conversion* De Forest offers one of the most stomach-
churning passages to appear anywhere in Civil War literature. Describing
a scene at a field hospital at Port Hudson, he writes, "One man, whose leg
was amputated close to his body, uttered an inarticulate jabber of broken
screams, and rolled, or rather bounced from side to side . . . with such violence that two hospital attendants were fully occupied in holding him." The
raw agony of this soldier is on full display, and his suffering, most probably,
is futile. For, as De Forest comments, "nearly all the leg amputations at Port
Hudson proved fatal." In De Forest's account, the horrible and the pathetic
intermix, and there is no comforting palliative. There is no mention of glory,
heroism, or valor.[40]

The field hospital at Port Hudson that De Forest describes is a place
filled with appalling sights and terrible anguish. Elaborating upon the work-
ings of the hospital, De Forest does not omit even the most repellent of
topics. In the center of the improvised hospital, De Forest explains, stand
"several operating tables, each burdened by a grievously wounded man and
surrounded by surgeons and their assistants. Underneath [are] great pools
of clotted blood, amidst which [lie] amputated fingers, hands, arms, feet
and legs." The hospital, according to De Forest, is a "mass of suffering." And
the only thing worse than remaining in it is leaving it. When a wounded officer with a tremendously swollen and infected arm is transported by army
wagon—a "chariot of torture"—away from the hospital, he and the other
wounded men experience an agony that is so "nearly supernatural in its horror" that it seems "at times to his fevered imagination as if he were out of the
world, and journeying into the realms of eternal torment."[41]

De Forest's unflinching descriptions of exposed bones, severed limbs,
and excruciating pain have nothing in common with the vast collection of
Civil War works that carefully sidestepped such difficult issues. Indeed, De
Forest's field hospital seems the hellish antithesis of the hospital in which
the curly haired soldier dies his picturesque and painless death in La Coste's

"Somebody's Darling." Using his pen for a scalpel, De Forest cut into a raw nerve in the nation's literary body, and he did not deaden the pain with the opiate of comforting words. He did not offer any anodyne.

De Forest not only exposed the horrors of the battlefields and field hospitals but also the immorality of army life. One subject that he wrote about with unusual candor was the routine intoxication of soldiers and their superiors. Drinking was considered a major vice in mid-nineteenth-century America, and the years preceding the Civil War witnessed the flourishing of temperance societies. In keeping with their effort to present the fighting men as wholesome heroes, most war writers entirely avoided the issue of men and drink. They presented unsullied images of sober, upright soldiers. De Forest, however, in his letters and his war novel, deals openly with the subject of drunkenness in the military. "Since pay-day there has been a bacchanalia of whiskey drinking," he wrote home in the early summer of 1862. "One-fifth part of the regiment keeps drunk all the time."[42]

De Forest himself was abstemious, but he well understood the causes that drove the men under his command to drink. "If you could look into our tents," he explained in a letter to his wife in September 1862, "you would not wonder that consolation is sought for in whiskey. The never-ceasing rain streams at will through numerous rents and holes in the mouldy, rotten canvas." Nor, according to De Forest, was drunkenness confined to the soldiers. The officers, who were meant to serve as exemplars of good character for the men under their command, were often plainly drunk. As De Forest noted in his letter, "The officers are nearly as miserable, and are tempted to seek the same consolation." And De Forest recounted a tale of one of his own underlings. "Lately a lieutenant reeled into my tent, dropped heavily on a bed, stared at me a minute as if to locate me, and said in a thick voice, 'Capm, everybody's drunk today. Capm the brigade's drunk.'"[43]

De Forest saw a correlation between fighting and drinking, and it was a correlation that ran directly counter to the romantic notion that combat was an uplifting and ennobling experience. An "army of teetotalers," De Forest observed in another letter, would be a big improvement over an army containing "the usual proportion of hard drinkers." But De Forest noted that the experience of war had led the men of the Twelfth Connecticut, with whom he served, to engage more frequently in vice. The soldiers and officers, he explained, were "not so *good* as they were once; they drink harder and swear more and gamble deeper." The experience of combat and the tedium of the soldier's life had a detrimental effect on character. Or so, at least, De Forest suggested.[44]

In his most damning pronouncement on the subject, De Forest declared, "De Quincey is right in his statement that if homicide is habitually indulged in, it leads to immorality."[45] That the taking of life in war could be equated with homicide, and that the experience of soldiering could be held responsible for fostering vices rather than virtue, was antithetical to the standard understanding of the Civil War. But John William De Forest did not allow himself to be bound by standard constraints. He wrote what his contemporaries considered unthinkable, or at least unprintable.

Unsurprisingly, De Forest received little reward in the literary marketplace for his transgressions. The publication history of his war novel well reflects the inhospitable climate for nontraditional war works. Late in 1864 De Forest began writing *Miss Ravenel's Conversion from Secession to Loyalty,* for which he freely borrowed from his own war experiences. The lengthy novel that emerged charts the path through the war of a young lady, Miss Lillie Ravenel, her two suitors, her aunt, and her father. Along the way, Miss Ravenel marries, has a child, loses her no-good husband (a womanizer, embezzler, and drunkard), marries again, and goes from being a gloating Confederate to a good Unionist.[46] In addition to chronicling Miss Ravenel's matrimonial tribulations and her shift of allegiance, the novel also presents some stunningly realistic battle scenes and addresses such sensitive subjects as military mismanagement and graft.

In 1865 De Forest sold the novel to the publishing establishment Harper and Brothers, with the understanding that the novel would be published serially in *Harper's New Monthly Magazine* and then might appear as a book. But soon thereafter the editors of *Harper's* had second thoughts. They worried that the novel might offend the sensibilities of their magazine's readers. De Forest begrudgingly agreed to certain alterations, but he could not refrain from remarking on the cost to the semblance of truth—or *vraisemblance* —that such selective censoring entailed. In late December 1865 he wrote his editors, "I make no objection to your reform of the story. If it goes into the *Monthly* of course it ought to be made proper for families. Only I think it ought to be understood, for the sake of *vraisemblance,* that the Colonel did frequently swear and that the Louisiana lady [the seductress in an adulterous affair] was not quite as good as she should be."[47] In the end, *Miss Rav-*

enel's Conversion from Secession to Loyalty never was serialized in *Harper's New Monthly Magazine.*

When *Miss Ravenel's Conversion* finally was published by Harper and Brothers in 1867, unexpurgated as a full-length novel, it did not fare well. *Harper's New Monthly Magazine,* not without a measure of self-interest, hailed the book as "the best American novel published for many a year."[48] The *Atlantic* also praised it. Nonetheless, the novel sold poorly. More than sixteen hundred copies of the first edition remained unsold in 1884, and no second edition would be published before De Forest's death in 1906.[49]

The *Ladies' Repository,* which had relegated Melville's *Battle-Pieces* to a distant second place behind a Latin primer, primly stated of *Miss Ravenel's Conversion,* "This is a novel which, of course, we have not read, but which, from glancing at a few pages, we judge is intended to be quizzical, piquant, and racy in its thoughts with regard to both sections of our country."[50] If the anonymous contributor to the "Literary Notices" column had done more than glance at several pages of De Forest's novel, she was not prepared publicly to admit it. Ostensibly, just a few peeks between the book's covers had been enough to convince this demure reviewer that the novel, 521 pages long, was too "racy" to be read in full. Although De Forest's wife might have had the stomach to handle her husband's accounts of battle deaths and army life, most other contemporary readers found his style too "piquant" for their literary palates.

Far more appreciative and understanding of De Forest's novel have been modern scholars. In a preface to a volume on narratives of the Vietnam War, Thomas Myers observes:

> Although the preponderance of Civil War fiction attempted to reaf-
> firm collective romantic notions of the individual chivalric aspects of
> combat, to reify categories of noble action and just cause from both the
> northern and southern perspectives, De Forest endeavored in *Miss Rav-
> enel's Conversion from Secession to Loyalty* not only to treat the physical
> and psychological realities of mass industrial slaughter in a new way, but
> also to cast warnings similar to Melville's of the increasing militarism
> within American society.[51]

Another modern literary critic hails *Miss Ravenel's Conversion* as the "first important novel about the Civil War."[52] The precise qualities of the novel that proved so distasteful to contemporary readers in the 1860s have won praise for De Forest's novel from generations of more modern readers.

Interestingly, the public reassessment of *Miss Ravenel's Conversion* began on the very eve of World War II, prompted by the novel's rerelease in 1939 by Harper. A notably favorable review of the book in *Time* magazine in late August of that year concluded, "The story of this novel is unsparing enough now to disturb most modern readers. Seventy-two years ago it was so shocking it blew its gifted author into literary oblivion. One of the best war stories in U.S. fiction . . . it was also one of the greatest failures in U.S. publishing."[53] Only after the United States had weathered World War I and readers had come to revere the antiwar works by American, British, German, and other writers that were published in the postwar decades did De Forest's war novel finally receive a measure of public acclaim.

De Forest did not temper his observations on the subject of the Civil War. He did not, as the Yale professor who wrote the introduction for the 1939 edition of the novel observed, offer battles "tidied up for the drawing room."[54] Throughout his war writings, De Forest wrote about unusual and uncomfortable topics, such as blisters and card-playing soldiers. And he wrote about conventional war subjects, such as heroism and dying soldiers, in an unconventional way.

The uniform frankness of his letters, articles, and novel set De Forest apart from the ranks of Civil War writers of the 1860s. Although he was not opposed to the Civil War, he defiantly opposed the way in which it was represented in print. As his friend and great admirer the prominent magazine editor and novelist William Dean Howells later remarked, De Forest was "a realist before realism was named."[55]

Even so, De Forest did not write all the "veracities" about the Civil War that he might have liked to write. In a letter to Howells in 1887, De Forest admitted:

> Let me tell you that nobody but [Tolstoy] has written the whole truth about war and battle. *I* tried, and I told all I dared, and perhaps all I could. But there was one thing I did not dare tell, lest the world should infer that I was naturally a coward, and so could not know the feelings of a brave man. I actually did not dare state the extreme horror of battle, and the anguish with which the bravest soldiers struggle through it. . . .

Nothing is more confounding, fragmentary, incomprehensible than a battle as one sees it.[56]

De Forest wrote very candidly about the war. He probably recorded more of the "whole truth" than any other American of his day. He addressed such taboo topics as the use of alcohol in the army, the fear men felt going into battle, and the horrific ways soldiers were wounded and killed.

If, as De Forest imagined, there was a "head-quarters of the veracities" that rewarded brave displays of honesty, he certainly would have received a commendation. Yet, like Melville, De Forest did not "dare" tell all. Even so, he anticipated the direction that antiwar literature would take in the late nineteenth and early twentieth centuries and pushed America toward a new way of both reading and writing about war.

6

WALT WHITMAN:
"THAT HELL UNPENT"

Away with themes of war! away with War itself!
Hence from my shuddering sight, to never more return, that show of
 blacken'd, mutilated corpses!
That hell unpent, and raid of blood—fit for wild tigers, or for lop-ear'd
 wolves—not reasoning men!

—Walt Whitman, from "After All, Not to Create Only," 1871

either a distant onlooker, like Melville, nor an officer in the trenches, like John William De Forest, Walt Whitman experienced the Civil War as a civilian volunteer. As a visitor to wounded, sick, and dying soldiers in military hospitals in New York, Virginia, and Washington, Whitman actively participated in the war without taking up arms. Nonetheless, the war took its toll. He entered the war years hale and hearty and left them physically broken. He traded his health to partake of an experience that he found at once tremendously inspiring and terribly appalling.

In ways both similar to and distinctly different from Melville and De Forest, Walt Whitman struggled to come to terms with the Civil War. Unable to align himself wholeheartedly with northern enthusiasts, yet determined to believe that the conflict would benefit the nation by leading it closer to his own democratic ideals, he vacillated between supporting and questioning the war. In the summer of 1863, soon after the Battle of Gettysburg, he wrote home to New York from Washington: "Mother, one's heart grows sick of war, after all, when you see what it really is—every once in a while I feel so horrified & disgusted—it seems to me like a great slaughter-house & the men mutually butchering each other—then I feel how impossible it appears, again, to retire from this contest, until we have carried our points— (it is cruel to be so tossed from pillar to post in one's judgment)."[1] In his letters home and his personal diaries, Whitman candidly admitted his inner conflict. Not so in his published writings.

Though "tossed from pillar to post" in his private judgment, Whitman consistently strove to present an uplifting and inspiring image of the war, and of wartime America, to his public readership. In his personal writings, however, appear some of the darkest observations and verses to spring from the Civil War.

At the outset of the war Walt Whitman was already an established poet. The first edition of his ever-evolving opus *Leaves of Grass* had been published in 1855, and revised and expanded editions had followed in 1856 and 1860. Though he lacked broad acclaim, he had won the admiration of the northern luminary Ralph Waldo Emerson, among others. And using a line both longer and far less regulated than that preferred by his contemporaries, he was well on his way to introducing a new and radically unconventional poetic form into American literature.

The start of the war found Whitman living in Brooklyn, New York, and conforming, within the bounds of poetic license, to the description he offered of himself in *Leaves of Grass:*

> Walt Whitman, a kosmos, of Manhattan the son,
> Turbulent, fleshy, sensual, eating, drinking and breeding,
> No sentimentalist, no stander above men and women or apart from them,
> No more modest than immodest.[2]

Whitman, who sided with the Union, lived through the early period of the war in the comfort of his home. His brother George had enlisted in the spring of 1861, within a week of the attack on Fort Sumter, and was a first lieutenant in the 51st New York. Whitman, at forty-one years of age, apparently felt no such impulse to place himself physically in the fight. Instead, he pursued his poetry and made occasional visits to Union soldiers recuperating in local New York hospitals.

Although Whitman experienced the opening stages of the war as a civilian, he did find a way to lend his special talents to the cause. When the northern forces were first mobilizing, he used his poetic skills to help the recruitment effort. As he would later recall, "Aroused and angry, I'd thought to beat the alarum, and urge relentless war."[3] Having traveled not much closer to the distant battlefields than the south shore of his beloved "Mannahatta,"

Whitman wrote, "Beat! Beat! Drums!" The poem is an insistent and excited call to arms. Amid many exclamation marks, Whitman acknowledges the high personal costs of war service—bridegrooms separated from brides, farmers separated from fields—but argues that the entreaties of mothers, children, and old men should not deter young men from their patriotic purpose. The final stanza of the poem begins:

> Beat! beat! drums!—blow! bugles! blow!
> Make no parley—stop for no expostulation,
> Mind not the timid—mind not the weeper or prayer.[4]

The war, Whitman asserts, must take precedence over all workaday and domestic demands. Nonetheless, Whitman exempted himself from the obligation to heed the drums of war.

Ever fond of enumerations, Whitman listed—in "First O Songs for a Prelude," another of his early war poems—the many walks of life from which men were being swept toward the battlefields. Among the "young men falling in and arming" were mechanics, lawyers, wagon drivers, salesmen, bosses, bookkeepers, and porters. "Mannahatta [was] a-march," he claimed. More precisely, Manhattan was a-march with the exception of a certain poet. While new recruits were bound "for a manly life in the camp," Whitman remained in New York, monitoring and supporting the war from afar.[5]

However, in late 1862 Whitman was suddenly drawn to the very vortex of the war. A newspaper report in mid-December listed his brother George among those wounded in the Battle of Fredericksburg. Shouldering his familial responsibilities, Whitman hurried to Virginia. Quickly, the Civil War changed for Whitman from distant phantasm to immediate horror. He was relieved to find his brother "alive and well" and practically healed from a gash in the cheek, but the lurid sights and intense suffering that Whitman found at the front greatly affected him.[6]

In Virginia, Whitman was introduced to what he described in a letter as "*war-life*, the real article," and it proved to be a pivotal experience in his own life.[7] Despite having a strong numerical advantage, the Union troops under the command of General Ambrose Burnside had been defeated by General Robert E. Lee and his forces, and there had been severe Union casualties, totaling more than 12,500. One of the first sights that Whitman encountered on his arrival at the military camp near Falmouth, Virginia, was, as he recorded in his diary, "a heap of feet, legs, arms, and human fragments, cut, bloody, black and blue, swelled and sickening" that lay under a tree in front of an improvised hospital.[8]

Whitman remained in Virginia for more than a week, immersing himself in the activities and scenes of the war. He visited the hospitals of the Army of the Potomac, where he befriended a young, badly wounded prisoner from Mississippi. He talked and mingled with soldiers in camp. He went out on picket duty with the regiments. At the end of his stay, he wrote home, "I have lived for eight or nine days amid such scenes as the camps furnish . . . and realize the way that hundreds of thousands of good men are now living . . . not only without any of the comforts, but with death and sickness and hard marching and hard fighting."[9] When he at last took his leave of the army camp, Whitman did not return to New York. Instead, he traveled to Washington in charge of a trainload of the wounded, and there he remained.

In the Union capital Whitman found a part-time job in the army paymaster's office and devoted his free time to serving as a self-appointed "wound-dresser" by visiting the military hospitals.[10] In December 1864, for a piece that would appear in the New York Times, he attempted to quantify his work comforting soldiers in hospital, camp, and field over the course of the prior two years. He estimated that he had gone "among from 80,000 to 100,000 of the wounded and sick, as sustainer of spirit and body in some slight degree, in their time of need." And he calculated that he already had made more than six hundred separate visits, which lasted from "an hour or two, to all day or night." Sometimes he even "took up . . . quarters in the hospital, and slept or watched there several nights in succession."[11]

As a sympathetic friend and helper to legions of soldiers who passed through the hospital wards, whether they hailed from the North or the South, Whitman experienced the Civil War in an immediate and intimate way. "I adapt myself to each case," he explained to a correspondent midway through the war, "some need to be humored, some are rather out of their head—some merely want me to sit down [beside] them, & hold them by the hand." Whether the soldiers wanted a "letter written to mother or father," "a cooling drink," or writing paper, envelopes, and stamps, Whitman did his best to assist them. However, his greatest gift to the soldiers, he concluded, was not of a material nature. "I should say that I believe my profoundest help to these sick & dying men is probably the soothing invigoration I steadily bear in mind, to infuse in them through affection, cheering love, & the like, between them & me. It has saved more than one life."[12]

In time, however, the great strain of his work as a volunteer, ministering to the needs of hundreds and thousands of hospitalized men, affected Whitman physically. In December 1864 he offered the following report about his health the previous summer. "For the first time in my life, I began to be prostrated with real sickness, and was, before the close of the Summer, imperatively ordered North by the physicians, to recuperate and have an entire change of air."[13] After the war years he would never again enjoy the vigorous vitality that he had boasted of in "Song of Myself," in which he described himself as "thirty-seven years old in perfect health."[14] In 1873 he was stricken with paralysis. Other setbacks followed in later years. He died in 1892 a physically broken man, but his writings about the Civil War survive as a very personal record of his war experience.

It is an indication of Whitman's great industriousness during the war years that, in addition to fulfilling the demands of his salaried job (first at the Paymaster's Office and later in the Department of the Interior) and spending long and wearying hours tending to the wounded, he found time to write. During the years of what he referred to as the "War of Attempted Secession," Whitman recorded his impressions extensively in poems, letters, occasional dispatches to the *New York Times* and *Brooklyn Eagle,* and a series of private journals. Then, very soon after the war ended, he arranged for a collection of his Civil War poems to be published as the slim volume *Drum-Taps,* which he soon expanded to include eighteen additional poems and published as *Sequel to Drum-Taps.* Both *Drum-Taps* and *Sequel to Drum-Taps* were then enfolded within subsequent editions of *Leaves of Grass.*

Whitman's postwar response to the conflict, however, was not confined to poetry or to the 1860s. Throughout the following decades, up until his death, Whitman dwelled on the subject of the Civil War and continually reworked and added to his published record of the years of battle. In addition to the poems that eventually made their way into *Leaves of Grass,* Whitman published two autobiographical works of prose that took as their central focus his wartime experiences. *Memoranda during the War,* a volume based on his own notebooks, was published as a private edition in 1875. Then, in 1882, Whitman included *Memoranda* within a longer volume, *Specimen Days.* Whitman also published a selection of his reminiscences and wartime jottings in the *North American Review* in early 1887 and a sampling of his wartime notes and wartime letters to his mother in *Century* magazine in late 1888.[15] As his writing and statements attest, the Civil War was the single most compelling and important subject Whitman ever encountered.

Revealingly, Whitman came to identify the entirety of *Leaves of Grass* —both the war poems *and* the hundreds of other poems included in the volume—with his experiences during "the secession war." An inveterate text-tinkerer, Whitman frequently reworked, rearranged, and retitled his works. Even after poems were published, Whitman continued to adjust and embellish. A new edition of *Leaves of Grass* always loomed on the horizon (the final version is known as "the deathbed edition"), and each new edition included changes both subtle and seismic. In a line he added to the poem "By Blue Ontario's Shore" for the 1871 edition of *Leaves of Grass*, Whitman reflects, "As a wheel turns on an axle, so I find my chant turning finally on the war."[16] A decade later, during an interview he gave while at work on yet another edition of *Leaves of Grass*, Whitman explained, "I do not know whether it will appear to the casual reader, but to myself my whole book turns on the secession war. It is the poem of the war."[17] In 1888 Whitman even went so far as to claim—despite the fact that three editions of *Leaves of Grass* had been published before the start of the war—that "without those three or four years and the experiences they gave, 'Leaves of Grass' would not now be existing."[18]

In *Specimen Days* Whitman once again emphasized the enduring influence of the war in shaping his poetry and his life. Specifically, under the subchapter heading "Sources of Character—Results," he explained the war's momentous importance to him. "I estimate three leading sources and formative stamps of my own character, now solidified for good or bad, and its subsequent literary and other outgrowth." These three overarching influences were his parents, New York, and his experiences "in the secession outbreak."[19]

The Civil War, with all its strains and sorrows, marked the most important period of Whitman's life. With haunting prescience, Whitman wrote to an acquaintance in the autumn of 1863, "I feel to devote myself more to the work of my life, which is making poems. I must bring out Drum Taps. I *must* be continually bringing out poems—now is the hey day. I shall range along the high plateau of my life & capacity for a few years now, & then swiftly descend."[20] Whitman committed himself both physically and ideologically to the Civil War. He willed himself to believe in the war's merit despite his vexing doubts.

To understand Whitman's outlook on the Civil War, it is essential to understand his hopes for America. Whitman envisioned a nation in which his fellow citizens would be bonded together by self-sacrifice and shared commitment. He imagined a country purified of self-interest, hypocrisy, and hollowness. Despite misgivings stemming from his visit in late 1862 to the "war fields in Virginia," he struggled to hold on to this vision during what he would later describe as "all of the fluctuations, gloom, despair, hopes again arous'd, courage evoked . . . filling those agonistic and lurid following years, 1863-'64-'65."[21]

The war provided satisfying proof to Whitman that Americans could rise above petty self-interest in support of vital democracy. In *Specimen Days* he describes the "prompt and splendid" reaction of the North to the bombardment of Fort Sumter as "the best lesson of the century, or of America." He elaborates: "In my judgment [the North's mobilization] will remain as the grandest and most encouraging spectacle yet vouchsafed in any age, old or new, to political progress and democracy. It was not for what came to the surface merely—though that was important—but what it indicated below, which was of eternal importance." In Whitman's assessment, the North had met the threat of "secession slavery, the archenemy personified" without hesitation, and "there had formed and hardened a primal hardpan of national Union will."[22]

The selflessness of the soldiers, in particular, impressed Whitman. In Whitman's estimation, the self-abnegation that these men demonstrated was testament to the innate fineness and generosity of the American spirit. In *Specimen Days* he explains, "Two great spectacles, immortal proofs of democracy, unequaled in all the history of the past, are furnished by the secession war—one at the beginning, the other at its close. Those are, the general, voluntary, armed upheaval, and the peaceful and harmonious disbanding of the armies in the summer of 1865."[23] The soldiers, the very men he aided and comforted in wartime hospitals, were Whitman's heroes. They were the upholders of democracy, the standard-bearers of his ideals.

In the patriotic "spectacles" of the Civil War, Whitman divined a message that was deeply inspiring. Decades after the war's conclusion, he exulted, "Was there not something grand, and an inside proof of perennial grandeur in that war!" According to his interpretation, the Union had gone to battle "for a bare idea and abstraction—a mere, at bottom, heroic dream and reminiscence."[24] However, the same war that gave evidence of "political progress and democracy" and "proof of perennial grandeur" also offered more disturbing proofs.

Whitman found much that was encouraging in the Civil War and claimed it was "a mighty privilege to have been part of it," but he also was profoundly troubled by the war.[25] He had walked among the bloated bodies of the war dead. He had witnessed the awful variety of ways in which combat maimed and unmanned soldiers. He knew, although he never personally experienced, the horrors of heated combat. Yet he did not publicly acknowledge the extent of his dismay and ambivalence. The history of Whitman's war writings and revisions is revealing. It is a history of self-censorship and circumspection.

From the turbulent years of the conflict to the end of his life, Whitman grappled with the challenge of writing about the Civil War. As he drafted and amended his war writings, he made significant choices about what he wished to include and what he wished to exclude. In the end, he withheld his sharpest critique of the Civil War from his published works. Choosing to put forth an inspiring interpretation of the events of 1861 to 1865, he guaranteed that his angriest indictment of the war never made it into print.

Some aspects of the war, Whitman felt, were best left unpublished, and he trusted writers to know and respect the appropriate boundaries. The literary record, he assumed, would be part artful reconstruction and part omission. In his most famous passage on the subject, Whitman writes in *Specimen Days,* "Future years will never know the seething hell and the black infernal background of countless minor scenes and interiors (not the official surface courteousness of the generals, not the few great battles) of the Secession War; and it is best they should not—the real war will never get in the books." The Civil War was being cleansed in the retelling. The result, Whitman tartly observed, was that the written war more nearly resembled "a quadrille in a ballroom" than the "seething hell" and moral miasma that the actual war often was. But, even so, Whitman was not entirely disapproving. There were things about the Civil War, he believed, that would "never be written—perhaps must not and should not be."[26]

Whitman clearly was torn between a desire to help hide the most distressing aspects of the war and a desire to chronicle the "real war." Early in *Specimen Days* he rhetorically asks:

What history . . . can ever give—for who can know—the mad, determined tussle of the armies, in all their separate large and little squads
. . . each steeped from crown to toe in desperate, mortal purports? Who
know the conflict, hand-to-hand—the many conflicts in the dark, those
shadowy-tangled, flashing-moonbeamed woods—the writhing groups
and squads—the cries, the din, the cracking guns and pistols—the
distant cannon—the cheers and calls and threats and awful music of
the oaths—the indescribable mix—the officers' orders, persuasions,
encouragements—the devils fully roused in human hearts—the strong
shout, *Charge, men, charge*—the flash of the naked sword, and rolling
flame and smoke? . . . Of scenes like these, I say, who writes—whoe'er
can write the story?

The brave deeds of scores of thousands of northerners and southerners, the
common soldiers whom Whitman admired and to whom he ministered,
would go unrecorded. They would be "unwrit heroes" and their deeds "unknown heroisms." So, too, troubling aspects of the war would go unwritten.[27]

Despite his underlying ambivalence, Whitman decides in *Specimen Days*
to "furnish a few stray glimpses" into the lives of actual soldiers, to give his
readers a glance "into those lurid interiors, never to be fully conveyed to the
future." Yet he also insistently reminds his readers that the "many-threaded
drama" of the war never will be captured in print. And the "untold and unwritten history of the war," Whitman contends, is "infinitely greater . . . than
the few scraps and distortions that are ever told or written."[28]

With a final, frank acknowledgment of his and other war writers' limitations and their shared reluctance to divulge certain truths, Whitman concludes the section of *Specimen Days* titled "The Real War Will Never Get in
the Books" with a bit of cautionary advice for his readers. He warns, "Think
how much, and of importance, will be—how much, civic and military, has
already been—buried in the grave, in eternal darkness."[29] Important aspects
of the war would not be chronicled. Other aspects would be chronicled
only within Whitman's journals.

Whitman penned some of the most overtly antiwar lines of the entire Civil
War generation. He vented his horror at the sight of war's human wreckage.
He questioned the role of God in allowing such full-scale destruction to
take place. He compared war to hell and fighters to devilish participants.
But he did all of this almost entirely within the privacy of his own diaries.

If the Civil War record was whitewashed by contemporary writers, Whitman was complicit. He added his own artful strokes to the collaborative paint job. In the progression of several of his war poems from first drafts to published works, Whitman's process of shaping the Civil War into presentable poetic form is plainly evident. One poem that underwent a radical revision as it traveled from the pages of the poet's personal journal to the pages of *Drum-Taps* is a piece originally titled "A Battle." The first draft appears in the notebook that Whitman carried with him while visiting Virginia in late December 1862.[30]

In lines of handwritten verse that fill four pages, Whitman offers a sensory tour of warfare. He masterfully evokes the sounds, sights, and smells of combat. First focusing on the noise of the battlefield, he records the "varied sounds of the different missiles." There is the "short s-s-t of the rifled ball," the "hum and buzz of the great shells," the "peculiar shriek" of other shells, the "rattle of musketry," and "the thud of the round ball falling in the soft earth." Then Whitman's focus shifts from musketry to men, and he catalogs a range of human noises, euphoric to agonized, made by the fighters. There is the "wild cry of a regiment charging" and a "cheer for a fine movement or charge." There are the "groans of the wounded" and the "shouts and curses of men."[31]

Next, Whitman describes the sights of the battlefield, including "the sight of blood." He notes the "scene at the batteries—what crashing and smoking!" He details how the "chief gunner ranges and sights his piece." And he repeatedly draws attention to the proximity of the living combatants to their dead comrades.[32]

Then, in the final section of the poem, Whitman describes the battle's aftermath, including the smells of the field hospital. The surgeons and ambulances converge on the "crowd of the bloody forms of soldiers," and Whitman captures the telling details. He notes "the smell of ether, the odor of blood," "the death-spasm," "the beautiful hair, clotted," and the "glisten of the little steel instruments."[33]

In addition to capturing the sights, sounds, and smells of combat in "A Battle," Whitman also records his profoundly troubled reaction to war's bloodletting. Interspersed throughout the poem are lines in which he openly calls attention to what he perceives as the immorality of warfare. Most notably, near the end of the poem, within the section describing the wounded, Whitman inserts the following stingingly harsh assessment:

O the hideous damned hell of war.
were the preachers preaching of hell?
O there is no hell more damned than this hell of war.[34]

"War is hell," General Sherman would famously proclaim.[35] But Whitman acknowledged it first.

In the privacy of his journal, Whitman wavered in his support of the Civil War. He had toured the battlefield and assisted in the burial of dead soldiers, and his poem conveys his stunned horror at what he saw. In the "Song of Myself" section of *Leaves of Grass,* written before the war, Whitman exudes an easy comfort with the realities of life and death:

Has any one supposed it lucky to be born?
I hasten to inform him or her it is just as lucky to die, and I know it.[36]

But the deaths that Whitman witnessed in Virginia were not lucky deaths. They did not conform to his understanding of the "kosmos."

The lines in "A Battle" depicting the battle-dead are extremely graphic. Whitman describes the corpses with none of the lofty language so commonly found in Civil War verse. In his early, enthusiastic war poetry—written before his visit to Virginia—Whitman had listed the various professions of men bound for war. In "A Battle" he offers a very different sort of list. With transparent horror, he records the various ways men appear in death:

The positions of the dead, some with arms raised, poised in the air,
Some lying curl'd on the ground—the dead in every position . . .
(Some of the dead, how soon they turn black in the face and swollen!)[37]

The passage is both quintessential Whitman and rawer than anything Whitman ever published.

The sight of the swollen and blackened corpses haunted Whitman. Try as he might, Whitman could not escape his memories of "the dead lying thick!" Near the end of "A Battle," Whitman writes, "Then after the battle, what a scene! O my sick soul! how the dead lie." In his journal jottings, Whitman revisits the subject. "After a severe battle," he notes, "the dead lie mostly on their backs—they swell & bloat—they turn very black & discolored." Whitman felt sickened and shaken by what he saw on the fields of Virginia. The wounded and the dead, the surgeons and ambulances, were like figures out of a ghoulish dream.[38]

Written while Whitman's initial impressions of combat were still fresh in his mind, "A Battle" reflects Whitman's surprised reaction to the Civil War's destruction. It is an uncensored work filled with images and sentiments that would have been repugnant to contemporary readers. Rather than offer decorous descriptions of soldiers mortally wounded, tearfully mourned, and tidily buried, Whitman wrote of the "delight infernal" of battle, of the soldiers' death spasms, and of the black and swollen dead.[39]

Whitman ventured well beyond the bounds of tidy romanticism and well into the realm of graphic realism. Yet he did so only within the assured privacy of his journal. The general public would not be privy to Whitman's dark thoughts on the subject of war.

Interestingly, a passage that is remarkably similar to Whitman's anguished description of the war dead would eventually appear in the autobiography of the Union army general Carl Schurz. In the final volume of his memoirs, the *Reminiscences of Carl Schurz*, the aged general would recall the ordeal of being under artillery fire on Cemetery Hill at Gettysburg. He would record that, after the great battle was finished, the Union dead "lay still in ghastly array on the ground where they had fallen." And he would recall his revulsion at the spectacle:

> There can be no more hideous sight than that of the corpses on a battlefield, after they have been exposed a day or more to the sun in warm weather—the bodies swollen to monstrous size, the faces bloated and black, the eyes bulging out with a dead stare, all their features puffed out almost beyond recognition, some lying singly or in rows, others in heaps, . . . others with arms raised, others in sitting position, others on their knees, others clawing the earth, many horribly distorted by what must have been a frightful death-struggle.[40]

Although Schurz described the battlefield at Gettysburg and Whitman described the one at Fredericksburg, their texts are strikingly similar. Both men list what Whitman terms the "positions of the dead." Both men focus on signs of mortal decay. Even the two writers' word choice overlaps. Indeed, it almost seems as if the general plagiarized the poet. Whitman described corpses "with arms raised." Schurz described corpses "with arms raised." Whitman described the dead "black in the face and swollen." Schurz described "faces bloated and black."

The volume of the *Reminiscences of Carl Schurz* that includes the description of Gettysburg was not published until 1908, more than forty-five years after Whitman penned the lines of "The Battle" in his journal. The shocked poet wrote his impressions of the battle-dead at Fredericksburg while the Civil War was still being waged. In the 1860s, to publish poems about swollen and blackened bodies would have been to defy the powerful conventions of romanticism. By contrast, Schurz wrote his memoirs in the final years of his life. By the time *Reminiscences* was published, Schurz was already dead and realism had long since gained solid ground in the literary marketplace.[41] The grisly realities of combat, so carefully suppressed in literature during and following the Civil War, were exposed only long after the fact.

In the 1860s, as the war was still being waged, Whitman kept his darkest thoughts to himself. On the page of his journal on which the conclusion to "A Battle" appears, Whitman first wrote the line, "O the hideous horrid hell of war." Then he drew a line through "horrid" and wrote above it "damned." It is a revealing change. Breaking the alliteration of "hideous horrid hell," Whitman decided on a more powerful invective. But his sharp judgment nowhere appears in the published version of the poem. In the lines of the poem set before the public, the Civil War is described as neither "horrid" nor "damned."[42]

In the published poem, instead of ruminating on war's hellish qualities, Whitman downplays the disturbing aspects of battle. Excising the most shocking lines from the original work, he conveys a sanitized image of combat. Gone from the poem is all mention of corpses swollen or discolored. Gone are the surgeons and ambulances. Gone, in fact, is any explicit mention of the war dead. The heavily revised poem—which appeared in *Drum-Taps* as "The Veteran's Vision" and in postwar editions of *Leaves of Grass* as "The Artilleryman's Vision"—lacks both the polemical punch and the immediacy of the original work. The "sounds of the different missiles" and "scenes at the batteries" remain. However, the battle is transformed from a lived reality into a safe but tantalizing "vision."

The published poem is set long after the war's conclusion and is told from the perspective of a war veteran. Lying in bed one night, the former artilleryman awakens from a dream to recall the sounds and scenes of the bygone war:

While my wife at my side lies slumbering, and the wars are over long,
And my head on the pillow rests at home, and the vacant midnight
    passes,
And through the stillness, through the dark, I hear, just hear, the breath
    of my infant,
There in the room as I wake from sleep this vision presses upon me.

In the middle of the night, as his wife and his child continue to sleep, the former artilleryman relives his wartime experiences. He explains, "All the scenes at the batteries rise in detail before me again." His memory of battle is vivid, but it is only a memory. He has outlived the danger posed by combat. He has survived the war.[43]

In Whitman's revised version of the poem, the Civil War has been tucked into the distant, hence safe, past. The war is recalled from the cozy comfort and assured safety of a matrimonial bed. Quite literally, the war has been domesticated. It has been transferred from the battlefield to the bedroom. And the attendant risks have been erased. Additionally, in the published poem, Whitman downplays the carnage and accentuates the thrill of combat. As the artilleryman relives the battle scene from long ago, he chooses to ignore the pain and suffering of those who were around him. Whitman has the artilleryman explain, "(The falling, dying, I heed not, the wounded dripping and red I heed not, some to the rear are hobbling)." In the version of the poem intended for the public, Whitman thus relegates the suffering of dying and wounded soldiers to a parenthetical aside. Moreover, he introduces lines emphasizing the peculiar exhilaration of combat. The artilleryman admits that the battle rouses "even in dreams a devilish exultation and all the old mad joy in the depths of [his] soul."[44] Why did Whitman retreat from his earlier, harsher assessment of the war? Why did he transform "A Battle" from a hellish nightmare to a dream of "mad joy"?

In his published poetry of the mid-1860s, Whitman insists on a version of the Civil War that conforms more neatly to his ideals than to the horrors he witnessed at Fredericksburg. Like the veteran artilleryman, he opts not to "heed" certain disturbing aspects of the war. However, in his published prose of the mid 1870s and 1880s, most notably in *Memoranda during the War* and *Specimen Days,* Whitman offers a more candid look at the war's carnage and expresses his own shocked and sickened reaction to the violence of the war.

In particular, on the pages of both works, Whitman describes in disturb-ing detail the battle at Chancellorsville. Although he did not witness the battle, which took place in the spring of 1863, Whitman learned about it from the wounded soldiers he cared for in Washington, and his writing has the vivid quality of a firsthand account.[45] As he had in "A Battle," Whitman candidly describes the sounds, sights, and even the smells attendant on war-fare. Moreover, Whitman freely admits his own feelings of outraged horror. "O heavens, what scene is this?—is this indeed *humanity*—these butchers' shambles? . . . There they lie . . . in an open space in the woods, from 200 to 300 poor fellows—the groans and screams—the odor of blood, mixed with the fresh scent of the night, the grass, the trees—that slaughterhouse!" In sharp contrast to the demure images of soldiers dying silent and stoic deaths that filled most Civil War works, Whitman offers an appalling im-age of bleeding, screaming "poor fellows" who lie by the hundreds on the bare ground. "Some have their legs blown off—some bullets through the breast—some indescribably horrid wounds in the face or head, all muti-lated, sickening, torn, gouged out." Whitman asks, "Is this indeed *human-ity*?" It is a profound question, and the answer is not entirely clear.[46]

By comparing war to a "slaughterhouse" and cataloging the "sickening" ways in which the soldiers are wounded, Whitman forthrightly challenges the romantic vision of warfare and the moral underpinning of battle. The image of butchery is one that recurs in Whitman's private wartime writings. In the wake of Gettysburg, he had admitted in a letter to his mother, "one's heart grows sick of war . . . it seems to me like a great slaughter-house & the men mutually butchering each other." In another letter home he lamented, "What an awful thing war is—Mother, it seems not men but a lot of dev-ils & butchers butchering each other."[47] That war is comparable to a giant slaughterhouse, an analogy suggested by Melville in *White-Jacket*, is an un-settling trope that would gain great currency in the twentieth century.[48] But it is a trope that Whitman, like Melville, used only selectively.

In his published war poetry of the mid-1860s, Whitman makes no men-tion of "butchers butchering" or slaughterhouses. He uses a far more deco-rous vocabulary. In his description of the mangled wounded at Chancel-lorsville in *Specimen Days,* Whitman writes of "the red life-blood oozing out from heads or trunks or limbs upon that green and dew-cool grass."[49] By contrast, in his poem "The Wound-Dresser," published in *Drum-Taps,* he describes injured soldiers, "Where they lie on the ground after the battle brought in, / Where their priceless blood reddens the grass the ground."[50] No blood oozes. No one screams. No one is described as "mutilated," "torn," or "gouged." And "The Wound-Dresser" is the most graphic of the *Drum-Tap* poems.

In *Drum-Taps* Whitman acknowledges the more unpleasant aspects of the war only very infrequently and very fleetingly. In "The Wound-Dresser" he describes wounds infected with a "gnawing and putrid gangrene" that is "sickening" and "offensive." In the brief poem "Look Down Fair Moon" he commands the moon to, "Pour softly down night's nimbus floods on faces ghastly, swollen, purple." But these are the rare exceptions. Overall, in *Drum-Taps* Whitman offers a cleansed, poignant, and uplifting interpretation of the years of fighting and sorrow. When a farmer's son dies in the poem "Come Up from the Fields Father," he does so not from an "indescribably horrid" wound, such as those Whitman would present in *Specimen Days*. Instead, he dies from that most conventionally heroic of Civil War deaths, a tidy "gunshot wound in the breast."[51]

Despite his misgivings, Whitman was determined in the mid-1860s to read—and to write—the war in a way that registered his hopes and optimism rather than his doubts and disgust. In early January 1865, several months before the Civil War would end, Whitman pronounced himself thoroughly satisfied with his war poems as they appeared in his manuscript of *Drum-Taps*. He wrote to a close friend, "Drum-Taps . . . delivers my ambition of the task that has haunted me, namely, to express in a poem (& in the way I like, which is not at all by directly stating it) the pending action of this *Time & Land we swim in,* with all their large conflicting fluctuations of despair & hope . . . with the unprecedented anguish of wounded & suffering, the beautiful young men, in wholesale death & agony, everything sometimes as if in blood-color, & dripping blood." The book was "unprecendently sad" he acknowledged, but it also had "clear notes of faith & triumph."[52]

Whitman's reaction to the Civil War was complex. The native New Yorker was a dedicated Unionist. Writing in the spring of 1863 to one of the wounded men whom he had cared for—and whom he had come to care for—he confided, "I believe this Union will conquer in the end, as sure as there's a God in heaven. This country can't be broken up by Jeff Davis, & all his damned crew."[53] Nonetheless, Whitman was profoundly shocked by the actuality of war. The bloated dead in no way conformed to his democratic ideals. The numerous, slim journals he filled during the war years became the repositories of his anguished thoughts about what he at one point termed, "these hells, these thrice hot hells of civil war."[54] But what he recorded in his diary remained private.

It is poignant to read Whitman's wartime writings and to realize how determinedly he kept his misgivings to himself. Regarding the war's fundamental morality, Whitman clearly was of two minds. Yet he guaranteed that his readership of the late 1860s never knew it. Why did he censor his response to the war? Ultimately, a combination of factors may have led Whitman to remove details about death and mangled soldiers from his poems and to conceal his own shock and horror.

Whitman certainly was not adverse to the prospect of making money from his war writings, and he was well aware of the conservative tastes of his potential readers. In the fall of 1863 he had contemplated writing a "book of the time"—based on his own experiences and hospital work in Washington —for the "larger American market." He had proposed the project, to be titled *Memoranda of a Year,* to a Boston publisher, James Redpath, who showed some interest. There would be a ready market for the volume in Washington and elsewhere, Whitman had claimed; the book "would please women" and be popular. An elegantly bound edition of the book, Whitman had even suggested, would be "very appropriate" as a present "for the holidays." Whitman had calculated the cost of publishing the book as well as the retail price and concluded, "It would be a very handsome speculation." Redpath, however, decided that the book would be too much of a financial strain for him, and the project moved no further toward publication. Whitman was not deterred. By the following spring, his thoughts had turned to bringing out a collection of his war poems, and again he focused on the potential profit of such a work. In a letter to his mother, he noted, "'Drum Taps' . . . may be a success pecuniarily."[55] And later that same year, while convalescing in Brooklyn, Whitman wrote, "I intend to move heaven and earth to publish my *Drum-Taps* as soon as I am able to go around."[56]

Popular and pecuniary success, however, eluded Whitman. Unable to find a willing publisher, he finally published *Drum-Taps* in April 1865 at his own expense. The volume, which was soon expanded to include *Sequel to Drum-Taps,* received scant notice and scanter praise. As the *Boston Commonwealth* reported in February 1866:

Having served in his chosen work through the war, both before and after his appointment and dismissal from a clerkship at Washington, [Whitman] sought in his native city a publisher for his patriotic verses, but he found none willing to put his name to the volume. Messrs. Bunce & Huntington finally printed it, but without their name, and without taking any of the customary steps to introduce the book to the reading public. It is scarcely to be got at a bookstore, has hardly been noticed by a newspaper, and, though full of the noblest verses, is utterly unknown to the mass of readers.

Others were far less flattering in their appraisal of Whitman's work. A review in the *Nation* that has been attributed to a youthful Henry James begins, "It has been a melancholy task to read this book; and it is a still more melancholy one to write about it." And an assessment of the volume printed in the *New York Times* judged:

Mr. Whitman has strong aspirations toward poetry, but he is wanting entirely in the qualities that [the popular English poet Winthrop Mackworth] Praed possessed in such large measure. He has no ear, no sense of the melody of verse. His poems only differ from prose in the lines being cut into length, instead of continuously pointed. . . . Considered as prose, then, we find in them a poverty of thought, paraded forth with a hubbub of stray words, and accompanied with a vehement self-assertion in the author, that betrays an absence of true and calm confidence in himself and his impulses. Mr. Whitman has fortunately better claims on the gratitude of his countrymen than any he will ever derive from his vocation as a poet.

Whitman's "ragged and broken" lines, so called by the *Independent*, little appealed to most contemporary readers. Revealingly, only outlying publications, such as the *Radical*, praised Whitman's efforts. A review that ran in that magazine in March 1866 noted, "And yet the author of *Leaves of Grass*, is as unquestionably a true poet, as the greatest of his contemporaries. He seems to us more purely permeated with the subtile essence of poetry than almost any other." Removing graphic details about corpses and hospital camps from his poetry had not sufficed to win Whitman an enthusiastic audience.[57]

In any case, it seems improbable that the revisions of his Civil War poetry were undertaken simply to guarantee public approval. That Whitman would have been willing to compromise his artistic principles and self-censor his poetry simply for profit or to conform to literary norms is un-likely. After all, he had refused to do so in the past. The early editions of *Leaves of Grass* had been sharply censured for including some highly sexual poems. But despite Ralph Waldo Emerson's entreaties, Whitman had in-sisted that these poems remain in the 1860 edition. Whitman was not in-clined to pander to public taste.

More likely, Whitman reshaped his poems to serve his patriotic purpose. The self-designated "wound-dresser" may have concluded that a series of poignant and inspiring war poems would be best suited to help ease the na-tion's pain. Moreover, by omitting detailed descriptions of carnage from his works, Whitman helped protect his readers, especially his female readers. When describing the suffering of the injured men at Chancellorsville on the pages of *Specimen Days,* Whitman would write, "O well is it their moth-ers, their sisters cannot see them—cannot conceive, and never conceived, these things."[58] As he prepared *Drum-Taps* for publication, Whitman likely concluded that there were certain things, certain horrors of battle, that were best left unexposed and unexpressed. Despite his moral misgivings, Whit-man evidently determined to make his poetry uplifting. Demonstrating his compassion, he would spare the war-weary nation unnecessary pain.

Ultimately, Whitman's shaping and reshaping of his war verses may have had the most to do with his own urgent need to view the war as proof that the democratic impulse beat strongly in the breast of all Americans. As George M. Fredrickson persuasively argues in *The Inner Civil War,* "[Whit-man] could give no formal expression to his sense of the war as an anony-mous 'slaughterhouse,' not only because his readers could not assimilate such an insight, but because, ultimately, he could not accept it himself."[59] Through his published war poems, Whitman endeavored to convince himself, and to convince posterity, that the war was not fought in vain. He desperately wanted to believe that America would not slip back into self-interested materialism once the war was over. He dreamed that a purified democracy would rise like a phoenix from the ashes of the war.

Sadly, in his wish to see America rise reborn and cleansed of all mean-ness and pettiness after its four-year struggle, Whitman was to be sorely disappointed. In his essay *Democratic Vistas,* published in 1871, he bemoans, "Never was there, perhaps, more hollowness at heart than at present, and here in the United States."[60] Whitman was disheartened, but he continued to put forth, in the revised editions of *Leaves of Grass,* an image of the Civil War in keeping with his faith that the war provided "immortal proofs of democracy."

Only in his writings published long after the war, most extensively in *Specimen Days,* did he publicly weigh other interpretations of the conflict and hint at his own dismayed response to the carnage. The seething hell of the real war—the realist's war—would never get in the books. At least, it would never appear in Walt Whitman's *Leaves of Grass.*

7

THE CIVIL WAR REWRITTEN IN
THE POSTWAR DECADES

But to lie inglorious beneath showers of shrapnel darting divergent from the
unassailable sky—meekly to be blown out of life by level gusts of grape—to
clench our teeth and shrink helpless before big shot pushing noisily through
the consenting air—this was horrible!

—Ambrose Bierce, "What I Saw of Shiloh," 1881

 near uniform reluctance to challenge the idealized representation of the Civil War shaped American literature published
during the 1860s. Even in the 1870s and early 1880s, the voice
of dissent remained nearly silent. However, as the war receded into history,
American writers gradually became more outspoken, and more overtly antiwar works began to appear in print.

Herman Melville, John William De Forest, and Walt Whitman all questioned the basic morality of armed battle and defied, at least in their private
works, the prevailing literary conventions for writing about the Civil War.
According to the romantic norm, soldiers marched fearlessly into the fray.
They squarely and fairly met their foe. If they were shot, they usually were
shot in the breast. If they died, they were buried in tranquil, wooded glades.
Hundreds upon hundreds of Civil War writers, amateurs and professionals,
helped perpetuate this highly pleasing image of warfare. The three northern
authors presented familiar subjects of war literature—soldiers, casualties,
hospitals—in new and disturbing ways. They offered a graphic and grisly
picture of what took place on the battlefield. Diverging from what was
deemed to be in good taste, they showed the brutal damage that war could
wreak upon the bodies of men. They presented corpses bloated, blackened,
mutilated, frozen, burned, and barely recognizable as human.

Melville, Whitman, and De Forest ventured onto dangerous literary
ground; nonetheless, they all supported the Union cause. They depicted
the horrors of combat and criticized military mismanagement, and in their

diaries, letters, poems, memoirs, and novels shine glimmers of a bold, shockingly explicit way of writing about war. But none of the authors took a steady stance against the Civil War. Despite their intermittent doubts, they shared a common sense that the North's call-to-arms was, in Melville's words, a "sanctioned sin."

Even so, the published works of these three iconoclastic writers were not well received in their day. Melville's *Battle-Pieces* sold poorly, as did De Forest's novel *Miss Ravenel's Conversion*. Whitman, who of the three seems to have practiced the greatest degree of self-censorship, reported in the late 1880s that *Leaves of Grass*, of which the *Drum-Taps* sequence had become an integral part, was "from a worldly and business point of view . . . worse than a failure." As Whitman wrote, "I have not gain'd the acceptance of my own time."[1] To break from literary conventions and question, even indirectly, war's morality during the sensitive decade of the 1860s was to court professional failure.

Other potential antiwar writers did not challenge the standard representation of the Civil War at all. Even traditional peace advocates, who might have been expected to present a moral argument against the pursuance of the war, largely fell silent during the war years.[2] The American Peace Society, which had opposed the Mexican War in the 1840s, was essentially inoperative during the early 1860s.[3] In any case, the organization did not even recognize the Civil War as such. As Charles Chatfield explains in *Peace Movements in America*, "The official line of the Society was that the Civil War was not a proper war at all; it was a rebellion against rightful authority or an assertion of Southern iniquity which would have to be quashed in order to make peace possible."[4]

Nor did other war opponents step forward during the four years of the war to shape a body of antiwar literature. Aside from overtly political tracts written by "Peace Democrats" in the North and "Croakers" in the South, who opposed the Civil War but not war per se, and religious tracts written by Quakers, Mennonites, and members of other historically pacifist religious sects, almost no explicitly antiwar literature was published during the war.[5] And as Peter Brock observes in *Pacifism in the United States*, even new literature on "the [Christian] peace testimony"—pamphlets bearing such titles as "War and Christianity Irreconcilable: An Address to Christians" and "On the Incompatibility of War with the Spirit of Christianity"—was meager during the war years.[6]

Notably absent from the thin ranks of religious writers who protested the war was the well-established Quaker poet John Greenleaf Whittier. An ardent abolitionist, he advised his readers to wait out the conflict without protest:

> Then let the selfish lip be dumb,
>   And hushed the breath of sighing;
> Before the joy of peace must come
>   The pains of purifying.
>   God give us grace
>   Each in his place
>   To bear his lot,
>   And, murmuring not,
>   Endure and wait and labor![7]

Along with most other abolitionists, Whittier viewed the war as a necessary evil that would lead to a worthy end, and he did not use his popularity or considerable poetic talent to protest the war. To the contrary, Whittier actually won recognition during the war years for his patriotic verses. His volume *In War Time, and Other Poems,* published in 1863, served to boost northern morale and even garnered the poet an invitation to visit the Army of the Potomac. While making that visit in 1864, Whittier won the praise of a brigadier general, who proclaimed, "Your loyal verse has made us all your friends, lightening the wearisomeness of our march, brightening our lonely campfires, and cheering our hearts in battle."[8] And that same year a literary critic for the *North American Review* approvingly commented, "Whittier is the only one of our older poets whom the war seems adequately to have inspired."[9]

Members of America's traditional peace churches either decamped to join the army—the poet Bayard Taylor, himself of Quaker stock, reported a few days after the attack on Fort Sumter, "All the young Quakers have enlisted"—or else remained largely silent during the Civil War years.[10] In any case, they made virtually no contribution to secular, antiwar literature.

Throughout the late 1860s, 1870s, and early 1880s, Americans showed a reluctance to publish or read about the Civil War.[11] Apart from a smattering of southern romances, fresh works about the war years were few. Revisiting the trauma of the conflict was still too painful to be appealing. As the century neared its close, however, a renewed literary interest in the Civil War became manifest. As the novelist and Union veteran Albion W. Tourgée aptly observed in early 1887, "One of the most notable features of our recent literature has been the revival of interest in matters connected with the war of rebellion."[12]

Between 1884 and 1887, the *Century* magazine ran its very successful "Battles and Leaders of the Civil War" series, and there was an outpouring of new romances about the war. More critical, ironic, and realistic depictions of the war also began to appear and gradually pushed back the boundaries of what was acceptable to write about the conflict. Civil War sentimentalists still abounded, but in the late 1880s and 1890s a new breed of war writers—including Stephen Crane and Ambrose Bierce—was published and well received.

In this later, postbellum period, one of these authors who challenged the traditional representation of what he called "the American War" was the journalist and novelist Harold Frederic. His novel *The Copperhead* appeared in 1893 and cast in a favorable light an upstate New York farmer who staunchly opposed the war. Frederic has his farmer protest, "This war—this wicked war between brothers—must stop." And he has the farmer, a man ostracized and relentlessly persecuted by his zealously patriotic neighbors, deliver such morally righteous speeches as, "Why, just think what's been a-goin on! Great armies raised, hundreds of thousands of honest men taken from their work an' set to murderin' each other, whole deestricks of country torn up by the roots, homes desolated, the land filled with widows an' orphans, an' every house a house of mournin'."[13] The farmer's broken dialect and the angry sentiments he expresses signal Frederic's disdain for florid romanticism. In *The Copperhead* and other of his war stories, Frederic upturned the standard understanding of the Civil War. Writing in the early 1970s, Edmund Wilson observed, "[Harold Frederic's stories] avoid Civil War clichés, and they stand as acrid first-hand testimony to the delusions and lasting grievances inflicted on American society by that fracture."[14]

On the subject of the Civil War, Frederic clearly was a renegade writer, but his war stories were written at a significant remove—both temporal and physical—from the war. By the time *The Copperhead* appeared, nearly three decades had passed since the fighting had ended and Frederic himself had long since moved to England to serve as the London correspondent for the *New York Times*. Frederic belonged to the postwar generation. He was a young boy when the fighting began, and living in upstate New York, he experienced the war far from the fray. Describing his Civil War stories, Frederic once explained, "They are in large part my own recollections of the dreadful time—the actual things that a boy from five to nine saw or heard about him, while his own relatives were being killed, and his school-fellows orphaned, and women of his neighborhood forced into mourning and despair—and they had a right to be recorded."[15]

Stephen Crane, whose own slim novel *The Red Badge of Courage* verily shook the field of war literature when it appeared in 1895, was born too late to experience the war at all. Whether Crane's book constitutes an antiwar novel has been much debated. What is clear is that it presented a new direction in war writing and even anticipated the antiwar works that would be written about World War I.[16]

The plot of Crane's work pivots on a young soldier's transformation from idealistic civilian to disillusioned veteran. Henry Fleming is a farm boy who, shivering "in a prolonged ecstasy of excitement," decides to enlist. He heads off to war, brimming with patriotism and a boyish enthusiasm for glory. "Tales of great movements shook the land. They might not be distinctly Homeric, but there seemed to be much glory in them. He had read of marches, sieges, conflicts, and he had longed to see it all. His busy mind had drawn for him large pictures extravagant in color, lurid with breathless deeds." However, what he finds at the battlefront is nothing like his idealized image of combat. When his best friend dies of a chest injury that leaves his side looking "as if it had been chewed by wolves," Henry feels "sudden, livid rage" and utters a single word, "Hell—."[17]

The Civil War, as imagined by Crane, is indeed hellish. At one juncture, Henry feels a "dull, animal like rebellion against his fellows, war in the abstract, and fate," and his brain is in "a tumult of agony and despair." He seeks comfort in nature, which he conceives of as a "woman with a deep aversion to tragedy." Fleeing from the chaos of combat, Henry discovers a place where arching boughs create a space like a chapel that is filled with a "religious half light." But even nature betrays him. The spectacle that greets Henry is anything but inspiring. He stops at the threshold "horror stricken":

> He was being looked at by a dead man who was seated with his back against a columnlike tree. The corpse was dressed in a uniform that once had been blue, but was now faded to a melancholy shade of green. The

eyes, staring at the youth, had changed to the dull hue to be seen on
the side of a dead fish. The mouth was open. Its red had changed to an
appalling yellow. Over the gray skin of the face ran little ants. One was
trundling some sort of a bundle along the upper lip.

The graphic detail of Crane's description seems almost gratuitously horrific,
but it did not deter readers.[18]

The Red Badge of Courage proved to be a hugely popular and influential
work. Even though Crane never had experienced war, he quickly became
the most famous American war writer of his day. Indeed, his book's publisher had trouble meeting the great demand for the work, and in the first
ten months of 1896, the novel went through thirteen American printings.
Praising the book on the pages of the *New York Times* in January 1896—in a
piece titled "Stephen Crane's Triumph"—Harold Frederic remarked on the
enthusiastic reception the work was receiving in both America and England. He noted, "Reviews burst forth in a dozen different quarters, hailing it
as extraordinary." And Frederic further observed, "It is evident that for the
next few months it is to be more talked about than anything else in current
literature. It seems almost equally certain that it will be kept alive, as one
of the deathless books which must be read by everybody who desires to
be, or to seem, a connoisseur of modern fiction." Crane's work, as Frederic
and other contemporary literary critics were quick to note, was "something
not like other things." It thrust aside all of "the historic and prescribed machinery of the romance." Summarizing what made the new book seem so
extraordinary, Frederic wrote, "The 'Red Badge' impels the feeling that the
actual truth about a battle has never been guessed before."[19]

Crane's book not only reshaped the reading public's perceptions of battle but also served for later generations of war writers as a model of their
craft. While waiting to be shipped to Europe in the fall of 1918, John Dos
Passos—who, after World War I, would emerge as one of America's most
prolific and prominent antiwar writers—read *The Red Badge of Courage*.[20]
So, too, Dos Passos's friend and fellow war writer Ernest Hemingway read
the novel and hailed it as "one of the finest books of our literature."[21]

In the progression of Civil War literature, and of American war literature as a whole, *The Red Badge of Courage* proved to be a seminal text. As
one of Crane's biographers writes, "Appearing at a time when the war was
still treated primarily as the subject for romance, [*The Red Badge of Courage*] turned the tide of the prevailing convention and established a new if

not unprecedented one."[22] Nevertheless, Crane was a student of the Civil War not a survivor. He was born in 1871, six years after Lee's surrender at Appomattox.

As the century neared its close, one war veteran did step forward to forcibly challenge the romantic literary norm. Melville, De Forest, and Whitman had been in their late thirties or forties during the war years. Ambrose Bierce had entered the war years as a teenager. In mid-April 1861, at the age of eighteen, he joined the Ninth Indiana Volunteers, and he participated in almost every major battle in the western theater until he was released from active duty, on medical grounds, in late January 1865. Decades later, Bierce began to write about the Civil War in a style that was more flagrantly graphic and gruesome than any of the early realists of the 1860s had attempted. Whereas typical Civil War works elicit the reader's empathetic or patriotic response, Bierce's works evoke in the reader shock, disgust, and dismay.

In numerous short stories Bierce mapped out, as perhaps only a veteran could, the myriad distortions of mind and body that months and years of fighting could wreak upon a soldier. Between 1887 and 1893 Bierce produced the majority of his most famous war stories and *Tales of Soldiers and Civilians,* a volume containing many of these works, appeared in 1891. Included in it was "Chickamauga," as well as another horrifying story titled "One Officer, One Man." A scene from "One Officer, One Man," in which a Captain Graffenreid is initiated into battle, well displays Bierce's style. He writes: "Captain Graffenreid lay alongside the dead man, from beneath whose breast flowed a little rill of blood. It had a faint, sweetish odor that sickened him. The face was crushed into the earth and flattened. It looked yellow already, and was repulsive. Nothing suggested the glory of a soldier's death nor mitigated the loathsomeness of the incident."[23] Bierce's rejection of romanticism is obvious, even heavy-handed. He takes the old convention of a soldier shot in the breast and gives it a "sickening" and "repulsive" new twist. And he does not stop there.

Captain Graffenreid is an officer who eagerly entered into battle, yet by battle's end he deliberately kills himself. Bierce writes, "Of all the Federal Army on that summer morning none had accepted battle more joyously than Anderton Graffenreid. His spirit was buoyant, his faculties were riotous. He was in a state of mental exaltation and scarcely could endure the enemy's tardiness in advancing to the attack." Foremost in Captain Graffenreid's mind as he prepared for the fray was that "he should prove himself a soldier and a hero." But the captain's "conception of war" undergoes "a profound change" during the battle. He feels fear and jumps when a shell passes a hundred feet to his left. He imagines that his first lieutenant and the men in the front ranks are laughing at him. Awaiting an order to attack, Graffenreid is "unnerved" and experiences a "strain upon his nervous organization" that is "insupportable." Convinced that his honor has been irrevocably compromised and that he has completely failed to prove himself a fearless leader, Captain Graffenreid thrusts his "naked sword" into his breast, falls on the corpse with the crushed face, and dies.[24]

Rather than depict a gallant man who fearlessly confronts battle's waves with sword upraised, Bierce presents an officer committing suicide mid-battle. It is a testament to the change in literary sensibility that Bierce's story found a receptive readership. Applauding Bierce's attempt to explore the psychological realm of battle, one contemporary essayist observed in the *North American Review*, "Mr. Ambrose Bierce has portrayed for us with remorseless exactness the experience of an untried officer in his story, *One Officer, One Man*. On reading it one has a most uncanny fellow feeling with Captain Graffenreid."[25]

Other of Bierce's stories focus on the perversion of normal human relations in wartime. In "A Horseman in the Sky" a Federal soldier shoots his Confederate father out of the saddle. In "The Affair at Coulter's Notch" a Union artillery officer obeys commands to take aim at his own home and effectively orders the deaths of his own wife and child. In "One of the Missing" a Union soldier stops to consider "where he could plant his shot with the best hope of making a widow or an orphan or a childless mother,—perhaps all three."[26] As Bierce strains to demonstrate in these and other tales full of graphic realism and psychic horror, acts that would be morally reprehensible and criminal in peacetime become, if not laudable, at least legally sanctioned in times of war.

Most writers of the Civil War tactfully underplayed the unpleasantness of combat, but Bierce focused on the ugly and disturbing aspects of war to the near exclusion of all else. In his first published reminiscence about the war—an article titled "What I Saw of Shiloh" that was published at the end of 1881—Bierce records that "in many of the engagements of the war the fallen leaves took fire and roasted the fallen men. At Shiloh, during the first day's fighting, wide tracts of woodland were burned over in this way and scores of wounded who might have recovered perished in slow torture."[27]

There is something familiar about the passage. Melville hinted in his poetry that soldiers perished in the flames of the Battle of the Wilderness. Whitman would record in *Specimen Days* that patches of the woods caught fire at Chancellorsville, taking the lives of wounded men and "burning the dead also."[28] But Bierce goes far beyond what even the most candid of the first generation of Civil War writers ever published.

Not content to leave the image of the men who died in the Tennessee forest to his reader's imagination, Bierce describes the "postures of agony that told of the tormenting flame" in which the bodies, "half buried in ashes," lay. "Their clothing was half burnt away—their hair and beard entirely; the rain had come too late to save their nails. Some were swollen to double girth; others shriveled to manikins. According to degree of exposure, their faces were bloated and black or yellow and shrunken. The contraction of muscles which had given them claws for hands had cursed each countenance with a hideous grin." Bierce dwells on the appalling distortions to the human body and the human psyche that were caused by the war. He offers war's damage as prima facie evidence of war's evil. There is nothing reassuring about Bierce's tales of war. There is nothing redemptive about the experience of battle. After his stomach-churning description of the burnt soldiers, Bierce concludes, "Faugh! I cannot catalogue the charms of these gallant gentlemen who had got what they enlisted for."[29]

Bierce rewrote the story of the war as much bleaker and rawer than it had previously been presented. Yet the very qualities that would have disqualified Bierce's work for popular appeal in the 1860s were used to market his books to a mass audience in the 1890s. A quotation from the *Scottish Leader* used in an 1898 publisher's advertisement for *In the Midst of Life: Tales of Soldiers and Civilians* (a revised and expanded collection of Bierce's stories) reads, "Mr. Bierce portrays the most appalling scenes with a deliberation, a force, and a precision that are rarely seen. A remarkable literary feat."[30] Verisimilitude had become a selling point, and Bierce's war stories won the plaudits of his contemporaries. As the author of *Ambrose Bierce: The Making of a Misanthrope* notes, Bierce's unsettling tales of soldiers and civilians "were praised by the majority of critics as highly unique, novel and boldly experimental."[31]

However, Bierce's exploration of war's horrors also clearly threatened the status quo. During World War I, two of Bierce's collections—*In the Midst of Life* and *Can Such Things Be?*—would be placed off-limits to American soldiers. Military censors, fearing that the works might destroy the morale of the troops, added the titles to an army index of "improper books" containing "dangerous thoughts" that were banned from army camps and from all posts where American soldiers were located.[32]

Bierce outdistanced his literary predecessors in writing about the Civil War's unseemly spectacles. He broke new ground in describing combat's physical and psychological toll. He led the way for future antiwar writers. But he did so only decades after the war, long after the fighting at Chickamauga and elsewhere had ended. His was a retrospective reinterpretation of the war.

Daniel Aaron contends in *The Unwritten War*, a comprehensive study of American Civil War literature, that the great Civil War novel was never written. Even more certain is the fact that the great antiwar novel was never written, or at least it was not written by anyone who lived through the war. De Forest's *Miss Ravenel's Conversion* comes closest, with its critique of military men and its brutal candor about war's fundamental horror, but it does not pack a solidly antiwar punch. And *The Red Badge of Courage,* the book now most frequently remembered as the greatest Civil War novel and antiwar novel, was written by an author who did not experience the Civil War firsthand. Although no great antiwar novel was written either during or soon after the war, other works were written that boldly questioned the consensus view of the war as morally righteous.

The letters, journal entries, poems, and fiction that Herman Melville, John William De Forest, and Walt Whitman wrote in the 1860s most nearly anticipated the antiwar literature that emerged in the final decades of the nineteenth century and flourished in the twentieth century. Yet these writers of the 1860s each practiced a form of self-censorship. Whether yielding to social pressure or their own sense of propriety, they did not allow into print the full extent of their dark thoughts. They did not share with the reading public their most vehement condemnations of the war.

In the 1860s, to describe the details of war's violence with great candor, much less to publicly question war's morality, was still a daunting task. Both privately and publicly, authors worried about overstepping the acceptable bounds for war writing. De Forest stated in a letter to William Dean Howells in the late 1880s that nobody but Leo Tolstoy had "written the whole truth about war and battle." Yet even Tolstoy worried about the consequences of unrestrained truth-telling. In 1855 and 1856 the Russian author wrote a series of sketches about the Crimean War. At the end of one of these pieces—in which, among other things, he described a ten-year-old boy's encounter with a "terrible, headless" corpse—Tolstoy muses, "Now I have said all that I wished to say on this occasion. I am, however, beset by a painful thought. Perhaps I ought not to have said it. Perhaps what I have said belongs to the category of those harmful truths each of us carries around in his subconscious, truths we must not utter aloud lest they cause active damage."[33] As authors of the mid- and late nineteenth century realized, words had the power to change people's perception of warfare. As gatekeepers to the "truths," writers took their responsibilities for maintaining public morality and morale very seriously. Avoiding "active damage," most contemporary writers attempted to use their poetry and prose to positive ends. They offered their fellow citizens patriotic and sentimental war works. Other writers would reveal more "harmful truths."

THE CHANGING WAYS OF FIGHTING AND WRITING WAR

It is not an uncommon observation that all the great inventions and discoveries which have contributed to mark the present century as the most extraordinary in the history of the world's progress have been immediately employed, so far as possible, to the "abominable end of annihilating mankind."

—John Millis, "Electricity in Land Warfare," 1889

8

THE RAPID MODERNIZATION OF
WEAPONRY AND WARFARE

So rapid has been the advance in military science that the weapons of a generation ago are to-day only fit for decorations,—of doubtful artistic value,—in
our public parks. The best guns of the Civil War period, made of cast-bronze or
wrought-iron and strengthened with metal bands, are as extinct as the stage-
coach. Even the field-guns of the Spanish War are hopelessly outclassed.

—Francis A. Collins, *The Fighting Engineers*, 1918

 ach new generation of American soldiers has marched to war
shouldering a new generation of firearms, and it is impossible
to understand American war literature of the late nineteenth
and early twentieth centuries without taking into consideration the corresponding changes in the technology of warfare. Unquestionably, the rapid
pace of change during the era was quite astonishing. Thanks in large part to
American ingenuity, the progression from smoothbore musket to machine
gun took place in less than fifty years.

New forms of weaponry fundamentally altered the way that combat was
conducted. Although some Americans welcomed the steady trend toward
modernization in warfare, most writers viewed it with alarm. Indeed, from
the late nineteenth century onward, an ever growing number of authors
came to consider the new generations of "killing machines" as proof of war's
immorality or, at least, as evidence of modern war's profoundly alienating
and unromantic dimensions. Although the heroic conception of war did
not disappear, a countering conception of war as slaughter steadily gained
acceptance. In order fully to appreciate the magnitude of change that occurred between the mid-nineteenth and early twentieth centuries, it is help-
ful to begin with a quick overview of the weaponry and ways of warfare
from the American Revolution up to World War I.

The Revolutionary War was fought with essentially the same type of
guns that had been in service for two hundred years. The soldiers of Gen-

eral Washington's army took aim at their British enemies with flintlock muskets—large caliber, smoothbore guns with socket bayonets. Theoretically, the unwieldy muskets were capable of killing at a range of up to two hundred yards, but in practice the likelihood of a soldier hitting a given target at a distance of even a hundred yards was slim to nil. In his authoritative history *Arms and Men,* Walter Millis notes that the muskets were "so wildly inaccurate that aimed fire against a man-sized target was of little use at even fifty yards."[1] Additionally, the flintlock muskets frequently misfired, and in bad weather, especially during heavy rain, the slugs of powder and ball, which were wrapped in paper and rammed down the musket muzzle, became sodden and useless.

The limitations of the flintlock muskets dictated how the Revolutionary War was fought. "Don't fire until you see the whites of their eyes," was no mere maxim. The fact that it was impossible to aim the muskets accurately at any great distance meant that defending soldiers usually did not open fire until their advancing enemy stood practically in front of them. Once the defending soldiers did fire, rarely was there enough time for them to go through the slow process of reloading their guns before their attackers were upon them and they were drawn into hand-to-hand combat. Instead of shooting a second round, soldiers battled their enemy with bayonet and musket butt.

In addition to affecting the way in which combatants engaged one another, the fault-prone flintlocks also determined the seasons and weather conditions in which men could fight. The fact that the muskets were utterly ineffective in rain or snow meant that battles primarily took place in certain seasons. Washington's ragged Continental Army retired into winter quarters at Valley Forge in Pennsylvania on December 17, 1777, to drill and train and emerged the following spring a better disciplined and more cohesive fighting force.

The smoothbore musket dominated warfare from the late sixteenth century through the eighteenth century, but in the nineteenth century it was soon outmoded. Eli Whitney, now commonly remembered as the inventor of the cotton gin, was responsible for one of the most significant innovations in the production of modern firearms. Prior to Whitney, the manufacture of guns had been time and labor intensive. The parts of each gun were made individually and assembled by an expert craftsman. Whitney offered a far more efficient and cost effective alternative. As a teenager during the Revolutionary War, he had turned his father's toolshed into a small nail factory, and as an adult he conceived of the use of interchangeable parts in guns. He invented guns so accurately and uniformly made that any part of one gun could be fit into another. Moreover, all parts of his guns could be pieced together using an assembly-line style of production. During the War of 1812 Whitney's muskets won great acclaim, and in time, his fundamental principle of interchangeable parts and assembly-line production was put into practice by all realms of modern industry. It made possible the age of mass production as well as mass warfare.

On the heels of Whitney's innovations, others quickly followed. The invention of the fulminate of mercury percussion cap greatly improved the functioning of the smoothbore musket. Replacing the old flintlock device, the new percussion cap was not affected by wetness. Consequently, it became possible for soldiers to fire their arms reliably in rain or snow. The Model 1841 cap lock became the standard military musket, and in 1842, four years before the start of the Mexican War, U.S. government arsenals ended production of flintlock muskets. In addition, guns with cylindrically grooved barrels began to replace guns with smoothbore barrels. This new generation of weapons gave bullets a horizontal spin, thereby increasing the long-range accuracy of firepower. Once the problem of designing a bullet to suit this "rifled" barrel was solved in the late 1840s by a French officer with the invention of the "minié ball" (a conical bullet that expanded to lock with the grooves in the barrel), the U.S. Army began switching to rifled muskets.

By the mid-1850s the army had fully adopted rifled muskets as the soldier's standard arms and had stopped manufacturing smoothbore muskets. The weaponry of war was rapidly changing, and contemporary observers took note. As the Civil War loomed, the military and tactical theorist Dennis Hart Mahan (whose son Alfred Thayer Mahan a generation later would write the broadly acclaimed study *The Influence of Sea Power Upon History*) commented, "At no past period has mechanical invention, in its bearing on the military art, been more active than at the present day. . . . The great destruction of life, in open assaults, . . . must give additional value to entrenched fields of battle."[2] However, the generals of the Civil War—North and South—were slow to realize the implications of the new technology. Schooled at West Point to revere the writings of such highly regarded military critics as the Prussian Carl von Clausewitz and the Swiss Antoine Henri Jomini, they remained convinced of the incomparable merit of the offensive approach to warfare. But if frontal assaults and bayonet charges had constituted sound military tactics in the age of the Napoleonic Wars about which Clausewitz and Jomini theorized, they were not well suited to the realities of mid-nineteenth-century weaponry. The new cap lock rifled muskets, which had a killing range of five hundred yards, made offensive charges suicidal.

When frontal assaults were attempted during the Civil War, they almost invariably met with disastrous results. At Antietam in September 1862, ranks of attacking Union soldiers were shot down in marching formation. At Fredericksburg in December 1862, casualties in the attacking Union army outnumbered Confederate casualties by more than two to one. At Gettysburg in July 1863, over 50 percent of the thousands of Confederate fighters ordered across a mile of open ground to attack Union infantry positions supported by cannons, numbered as casualties. And at Cold Harbor in June 1864, as many as seven thousand Union soldiers were killed or wounded in the course of a few hours as they tried to attack the fortified Confederate lines. One survivor who took part in the ill-fated Pickett's Charge at Gettysburg described the experience with chilling immediacy. "Volley after volley of crashing musket balls [swept] through the line and mow[ed] us down like the wheat before the scythe."[3]

The new guns gave unprecedented power to the tactical defense. As the Civil War demonstrated, it was no longer practical to lead soldiers into battle shoulder-to-shoulder in orderly lines. Close-order infantry tactics simply were not suited to the precision and volume of mid-nineteenth-century firepower. Rifled muskets had become so accurate at long range that they could be loaded and fired multiple times as the enemy attacked. By contrast, the exposed attacking forces could not easily stop to take careful aim or to reload, and if the defending forces were entrenched or otherwise protected, their opponents were unable to target them at all.

New technology demanded new tactics. The rifled musket clearly favored the defense and, as Mahan had astutely predicted, ushered in the age of trench warfare. At the outset of the Civil War it was thought cowardly to hide in a ditch. By the end of 1862 both armies routinely dug in whenever they halted. A passage from a postwar novel by Joseph Kirkland, *The Captain of Company K,* demonstrates the new importance of trenches and the failure of military regulations to keep apace of the times. Before the Battle of Shiloh, a soldier engages in a conversation with an officer about the building of breastworks. The soldier picks up his well-worn copy of "army regulations" and reads aloud, "Section 643. Unless the army be acting on the defensive, no post should be intrenched." The officer responds, "Ya-as, I know old Section 643 by heart, and I'd make a special intrenchment expressly to bury Section 643 in." The officer then explains to the novice soldier that men anticipating an attack will use anything they can to build trenches. They will make use of such specialized tools as picks and shovels and, if need be, of such improvised tools as "bayonets, musket-butts, rails, branches, tin-cups, dinner-plates, caps, shoes, feet, fists, fingers and finger-nails." Kirkland, a veteran as well as a novelist, well knew of what he wrote.[4]

Trench warfare changed both the landscape of war and the day-to-day life of soldiers. The summer of 1864 found the deadlocked armies of Grant and Lee entrenched in well-fortified lines outside Petersburg, Virginia. As this new form of warfare gradually became a way of life, night attacks became commonplace, and a new style of continuous fighting emerged. Whereas Union soldiers were rotated in and out of their trenches, the un-lucky men of the depleted Confederate regiments often spent months at a stretch in theirs.

Trench warfare also invited other changes. The mortar—a stubby, short-barreled cannon used to hurl shells short distances—became a popular weapon. Fighting was also taken substratum. Mining and underground explosions were attempted, although they did not necessarily bring the desired results. (The Union forces detonated eight thousand pounds of gun-powder beneath the Confederate works southeast of Petersburg on July 30 and then sustained nearly four thousand casualties in a failed attack following the explosion.)

Changes in weaponry also resulted in changes in attitudes about proper war conduct. The practice of sharpshooting, considered distasteful and ungallant at the beginning of the Civil War, had become commonplace by the war's close. Artillerymen who attempted to move forward with infantry troops were targeted by sharpshooters. Likewise, officers on the battlefield were singled out by enemy sharpshooters (and soon learned to stop displaying their insignia). Even soldiers who ventured out of their trenches to answer the call of nature risked being shot by eagle-eyed marksmen. So too was war brought to bear directly against a civilian population, most famously in Sherman's destructive March to the Sea in late 1864.

Several major technological advances of the first half of the nineteenth century—the telegraph, railroad, and steamship—also had major effects on the tactics and scale of the Civil War and proved of key importance to the North's victory. These new modes of transportation and communication made it possible for troops and supplies to be moved quickly and reliably from place to place. For the first time in the history of American warfare, vast armies of hundreds of thousands of soldiers could be maintained and maneuvered in the field.

The expansion in the size of armies and the introduction of new weaponry imperiled the romantic view of war as a sphere for demonstrating individual heroism. As armies grew ever larger, the relative significance of each individual soldier grew smaller, and the war he participated in grew ever more sprawling and anonymous. Washington commanded an army of a mere nine thousand men at the Battle of Yorktown in the fall of 1781. Less than a century later, Generals Grant and Sherman each commanded more than one hundred thousand soldiers. Overall, the Civil War saw the disappearance of tightly massed charges and witnessed the gradual emergence of a form of "modern" warfare in which battles were more frequent, more spread out, and less decisive.

The "devolution from warfare-as-duel," a phrase coined by John Limon, was well under way by the end of the Civil War, and the next few decades quickened the process.[5] Indeed, compared to the rate of change in earlier American military history, the rapidity with which new weapons were introduced in the late nineteenth century and then quickly became outmoded was astounding. The flintlock musket had reigned supreme as the standard military weapon for more than two hundred years. Within the span of just thirty years, from 1873 to 1903, the U.S. Army went through four different generations of rifles. First, the army replaced the slow-loading rifle of the Civil War era with the quick-firing Model 1873 Springfield rifle. But, before long, the Springfield breechloader also became obsolete.

The development of smokeless powder, called cordite, by the British at the end of the century had a dramatic effect on the course of modern warfare. It eliminated the telltale clouds of smoke that previously had revealed the location of battlefield artillery. In recalling how it felt to be under fire at Shiloh during the Civil War, Ambrose Bierce wrote that the Union artillery guns "seemed to raise their 'cloud by day' solely to direct aright the streaming procession of Confederate missiles."[6] The new smokeless powder proved indispensable to armies hoping to avoid enemy detection on the battlefield.

Another consequence of the powder was that it rendered battlefields more visible to combatants. Whereas clouds of dense smoke formerly had hung over entire battlefields, the new battlefield was relatively smoke free. As the Polish writer Jean de Bloch noted in his influential work *The Future of War*, which was translated into English in 1899, "Now armies will no longer fight in the dark. Every soldier in the fighting line will see with frightful distinctness the havoc which is being made in the ranks by the shot and shell of the enemy. The veil which gunpowder spread over the worst horrors of the battlefield has been withdrawn for ever."[7] Echoing Bloch, the author Jack London, whose writing career was just getting under way, noted in early 1900, "The battles of the future must be fought without the merciful screen of smoke, which in the past hid the shock of the charges, the wavering and indecision, the ghastly carnage."[8]

By 1897 the black-powder Springfield had been replaced in the small, peacetime U.S. Army with the Norwegian Krag-Jorgensen rifle, which fired smokeless powder. However, there would not be enough of the new guns or the smokeless powder to supply the much larger, volunteer American army that would fight the Spanish-American War. Hence, Theodore Roosevelt would have cause to complain in his memoir *The Rough Riders* about "the inestimable advantage" that smokeless powder gave to the Spaniards. "The effect of the smokeless powder was remarkable," he explained. It made the enemy riflemen "entirely invisible." And Stephen Crane, who was in Cuba as a war correspondent, elaborated on the subject in one of his dispatches for the *New York World*. "The Springfield, 1873, was undoubtedly a good weapon in its time, and certainly it is even now a very strong shooting rifle, but if we are conducting a modern war on modern lines we may just as well understand once for all that black powder will not do." According to Crane, "The Spaniards were able not only to locate the [American] line exactly but to estimate from the puffs of smoke how many men were engaged." The American volunteers fighting in Cuba may have longed for the smokeless Krag-Jorgensen. However, even the coveted Krag-Jorgensen soon grew outdated. Several years after the war in Cuba, it was replaced in the U.S. Army by the Model 1903 Springfield.[9]

Assessing the increased deadliness of the new generations of rifles and how they shaped what transpired on the modern battlefield, Jack London wrote:

> The modern rifle has a range of from two to three miles; for the first mile and a half it is deadly. Because of this, attacks must be made in loose

formation. . . . No longer is it possible to fight men in masses, nor can battles be opened up at close range; and if an attack be insisted upon, the increase in casualties will be frightful. During the time a body of men are attacking a modern battery across a distance of a mile and a half it is estimated that that single battery would fire fourteen hundred and fifty rounds of shell, scattering 275,000 fragments of death among the soldiers of the assaulting party.

Certain experts predicted that future wars, if they were fought at all, would result in deadlocks. Paraphrasing the argument of the military theorist Jean de Bloch, London explained, "Future wars must be long. No more open fields; no more decisive victories." Neither army would be able to "develop a general attack and escape extermination," and neither army would be "very apt to advance to suicide." The only alternative would be extended warfare that could only be, Bloch claimed, "terminated by famine." Reflecting the general public's ready acceptance of such thinking, the *San Francisco Town Talk* complimented London's "scholarly and well-considered article on the subject of 'The Impossibility of War.'"[10]

Technological innovations also led to dramatic changes in other forms of weaponry. In the early 1880s, Hiram Maxim, an inveterate inventor from Maine who had moved to England, patented a revolutionary machine gun. Unlike its inferior predecessors—the Gardner, Gatling, and Nordenfelt guns—that operated on the principle of a turning crank and often jammed, the Maxim machine gun avoided jamming by using the recoil of the gun to move the cartridge belt. Moreover, the Maxim machine gun was able to fire four hundred rounds a minute. As historians have noted, "As a mechanical invention it was a stroke of genius, as a slaughtering machine it was unspeakably effective."[11]

Indeed, the devastating power of Maxim's machine gun was soon demonstrated when British troops battled Arabs of the Sudan at Omdurman in 1898. Contemporary newspapers recorded that when the British turned their Maxim guns on the Arabs, "a visible wave of death swept over the advancing host." As Sir Edward Arnold, the chief editor of the *Daily Telegraph* of London, astutely observed, "In most of our wars it has been the dash, the skill, and the bravery of our officers and men that have won the day, but in this case the battle was won by a quiet scientific gentleman living down in Kent." The inventor, safe at home in England, was the hero of the modern battlefield.[12] And in recognition of his contributions, Maxim, who took British citizenship, was knighted.

By the dawn of the twentieth century, machines seemingly had gained primacy in battle over man. Reflecting the dreadful awe with which the public had come to regard military technology was a darkly comical sequence of events that transpired during the Spanish-American War. Wild rumors began to circulate that Hiram Maxim was prepared to supply the U.S. Navy with a cruiser armed with a gun of such incomparable power that it would instantly wipe out the entire Spanish navy at a distance of nine miles. Telegrams sped across the Atlantic and Europe seeking confirmation. The frazzled inventor was roused from his sleep at two o'clock in the morning, whereupon, clad in his dressing gown, he drowsily denied that there were any grounds for the rumors and swore that no such weapon existed.[13] Although the news of Maxim's extraordinary gun was false, the fact that it seemed plausible—and was reported in American papers as fact—points to a greater underlying truth. As the nineteenth century drew to a close, people increasingly were looking to machines to fight and win their wars for them.

The great advances in technology that occurred in the decades leading up to World War I meant that more soldiers could be killed more quickly and at greater distances than ever before. Not everyone welcomed the changes. Dire prognostications for the future of warfare abounded. As early as the 1880s one retired Union army general predicted:

> The next war will be marked by terrific and fearful slaughter. So murderous have warlike weapons become, and so fertile has the inventive power of man grown in producing means of killing his fellows, that the Rebellion and the Franco-Prussian war of 1870–1871 will seem mild in comparison with it. Machine cannon, dynamite guns, and magazine rifles now do in the space of a minute what formerly required hours; while steam, electricity, chemistry, and all the agents which man has called to his aid will be utilized in the work of destruction.

War writers, too, took note of war's new weaponry, and they made their own forecasts about the future.[14]

World War I would fulfill many of their darkest fears. Even a consummate romantic such as the American poet Alan Seeger, whose rhapsodic poem "I Have a Rendezvous with Death" would become hugely popular after he was killed at Belloy-en-Santerre, could not help but concede the

alienation that soldiers felt on the modern battlefield. In the lines of his wartime poetry, Seeger depicted men marching into battle with "heads high
and hearts aflame and bayonets bare." But in the letters and diary entries
he wrote while serving as a volunteer with the French Foreign Legion, he
painted quite a different picture.

In a letter Seeger sent from the trenches to the *New York Sun* in late 1914
he reported:

> This style of warfare is extremely modern and for the artillerymen is
> doubtless very interesting, but for the poor common soldier it is any-
> thing but romantic. His rôle is simply to dig himself a hole in the ground
> and to keep hidden in it as tightly as possible. Continually under the
> fire of the opposing batteries, he is yet never allowed to get a glimpse
> of the enemy. Exposed to all the dangers of war, but with none of its
> enthusiasms or splendid *élan,* he is condemned to sit like an animal in
> its burrow and hear the shells whistle over his head and take their little
> daily toll from his comrades.

Beyond a doubt, World War I would prove to be "extremely modern" and
also, for many writers, extremely disillusioning. The war that Seeger described was still in its early stages. Shells would whistle and soldiers would
die for nearly four more years.[15]

The war literature of the late nineteenth and early twentieth centuries reflects Americans' struggle to come to terms with the meaning and morality
of modern warfare. Alternately praising, damning, denying, and vacillating,
a wide range of writers—including authors as diverse as Mark Twain, Theodore Roosevelt, and William James—strove to interpret for their readers
the implications of "modern" war. While some observers enthusiastically
and unhesitatingly applauded the new technology, believing that more efficient weaponry was more humanitarian because it would result in smaller
armies and shorter wars, most authors, especially antiwar authors, were far
more skeptical. They worried about the dehumanization of the modern soldier and the apocalyptic potential of modern warfare.

Even as early as the Civil War, certain authors expressed their concern
about the increasing mechanization of combat. Nathaniel Hawthorne and
other writers' reaction to the famous confrontation of the Union's *Monitor*
and Confederacy's *Merrimac,* for example, reflects a mounting anxiety that

war was becoming ever more impersonal and inglorious. Indisputably, the ways of warfare were rapidly changing in the half century preceding World War I, and even those who wished to believe in the romance of the fray found it hard to overlook the obvious implications.

9

NATHANIEL HAWTHORNE, THE *MONITOR*, AND THE MORALITY OF WAR

There is no remoteness of life and thought, no hermetically sealed seclusion, except, possibly, that of the grave, into which the disturbing influences of this war do not penetrate.

—Nathaniel Hawthorne, "Chiefly about War Matters," July 1862

efore the Civil War staggered to its conclusion, the prominent New England novelist and short story writer Nathaniel Hawthorne was destined to enter the lone seclusion of the grave. However, while he lived, Hawthorne took careful measure of what he referred to as "the present stage of our national difficulties" and wrote about the war with surprising candor.[1] Through various of his wartime works— assorted letters, a long essay describing his visit to the vicinity of the battle-front, and an unfinished novel—Hawthorne registered his ambivalence about the Civil War, his condemnation of warfare in general, and his specific concern about modern weaponry. Along with Whitman, Melville, and De Forest, he stands as one of the earliest writers to question the morality of the Civil War.

At the start of the Civil War, Hawthorne was fifty-six years old with silver hair. He would die in mid-May 1864, nearly a year before the war's end. He had never been a soldier. And when a company of volunteers was sent off from Concord, Massachusetts, on April 19, 1861, with a cannon salute and a speech from Judge Ebenezer Hoar, Hawthorne's son, Julian, was too young to be among them. Nonetheless, Hawthorne was not immune to war fever.

It was not politics that initially attracted Hawthorne's interest in the war; it was the "invigorating effect" that the excitement and charged public mood had on him. Very early in the war, on May 26, 1861, Hawthorne wrote a letter to his friend Horatio Bridge, the paymaster general of the U.S. Navy, and confessed, "The war, strange to say, has had a beneficial effect upon my spirits, which were flagging woefully before it broke out. But it was delightful to share in the heroic sentiment of the time, and to feel that I had a country—a consciousness which seemed to make me young again. One thing, as regards this matter, I regret . . . that I am too old to shoulder a musket myself." Hawthorne was grateful that the excitement of the war had roused him from his torpor. But as he admitted in a letter he wrote the very same day to his close friend and publisher William Ticknor, "It is rather unreasonable to wish my countrymen to kill one another for the sake of refreshing my palled spirits; so I shall pray for peace."[2]

A consummate New Englander, Hawthorne sided unequivocally with the Union and showed a northerner's chauvinism.[3] However, despite what he called his "Yankee heart," Hawthorne could not bring himself to subscribe to the customary views of a stalwart Unionist.[4] "Meantime (though I approve the war as much as any man) I don't quite understand what we are fighting for, or what definite result can be expected," he confided to Bridge.[5]

Hawthorne considered the war ill-conceived and appallingly deadly. He wrote to Bridge in February 1862, "It would be too great an absurdity, to spend all our Northern strength, for the next generation, in holding on to a people who insist upon being let loose."[6] Indeed, Hawthorne calmly entertained the notion of disunion, as long as the resulting borders could be drawn to his satisfaction. Contrasting himself to those who were "bigoted to the Union" and who could see "nothing but ruin without it," Hawthorne claimed that he "should not much regret an ultimate separation . . . if we can only put the boundary far enough south." On this theme, Hawthorne even declared that he was glad that the South had chosen to secede from the Union. "I must say," he wrote to Bridge in late May 1861, "that I rejoice that the old Union is smashed. We never were one people, and never really had a country since the Constitution was formed."[7]

From his distant vantage point in New England, Hawthorne waited out the war's first spring, summer, and autumn—repeating from time to time his lament that he was too old to fight—and strove, without success, to complete a novel. Soon after the new year was ushered in, he was encouraged by his friend Bridge to pay a visit to Washington and see the war up close. But Hawthorne responded that certain obstacles stood in the way. "For instance, I am not very well, being mentally and physically languid; but, I suppose, there is about an even chance that the trip and change of scene might supply the energy which I lack. Also, I am pretending to write a book, and though I am nowise diligent about it, still each week finds it a little more advanced; and I am now at a point where I do not like to leave it entirely."[8] Eventually, Hawthorne did resolve to visit Washington. In the company of William Ticknor, he left frozen New England and headed south in March 1862. Arriving in Washington a day too late to watch sixty thousand troops, en route to Manassas, cross the Potomac, Hawthorne contented himself with visiting the capitol, meeting President Lincoln in the White House, and traveling to various forts, fortresses, and naval ports in Virginia.

In an article titled "Chiefly about War Matters" that appeared in the *Atlantic Monthly* in July 1862, Hawthorne recorded his impressions of the trip. The article is a peculiar piece, at once serious and self-mocking, and instead of signing his name to it, Hawthorne chose to have it simply run under the byline "By a Peaceable Man." The editors of the *Atlantic Monthly* trimmed some of Hawthorne's more "objectionable" matter—an unflattering description of Lincoln's physique and some overly sympathetic remarks about misguided southerners—but they left intact other of his irreverent, and at times highly critical, observations about the war.

Hawthorne questioned the war aims as well as the manner in which the war was being carried out. In particular, his fuming reaction to scientific innovations in naval combat reveals a profound uneasiness with the trend of modern warfare. Hawthorne dedicated a long section of "Chiefly about War Matters" to describing a visit he made to Fortress Monroe and to two warships anchored in nearby Norfolk Harbor, the *Minnesota* and the *Monitor*. Hawthorne pronounced the *Minnesota*, the flagship vessel among the "gallant array of ships of war and transports" thronging the fortress, "splendid." He praised "her gallant crew, her powerful armament, her mighty engines." But he had nothing complimentary to write about the famous *Monitor*. When he toured the vessel by Fortress Monroe, it had recently returned from its historic engagement with the Confederacy's *Merrimac*, the first battle ever fought between two ironclad warships. Hawthorne was distinctly unimpressed. "How," he wondered, "can an admiral condescend to go to sea in an iron pot?"[9]

Hawthorne, whose grandfather had commanded a ship during the American Revolution, held a traditional view of what constituted naval grandeur and gallantry, and the thoroughly modern, low-lying *Monitor* left him upset and confused. He disdainfully observed, "It could not be called a vessel at all; it was a machine. . . . It was ugly, questionable, suspicious, evidently mischievous,—nay, I will allow myself to call it devilish; for this was the new war-fiend." In short, Hawthorne declared that the ironclad looked less like a dignified warship than "like a gigantic rat-trap."[10]

Hawthorne's visit to Fortress Monroe and Norfolk Harbor forced him to confront the uncomfortable truth that the ways of warfare were quickly changing. As he unhappily noted, "Military science makes such rapid advances." He realized that wooden warships soon would become obsolete and despondently imagined a future in which men would go to battle "boxed up in impenetrable iron." Ruminating on the implications of the battle fought between the two ironclads, Hawthorne predicted that science, which he wrote with a capital "S," would spell the end to heroism:

> All the pomp and splendor of naval warfare are gone by. Henceforth there must come up a race of engineermen and smoke-blackened cannoneers, who will hammer away at their enemies under the direction of a single pair of eyes; and even heroism—so deadly a gripe [*sic*] is Science laying on our noble possibilities—will become a quality of very minor importance, when its possessor cannot break through the iron crust of his own armament and give the world a glimpse of it.

Science was spelling the end to pluck and daring. Hawthorne lamented, "There will be other battles, but no more such tests of seamanship and manhood as the battles of the past." The introduction of ironclad warships, he realized, would "not long be the last and most terrible improvement in the science of war."[11]

The old ways of naval warfare were rapidly disappearing, and Hawthorne offered a grim forecast for the future. Ever more sinister innovations, he suspected, would be introduced. "Already we hear of vessels the armament of which is to act entirely beneath the surface of the water; so that, with no other external symptoms than a great bubbling and foaming, and gush of smoke, and belch of smothered thunder out of the yeasty waves, there shall be a deadly fight going on below,—and, by and by, a sucking whirlpool, as one of the ships goes down." The "science of war," according to Hawthorne, would undermine the individual fighter's "pristine value." The "long procession of heroic sailors" would reach its end, and machines would replace gallant warriors. With more than a little irony, Hawthorne concluded, "The Millennium is certainly approaching, because human strife is to be transferred from the heart and personality of man into cunning contrivances of machinery, which by and by will fight out our wars with only the clank and smash of iron, strewing the field with broken engines, but damaging nobody's little finger except by accident. Such is obviously the tendency of modern improvement." Man would become the servant of the machine, and war would become a bloodless affair.[12]

Whereas Hawthorne's letters from early in the war show him eager to shoulder a musket, his curmudgeonly article for the *Atlantic Monthly* shows him grappling with the technological reality of "modern" war. The story-teller from New England was deeply disturbed by the new machinery of naval warfare. He worried that humans and heroism were being displaced by "cunning contrivances of machinery."

Interestingly, published in the very same issue of the *Atlantic Monthly* as Hawthorne's "Chiefly about War Matters" was an article that praised John Ericsson, the engineer who had designed the *Monitor*. The essay, "Ericsson and His Inventions," reads in part, "Ericsson is now zealously at work in constructing six new iron gun-boats on the plan of the Monitor. If that re-markable structure can be surpassed, he is the man to accomplish it. His ambition is to render the United States impregnable against the navies of the world."[13]

Changes in warfare would continue apace, and their moral meaning would remain open to interpretation. The wartime readers of the July 1862 installment of the *Atlantic Monthly* were presented, both figuratively and literally, with two very different readings of the merging of science and warfare.

As his wartime letters and his account of his visit to the war arena make clear, Hawthorne felt a profound ambivalence about the Civil War. He wrote in "Chiefly about War Matters" with revealing candor, "For ourselves, the bal-ance of advantages between defeat and triumph may admit of question."[14] Hawthorne was suspicious both of the war's means (the use of modern weaponry) and its ends (forcing the secessionist South into submission).

More fundamentally, Hawthorne questioned war's underlying morality. Halfway through "Chiefly about War Matters," he inserts his bluntest words on the subject:

Set men face to face, with weapons in their hands, and they are as ready
to slaughter one another now, after playing at peace and good will for

so many years, as in the rudest ages, that never heard of peace societies, and thought no wine so delicious as what they quaffed from an
enemy's skull. Indeed, if the report of a Congressional committee may
be trusted, that old-fashioned kind of goblet has again come into use,
at the expense of our Northern headpieces,—a costly drinking-cup to
him that furnishes it! Heaven forgive me for seeming to jest upon such a
subject!—only, it is so odd, when we measure our advances from barbarism, and find ourselves just here![15]

War is uncivilized slaughter, Hawthorne boldly suggests. The soldiers of the
Civil War are no better than the barbarians of old, who claimed skulls as
trophy drinking cups and dishonored the enemy dead.

Hawthorne was outspoken, but he was not out of touch. He knew that
his stark assessment of war as slaughter was provocative and would offend
the sensibilities of his readers. He wrote to the *Atlantic Monthly*'s publisher,
"I don't wish to foist an article upon you that might anywise damage the
Magazine."[16] Nevertheless, Hawthorne felt compelled to share his thoughts,
however unpopular, about the ongoing war. In the very body of the article, he offered the following self-justification for presenting his dissenting
views. "In writing this article, I feel disposed to be singularly frank, and can
scarcely restrain myself from telling truths the utterance of which I should
get slender thanks for."[17]

The Civil War, however, was not the only war about which Hawthorne
wrote in the early 1860s. He also turned his attention to writing about the
morality of an earlier conflict, the American Revolution. Killing, he seemed
to conclude, was never acceptable, even in the most ideal of wartime
circumstances.

In the fall of 1861, within half a dozen months of the outbreak of fighting
at Fort Sumter, Hawthorne began work on a new romance, *Septimius Felton.*
The book would remain unfinished, with a second draft halfway completed,
at the time of his death. The way in which Hawthorne presents war in this
odd romance, which was posthumously published in 1872, is very revealing.

Septimius Felton; or, The Elixir of Life is set in Massachusetts and begins
at the very start of the Revolutionary War. The plot, as the extended title
suggests, revolves around the eponymous protagonist's quest for an elixir
of eternal life. Of particular interest here is an early passage in which Septimius, a young New Englander, meets and kills a Redcoat. The scene occurs

on the first day of the war, April 19, 1775, when seven hundred British troops march on Concord.

Hawthorne presents a battle scene that is at once very intimate and idealized. As the fighting rages, Septimius and a handsome British officer—who several hours earlier had stolen a kiss from the girl Septimius loves—find themselves alone on a hillside. Septimius is hidden in a thicket when the young officer commands, "Stand out, or I shoot." Septimius obeys, yet he does so not simply to avoid being shot. Rather, he reveals himself "because his manhood felt a call upon it not to skulk in obscurity from an open enemy."[18] Septimius' actions, Hawthorne emphasizes, conform to a traditionally conceived code of chivalrous engagement.

As the two men face each other, each has the opportunity to appraise his opponent. Septimius can see the young British officer, "so handsome, so beautiful, in budding youth." The British fighter can plainly see "rustic Septimius." Theirs is a decidedly personal and private encounter amid a much larger battle. The two men speak the same language, and they talk to each other before any shots are fired. They even debate the merits of shooting one another. The British fighter declares, "Come, we have in the first place the great quarrel between me a king's soldier, and you a rebel; next our private affair, on account of yonder pretty girl. Come, let us take a shot on either score!" Septimius tries to decline, "I have no enmity towards you . . . go in peace." But the redcoat is insistent. Eventually, Septimius consents to fight.[19]

When the two men finally aim their firelocks at one another, they do so by mutual consent and according to strictly prescribed rules of conduct. It is war reduced to a duel. "Stand where you are," orders the British officer, "and I will give the word of command." In a show of perfect sportsmanship, neither man even raises his gun until the Redcoat commands, "Now; ready, aim, fire!" Only then do the two men lift their firearms to their shoulders, aim, and shoot. Septimius is only slightly grazed by the Englishman's bullet. The British officer is shot squarely in the breast.[20]

The scene of battle that Hawthorne crafts accentuates not only the connection between the two young men before their firing of arms but also the connection between them after their weapons have been fired. Septimius reacts to the sight of his mortally wounded enemy with horror and immediate regret. "Good God!" he exclaims, devastated to realize what he has done. "I had no thought of this, no malice towards you in the least!" Septimius helps the wounded officer to lie down. He fetches a jug of cold water. He obeys in turn each of the dying man's requests. "Is there anything more that I can do for you?" Septimius asks as he kneels "with genuine sympathy and sorrow . . . by his fallen foe's side." When the officer dies, Septimius digs a grave for his former enemy and asks the local minister to say prayers over it.[21]

Rather than a battle between unseen and unknown strangers, the fight between Septimius and the British officer is intensely personal. Septimius witnesses the consequences of his actions and experiences his enemy's death in a very immediate way. And Septimius' remorse is plainly evident. In "a dream of horror and pity," he rushes to fulfill the dying man's requests. The two men share a very special connection. The dying British officer calls Septimius, "my enemy that was, my friend that is," and Septimius, in turn, confesses to his former foe, "I grieve for you like a brother." Not insignificantly, Hawthorne reveals later in the work that the two men actually were distant relatives. War, Hawthorne suggests—perhaps with the Civil War in mind—is inherently fratricidal.[22]

Moreover, Hawthorne implies that war is inherently tragic and immoral. He paints a prettified image of battle. The chivalric codes of conduct are all respected. The fighters comport themselves with dignity. Even so, Hawthorne offers no celebratory prose or paeans to the glory of battle. Instead, he dwells on the British officer's loss of life and on Septimius' sense of personal responsibility and culpability. Septimius engages in war. He slays his foe. But afterward he wishes he could undo his deadly deed. Describing Septimius's emotions following the shooting, Hawthorne writes:

> He had taken a human life; and, however the circumstances might excuse him,—might make the thing even something praiseworthy, and that would be called patriotic,—still, it was not at once that a fresh country youth could see anything but horror in the blood with which his hand was stained. It seemed so dreadful to have reduced this gay, animated, beautiful being to a lump of dead flesh for the flies to settle upon, and which in a few hours would begin to decay; which must be put forthwith into the earth, lest it should be a horror to men's eyes.[23]

As Hawthorne makes clear, Septimius experiences a moral revulsion to the act of killing. And that revulsion is manifestly Hawthorne's own.

Modern contrivances, such as the *Monitor*, might change the ways of war, but to read Hawthorne's wartime romance is to realize that he did not really believe in the grandeur of battle at all. Even in the most idealized of wartime situations, Hawthorne shows, killing is still killing. The Redcoat dies, and not even the magical elixir of life that Septimius seeks could revive him.

The American Revolution, no less than the Civil War, involved reducing live men to decaying corpses for flies to feed on. Nonetheless, there was something particularly unmanning, Hawthorne suggests, about the new weaponry being introduced during the Civil War. It deprived fighters of control and threatened to convert them into an army of "engineermen" and "cannoneers" whose personal qualities mattered little.

Nor was Hawthorne the only wartime writer to worry about the direction in which science and warfare were headed. As other works about the *Monitor* confirm, Hawthorne's concern was shared by a wide range of contemporary authors, including his onetime close friend Herman Melville. Like Hawthorne, Melville lamented the new type of naval battle that was being ushered in by the ironclads and modern science. Indeed, Melville—who himself had served on a frigate—repeatedly addressed the subject of naval combat in *Battle-Pieces*. In a poem titled "A Utilitarian View of the *Monitor's* Fight," Melville gives his opinion of the ironclads' battle. Drawing a pointed comparison between the heroic contests of the past and the intense, yet peculiarly dispassionate, fight of the *Monitor* and *Merrimac*, Melville writes:

> Hail to victory without the gaud
>   Of glory; zeal that needs no fans
> Of banners; plain mechanic power
> Plied cogently in War now placed—
>   Where War belongs—
> Among the trades and artisans.

A few lines later, Melville argues that war is fast becoming a matter of cranks, pivots, screws, and scientific calculations. The warriors of old, he claims, are being replaced by mere "operatives." The poem concludes, "War's made / Less grand than Peace, / And a singe runs through lace and feather."[24]

In another poem, "In the Turret," Melville tries to imagine the thoughts that ran through the mind of Lieutenant John L. Worden, the commander of the *Monitor*. Did the dutiful Worden—who "bore the first iron battle's burden / Sealed as in a diving-bell"—worry that he would drown in "liquid gloom" sealed in a "welded tomb"? Drawing a powerful analogy, Melville writes of Worden:

> Alcides, groping into haunted hell
> To bring forth King Admetus' bride,
> Braved naught more vaguely direful and untried.

To venture into battle in an ironclad, Melville suggests, was comparable to venturing into hell. Combining the language of patriots with that of engineers, Melville imagines Worden's silent prayer before the battle began as, "First duty, duty next, and duty last; / Ay, Turret, rivet me here to duty fast!" *Riveted* to his post, Worden did his duty. But the definition of what constitutes duty had been reinvented to suit the "mechanic power" of modern warfare.[25]

In yet another poem, "The Temeraire," Melville describes an English sailor's reaction to the replacement of the old wooden fleets with the new ironclads:

> But Splendors wane. The sea-fight yields
> No front of old display;
> The garniture, emblazonment,
> And heraldry all decay.

The "navies old and oaken," of which the *Temeraire* was the "poetic ideal," are to be no more. Now the "rivets clinch the iron-clads," and as Melville ominously warns, "Men learn a deadlier lore."[26]

Other poets of the era expressed similar concerns. In his poem "The Cumberland," Henry Wadsworth Longfellow recounts how the wooden USS *Cumberland* futilely attempted to defend itself against the ironclad *Merrimac* in an encounter that took place the day before the *Merrimac*'s engagement with the *Monitor*. The clash—in which the *Cumberland* was shelled, rammed, and sunk—marked a turning point in the history of naval warfare. Longfellow writes:

> And we knew that the iron ship of our foes
> Was steadily steering its course,
> To try the force
> Of our ribs of oak.

The ironclad is, in Longfellow's imagination, a uniquely fearsome foe. He describes it alternately as like the legendary kraken sea monster "huge and black" and like a "floating fort." It is both animate and inanimate, both malevolent beast and unfeeling machine. The *Cumberland* fires at the iron-clad but to little effect.

> As hail rebounds from a roof of slate,
>   Rebounds our heavier hail
>   From each iron scale
>   Of the monster's hide.

The fire-breathing *Merrimac* ultimately crushes the *Cumberland*'s wooden "ribs in her iron grasp."[27]

In the lines of his poem, Longfellow at once acknowledges the change that had been introduced into naval warfare and tries to reconcile it with the poetic norms of the day. Paying tribute to the men who died on the *Cumberland,* he begins the poem's final stanza in a conventionally romantic vein, "Ho! brave hearts that went down in the seas, / Ye are at peace in the troubled stream." The old-fashioned words at the start of each line seem intended to link the poem to some earlier, idealized age of seamanship. But as Longfellow clearly realized, traditional wooden warships like the *Cumberland* were bound to be displaced by impregnable ironclads.[28]

As the Civil War progressed, it became increasingly difficult for poets and other writers to reconcile the new ways of warfare with their inherited notions of naval grandeur and bravery. Even so, the occasional poet tried to find cause for celebration in the handiwork of the engineers. "The Cruise of the Monitor" by George Henry Boker jubilantly toasts John Ericsson, the designer of the famous ironclad:

> Hurrah for the master mind that wrought,
> With iron hand, this iron thought!
> Strength and safety with speed combined,
> Ericsson's gift to all mankind;
> To curb abuse, and chains to loose,
> Hurrah for the Monitor's famous cruise![29]

Nonetheless, it was hard to deny that warfare—both on land and sea—was fundamentally changing in ways that threatened traditional concepts of battle and altered the role of the individual fighter.

One of the direst predictions about the future of warfare was put forth by Henry Adams, who served as private secretary to his father, the American ambassador to England, during the Civil War years. Upon hearing about the engagement between the *Merrimac* and the *Monitor,* Adams wrote to his brother Charles Francis Adams Jr., a captain in the Union army: "Man has mounted science, and is now run away with. I firmly believe that before many centuries more, science will be the master of man. The engines he will have invented will be beyond his strength to control. Some day science may have the existence of mankind in its power, and the human race commit suicide by blowing up the world."[30] The invention of nuclear weaponry still lay far in the future, but Adams's apocalyptic vision reflects an anxiety about science and warfare that was becoming quite palpable in the second half of the nineteenth century.

Not coincidentally, in the decades following the Civil War, war criticism moved from the periphery of American literature to the center.

WAR AS EXPERIENCED AND IMAGINED
BY MARK TWAIN

"Still, it is true, lamb," said Satan. "Look at you in war—what mutton you are, and how ridiculous."
—Mark Twain, "The Chronicle of Young Satan," 1900

ne extremely prominent American writer alert to the changing ways of war in the late nineteenth century was the inimitable Mark Twain, and his antiwar stance was unambiguous. With his signature wit and irreverent irony, Twain returned again and again in his fiction and correspondence to the theme of technology and warfare. He wrote not only about actual wars, past and present, but also about wars that were wholly imaginary. Among the bloodlettings with which he concerned himself were: the Roman, Greek, and Hebraic Wars, the Napoleonic Wars, the Civil War, the Spanish-American War, and a couple of sixth-century wars that had never taken place.

To understand the evolution of Twain's thoughts about the madness and modernization of warfare, it is important to begin with his actual military experience. Unlike Hawthorne, Twain did fight in the Civil War, albeit very briefly and on the losing side. In the summer of 1861 he was twenty-five years old, fresh from a stint piloting steamboats up and down the Mississippi River, and a new convert to the Confederate cause. Upon returning to his boyhood home of Hannibal, Missouri, Twain joined up with a group of fourteen other young men and for a few weeks played at being a soldier before his military zeal soured and he headed out West to join his brother, Orion, who had been appointed secretary to the governor of the Nevada Territory.

Nearly a quarter of a century later, Twain recalled his short-lived experience as a Confederate soldier in an autobiographical sketch titled "The Private History of a Campaign That Failed." Part fact and part fiction, this penitent and thoroughly self-ridiculing account of his misadventures appeared in the December 1885 installment of *Century* magazine's famous "Battles and Leaders of the Civil War" series. Though Twain strives for the comic tone of a mock epic, the piece is key to understanding his enduring abhorrence of war.

As "the first wash of the wave of war broke upon the shores of Missouri," Twain records, he and a ragtag group of Confederate sympathizers organized themselves into a military company. The self-dubbed Marion Rangers, Twain claims, were more clumsy than courageous, and by and large they treated their entree into militarism as a "holiday frolic." Full of horseplay and laughter, they traveled around the countryside doing their best to avoid the enemy and ran at the least sign of danger. "Our scares were frequent," Twain writes. "Every few days rumors would come that the enemy were approaching. In these cases we always fell back on some other camp of ours; we never [stayed] where we were."[1]

Their strategy of preemptive retreat served the novice soldiers well until one tragic, dimly lit night. In an incident that marks the climax of Twain's tale, the blundering Marion Rangers mistake a man on horseback for a Union soldier and shoot him out of his saddle. Twain recalls that, after feeling an initial surge of exhilaration, he was struck with remorse. "The thought shot through me that I was a murderer; that I had killed a man—a man who had never done me any harm. That was the coldest sensation that ever went through my marrow."[2]

Twain traces the conversion in his outlook on war to the death of the unknown horseman.

> The man was not in uniform, and was not armed. He was a stranger in the country; that was all we ever found out about him. The thought of him got to preying upon me every night; I could not get rid of it. I could not drive it away, the taking of that unoffending life seemed such a wanton thing. And it seemed an epitome of war; that all war must be just that—the killing of strangers against whom you feel no personal animosity; strangers whom, in other circumstances, you would help if you found them in trouble, and who would help you if you needed it.

The Civil War went on, but after the death of the stranger, Twain—who had served in an unofficial troop—opted out. He explains, "It seemed to me that I was not rightly equipped for this awful business; that war was intended for men, and I for a child's nurse. I resolved to retire from this avocation of sham soldiership while I could save some remnant of my self-respect."³

Implicit in Twain's self-deprecating assessment of his failings is a critique of modern battle, which demands that soldiers kill anonymously, often without even seeing the target of their deadly fire. Rather than producing a traditional tale of guts and glory, Twain reduces all of warfare to the murder of an innocent man by the ignorant Marion Rangers. It is absurd, Twain demonstrates, to try to give the death of the unknown horseman a transcendent meaning. Of the slain stranger, Twain writes, "He was killed in war; killed in fair and legitimate war; killed in battle."⁴ Twain lays out the words on the page and tries them on for size, but they are too large, too lofty. The result is ridiculous; it is like a child prancing around in his father's oversize shoes. Twain makes the language of valor and heroism laughable. He knows, and his readers know, that there is no glorious justification—no adequate justification at all—for the unlucky stranger's death.

Twain fled the war, but other of the Marion Rangers went on to become "valuable soldiers." They "fought all through the war," he records, "and came out at the end with excellent records." However, these men succeeded at "the grim trade" of warfare only after they forfeited their own sense of independence. They made good soldiers, Twain notes, once they had "learned to obey like machines." Twain's word choice is revealing. Machinelike soldiers who mechanically obey orders, he suggests, are the men best "equipped" for the "awful business" of modern war.⁵

In several of his later works, Twain further probes the link between soldiers, machines, and warfare. In these texts his denouncement of war becomes ever more explicit, just as his anxiety about modern weaponry becomes ever more evident. *A Connecticut Yankee in King Arthur's Court*, a pseudohistorical novel, is one such text. Twain's work on the book was spread over five years, and it was published in late 1889, after promotional excerpts appeared in the *Century* magazine.

Twain uses the pretext of inadvertent time travel to imagine what might happen if nineteenth-century technology, especially military technology, were visited upon the England of King Arthur's age. A young New Englander (identified as Twain himself in early notebook entries) is clobbered on the head with a crowbar at an arms factory in Hartford, Connecticut, and wakes to find himself transferred back in time to the sixth century. In the course of the far-fetched sequence of events that ensues, Twain royally ridicules the modern age's blind faith in military technology.

The time traveler, named Hank Morgan, is the quintessential child of America's industrial revolution. Indeed, he is a technological virtuoso. Morgan boasts:

> My father was a blacksmith, my uncle was a horse doctor, and I was both, along at first. Then I went over to the great arms factory and learned my real trade; learned all there was to it; learned to make everything; guns, revolvers, cannon, boilers, engines, all sorts of labor-saving machinery. Why, I could make anything a body wanted . . . and if there wasn't any quick new-fangled way to make a thing, I could invent one—and do it as easy as rolling off a log. I became head superintendent; had a couple of thousand men under me.

Cocky with Yankee self-assurance, he determines upon his arrival in Camelot to "boss the whole country inside of three months."[6]

Morgan has infinite confidence in the science of warfare. When nineteenth-century weaponry meets sixth-century chivalry, he is certain that there can be no real contest. On one occasion, Morgan kills a couple of armored knights-errant with a dynamite bomb. He records, "When they were within fifteen yards, I sent that bomb with a sure aim, and it struck the ground just under the horses' noses . . . and during the next fifteen minutes we stood under a steady drizzle of microscopic fragments of knights and hardware and horse-flesh."[7] Another day, five hundred knights charge en masse at Morgan only to be routed with a mere nine shots from his pair of revolvers.

Among the many modern-day institutions that Morgan imports into medieval England is West Point, and he proudly monitors the progress that the sixth-century cadets make in mastering the basics of late nineteenth-century warfare. After listening to one medieval West Pointer recite his lessons, Morgan rhapsodizes: "It was beautiful to hear the lad lay out the science of war, and wallow in details of battle and siege, of supply, transportation, mining and countermining, grand tactics, big strategy and little strategy, signal service, infantry, cavalry, artillery, and all about siege guns, field guns, gatling guns, rifled guns, smooth bores, musket practice, revolver practice." Morgan—whose very name sounds like a terse command, "more gun"—is absolutely enamored with modern weaponry and the infinite potential for innovation. Within three years of his arrival in Arthurian England, Morgan has introduced into that superstitious and pretechnologi-

cal land "the telegraph, the telephone, the phonograph, the type-writer, the
sewing machine, and all the thousand willing and handy servants of steam
and electricity" known to the late nineteenth century, including steam
warships.[8]

Morgan's escapade in the sixth century is nothing less than a dress re-
hearsal for the industrial revolution. And on Morgan's success or failure,
Twain implies, rides the fate of modern war and, not incidentally, the fate
of modern civilization. Old England replicates New England, and the destruction of the one portends the destruction of the other. The apocalyptic
ending of the novel, thus, is especially instructive.

Fully expecting to prevail, Morgan pits his wee army of fifty-four against
a vast enemy army of twenty-five thousand knights. Indeed, Morgan proclaims that he will settle for nothing less than the complete extermination of
his foe. "While one of these men remains alive, our task is not finished, the
war is not ended. We will kill them all." He surrounds his forces with twelve
concentric circles of wire fences, sets up a battery of thirteen Gatling guns,
and buries an abundance of "glass-cylinder dynamite torpedoes." When
the knights draw near, the first wave of them hits the torpedo-embedded
sand belt and is instantly reduced to "homogeneous protoplasm, with al-
loys of iron and buttons." Next, eleven thousand of the knights are stopped
dead in their tracks when Morgan sends a lethal electrical charge through
his wire fences. Finally, Morgan's thirteen Gatling guns commence "to
vomit death into the fated ten thousand" knights who remain. Morgan is
euphoric. "Within ten short minutes after we had opened fire," he gloats,
"armed resistance was totally annihilated, the campaign was ended, we fifty-
four were masters of England! Twenty-five thousand men lay dead around
us." Modern warfare, imported from the late nineteenth century, spells the
extinction of the enemy.[9]

The victory of technology, however, is short-lived. The conquerors are
in turn conquered, not by men but by an unanticipated result of the mass
carnage they created. Morgan's army is "enclosed with a solid wall of the
dead—a bulwark, a breastwork, of corpses."[10] The air becomes poisoned,
and the men of Morgan's army grow sick and die. Only Morgan survives.
Wrapped in a sound sleep like an extremely somnolent Rip Van Winkle, he
safely slumbers until the nineteenth century.

Twain's depiction of mass death by airborne contamination offers an
eerie preview of twentieth-century writers' and readers' preoccupation with

nuclear warfare and nuclear fallout. Indeed, in Nevil Shute's chilling novel of nuclear disaster *On the Beach,* published in 1957, the vanquished and victors all die. In both works, the weapons meant to destroy the enemy cause the air to become so poisoned that no one, or almost no one, can survive. "We were in a trap, you see," Twain writes, "a trap of our own making."[11] In Shute's novel, those who do not die from the nuclear bomb die from radiation fallout or choose to commit suicide by taking cyanide pills.

Twain paints a distinctly chilling picture of modern warfare, but his representation of the wars of the past is also grim. He shows that the knightly tournaments of preindustrial times were bloody, lurid affairs entirely lacking in the "chivalrous magnanimities" that nineteenth-century authors, led by Sir Walter Scott, were so fond of romanticizing.[12] The only difference between the wars of old and the wars of the present and future, according to Twain, is the scale of the killing. With increased mechanization, the death toll rises exponentially.

Nor was Twain the only observer of his day to take note of the increased deadliness of modern weaponry. In the years immediately preceding the publication of *A Connecticut Yankee,* rapid advances in military science had been reported and debated in assorted popular magazines, including the *Century* magazine (in which excerpts from Twain's novel were published in November 1889).

In October 1888, for example, the *Century* magazine published an article titled "American Machine Cannon and Dynamite Guns" written by Lieutenant William R. Hamilton. Paying tribute to the Gatling gun and other recent inventions, Hamilton argued that "the extreme mortality of modern war" offered "the only hope that man can have of even a partial cessation of war." And justifying the use of ever more deadly weaponry, Hamilton contended, "All means which will bring the enemy to terms in the shortest possible time—except such as are absolutely objectionable—are justified in war."[13] (Interestingly, Ambrose Bierce was among the readers of the article. In his essay "Modern Warfare," Bierce faults Hamilton's "smug and comfortable assurance." Challenging Hamilton's claim that deadlier weaponry will bring an end to war, Bierce describes militarists like Hamilton as "happily unconscious of the fact that men's sense of their power to make [war] dreadful is precisely the thing that most encourages them to wage it.")[14]

A year later *Scribner's Magazine* published a pair of articles on the theme of electricity in war, bearing the subtitles, "Electricity in Naval Warfare" and

"Electricity in Land Warfare." In the second of these pieces, John Millis, a first lieutenant in the Corps of Engineers contends:

> From a humane point of view, it is a gratifying reflection, and a fact fully established by history, that with the improvements and advancements in military science and art of modern times, warfare now consists of much shorter conflicts in arms than was formerly the case, and though the action is thereby rendered vastly more intense while it continues, it also becomes the more decisive, hostilities are terminated the sooner, and the loss of life is actually less; so that instead of contributing to the "abominable end" of exterminating the human race, the application of the most advanced discoveries and inventions to the art of war has in reality mitigated the distressing results of armed conflict.[15]

Modern weaponry, so a popular school of thought suggested, would spell the end of warfare.

Twain remained unconvinced. Certain of the efficacy of modern weaponry in killing and dubious that the killing would ever cease, he challenged the logic used by the advocates of new military technology.

Writing in early 1899 to William T. Stead, editor of the monthly *Review of Reviews,* Twain laid out his objections to war and modern weaponry even more openly than he had in *A Connecticut Yankee.* In response to a proposal for world disarmament made by the czar of Russia, Twain mused, "I feel sure that the armaments are now many times greater than necessary for the requirements of either peace or war." With a little bit of guesswork and a few calculations, Twain set about proving his point.

> Suppose circumstances made it necessary for us to fight another Waterloo. . . . I will guess that 400,000 men were on hand at Waterloo (I have forgotten the figures). In five hours they disabled 50,000 men. It took them that tedious, long time because the firearms delivered only two or three shots a minute. But we would do the work now as it was done at Omdurman, with shower guns, raining 600 balls a minute. Four men to a gun—is that the number? A hundred and fifty shots a minute per man. Thus a modern soldier is 149 Waterloo soldiers in one.

With stinging sarcasm, Twain concluded that it made sense to "retain one man out of each 150 in service" and "disband the others." For, as he explained, each modern soldier equaled "149 Waterloo men, in usefulness and killing capacity." But modern armies had continued to expand throughout the nineteenth century until they constituted, according to Twain's calculations, the force of some 350 or 450 million Waterloo men. Consequently, in the course of the seventy-five years since the Battle of Waterloo was fought in 1815, war had become vastly more lethal.[16]

Technology, Twain indicated, was the real enemy. Indeed, technology was proving disillusioning in his own life. Twain long had been fascinated with inventions and over the years had invested in dozens of them.[17] He was the first in Hartford to have a private telephone and among the first Americans to purchase a Remington typewriter. Had he not been a successful author, he might well have tried his hand at inventing.

As it was, in 1880, full of high hopes, Twain began investing in a typesetting machine being built by a man named James W. Paige. The device was supposed to set, justify, and distribute single-foundry types automatically "without human help or suggestion."[18] It would do the work of six human typesetters, and it would do it better. Twain felt sure that, once the machine was completed and orders were placed for it, he would rise to the ranks of the wealthiest men in America.[19] But Paige ran into a long and expensive series of setbacks constructing the massive, extremely intricate, contraption. Problems dragged on for nine long years.[20] At last, in early January 1889, Twain believed the typesetter finally was ready. He ecstatically wrote to a friend, "The machine is finished! . . . This is by far and away the most marvelous invention ever contrived by man. And it is not a thing of rags and patches; it is made of massive steel, and will last a century." In another letter Twain marveled, "All the other wonderful inventions of the human brain sink pretty nearly into commonplaces contrasted with this awful mechanical miracle."[21] However, shortly after Twain sent off these jubilant reports, the machine broke down again.

In the end, the typesetter never was rid of its many glitches, and Twain, nearly bankrupt, was obliged to give up on the machine. As his biographer and literary executor, Albert Bigelow Paine, would later observe, by early 1891 Twain "had spent in the neighborhood of one hundred and ninety thousand dollars on the type-setter—money that would better have been thrown into the Connecticut River, for then the agony had been more quickly over. As it was, it had shadowed many precious years."[22] The years overshadowed by the failure of the "awful mechanical miracle" were the very ones in which Twain wrote "The Private History of a Campaign That Failed" and *A Connecticut Yankee*. And his observations about the strength of Napoleon's soldiers versus modern ones were yet to come.

For Twain, in the 1880s and 1890s, the American industrial revolution promised much and delivered little. Perhaps, then, the story of Twain's frustration with the costly, problem-prone typesetter should be read as a companion piece to his mounting criticism of the mechanization of warfare. In fact, when Twain first went to inspect the typesetting machine, it was being built at the Colt arms factory in Hartford, Connecticut.[23]

As the 1890s drew to a close, Twain once again turned to fiction to condemn warfare and to voice his concern about the use of ever deadlier weaponry. In his darkly pessimistic "Chronicle of Young Satan," Twain imagines the visit of a "mysterious stranger" to a small Austrian village. The year is 1702, and the stranger goes by the name of Satan.[24]

After befriending a couple of teenage boys, Satan undertakes to educate them in world history, which is the same, in Satan's account, as the history of war. He traces for the boys the path from humankind's fall from grace in the Garden of Eden through the bloodshed of the ages. He concludes:

> You perceive . . . that you have made continual progress. Cain did his murder with a club; the Hebrews did their murders with javelins and swords; the Greeks and Romans added protective armor and the fine arts of military organization and generalship; the Christian has added guns and gunpowder; two centuries from now he will have so greatly improved the deadly effectiveness of his weapons of slaughter that all men will confess that without the Christian Civilization war must have remained a poor and trifling thing to the end of time.

The weaponry of warfare, as Satan illustrates, had become ever more deadly, but the immorality of war had remained unchanged throughout the ages. There has never been "a war started by the aggressor for any clean purpose," Satan informs the boys. "There is no such war in the history of your race."[25]

Not only does Satan recall the wars of the past but he also foretells the wars of the future. "Nine years from now a Prussian prince will be born who will steal Silesia; plunge several nations into bloody and desolating wars; lead a life of treachery and general and particular villainy, and be admiringly called 'the Great.'" Nor does Satan stop there. "All through the next century," he explains, "there will be wars—wars everywhere in the earth. Wars for gain—each a crime on the part of the provoker of it." And so it shall be, Satan predicts, for "a million years ahead."[26]

In the early years of the twentieth century—against the backdrop of
the ongoing Philippine-American War, the Boer War, the Russo-Japanese
War, and the Boxer Revolution in China—Twain continued to condemn
the perpetuation of war. In particular, he focused his attention on America's
own transgressions. As the vice president of the American Anti-Imperialist
League, a post he held from 1901 until his death in 1910, he was an unwaver-
ing opponent of America's transformation into a colonial empire. Notably,
in a lengthy article published in the *North American Review* in 1901, "To the
Person Sitting in Darkness," Twain made unmistakably clear his criticism
of America's actions in the Philippines. "We have stamped out a just and
intelligent and well-ordered republic; we have stabbed an ally in the back
and slapped the face of a guest; . . . we have robbed a trusting friend of his
land and his liberty; we have invited our clean young men to shoulder a dis-
credited musket and do bandit's work[;] . . . we have debauched America's
honor and blackened her face before the world."[27] War, Twain argued, is
inherently immoral, and he considered America's actions in the Philippines
particularly dishonorable.

Once again, in a brief sketch titled "The War-Prayer," which he clearly
wrote with the wars in Cuba and the Philippines in mind, Twain aired his
views on the subject of war. In the story, which was rejected for publication
by *Harper's Bazaar* in early 1905, Twain describes a time when the country
is "up in arms" and "in every breast" burns "the holy fire of patriotism." A
spirit of great exuberance and enthusiasm prevails, and those who venture
"to disapprove of the war and cast a doubt upon its righteousness" are in-
timidated "for their personal safety's sake" into silence. Amid this climate of
intolerance, one man dares voice his dissent.[28]

The pivotal scene occurs on a Sunday morning as a community's bat-
talions prepare to leave for the front. The local church is full of parishioners
whose heads are filled with thoughts of "flashing sabres," "bronzed heroes,"
and "golden seas of glory." The service begins, and God's help is invoked
to watch over the soldiers and "grant to them and to their flag and country imperishable honor and glory." Then in walks a tall stranger adorned
in a long robe. He is an old man, with billowy, white hair and a pale, wrin-
kled face. Claiming to be a messenger from God, the stranger rewords the
parishioners' prayers: "O Lord, our God, help us to tear their soldiers to
bloody shreds with our shells; help us to cover their smiling fields with the
pale forms of their patriot dead; help us to drown the thunder of the guns

with the shrieks of their wounded, writhing in pain; help us to lay waste their humble homes with a hurricane of fire." Boldly challenging the self-righteous rhetoric of the war supporters, the old man reinterprets the war as plain bloodlust.[29]

Wickedness, Twain contends, underlies all wars. Those who believe otherwise and profess to fight with God's blessings, Twain argues, only delude themselves. And those who use the mantle of patriotism to mask their imperialist or self-serving intentions invite Twain's particular scorn.

Twain was outspoken in condemning war, yet he doubted that his writings would have much effect. In "The Chronicle of Young Satan," Twain offers a long reflection on the role of war protesters. Whenever there is agitation for a war, he explains,

> A few fair men on the other side will argue and reason against the war with speech and pen, and at first will have a hearing and be applauded; but it will not last long; those others will out-shout them, and presently the anti-war audiences will thin out and lose popularity. Before long you will see this curious thing: the speakers stoned from the platform and free speech strangled, by hordes of furious men who in their secret hearts are still at one with those stoned speakers,—as earlier,—but do not dare to say so! And now the whole nation—pulpit and all—will take up the war-cry, and shout itself hoarse, and mob any honest man who ventures to open his mouth; and presently such mouths will cease to open.

War will forever be, Twain predicts, and the cautionary voices of war opponents and antiwar writers will forever go unheeded.[30]

Twain admitted the inherent ineffectualness and personal riskiness of the craft of an antiwar writer, yet at the same time he shaped a series of powerful, antiwar texts. He at once denied his ability to effect change and did his best to make sure that change was effected. "Now then," says Satan to the boys under his tutelage, "I will show you this long array of crimson spectacles, so that you can note the progress of civilization from the time that Cain began it down to a period a couple of centuries hence."[31] Similarly, through his writings, Twain shared with his readers his own grim view of the bloody spectacle of war—past, present, and future. In particular, he shared his concern about the use of new weaponry. His work as an antiwar writer might be futile, Twain admitted, but what was the alternative?

11

THE WAR NOVELS OF STEPHEN CRANE,
JOSEPH KIRKLAND, AND
FRANK STOCKTON

Probably no other invention of the age is the outcome of so much human thought and ingenuity [as the torpedo]; certainly none is the result of the expenditure of such vast sums of money.

—W. S. Hughes, "Modern Aggressive Torpedoes," April 1887

y the 1890s America had moved solidly into the industrial age. Andrew Carnegie had modernized the steel industry. John D. Rockefeller had revolutionized the oil industry. In 1890 a record twenty-five thousand patent applications were filed. American war literature also had moved solidly into the age of industry. American war writers—especially antiwar writers—increasingly came to borrow their language, imagery, and themes from the realms of the factory, the foundry, and the technological frontier.

In particular, the way in which war novelists imagined battle—as reflected in Mark Twain's *A Connecticut Yankee*—revealed the unprecedented influence of industrialization and mechanization in shaping Americans' understanding of warfare. Whereas certain writers viewed the invention of more powerful weaponry with trepidation, other writers believed that new war technology would bring about a more peaceful future. Three novels published between 1889 and 1895—Stephen Crane's *The Red Badge of Courage*, Joseph Kirkland's *The Captain of Company K*, and Frank Stockton's *The Great War Syndicate*—demonstrate the range of ways in which American war literature, including antiwar literature, responded to industrialization and the advent of modern, industrialized warfare.

American novelists who wrote about the Civil War during the decade of the 1890s showed a far greater awareness of the industrial dimensions of that war than had their literary predecessors who wrote during the 1860s,

1870s, and even the 1880s. Stephen Crane's fantastically popular novel *The Red Badge of Courage* stands as an excellent example.[1] Crane describes combat almost as if it were transpiring in a gigantic factory or foundry. He writes about "the furnace roar of the battle" and notes that, in the middle of fighting, his protagonist, Henry Fleming, wishes that his rifle was "an engine of annihilating power."[2]

The distinction between war and industry, Crane suggests, had become obscured even by the time of the Civil War. Further accentuating the point, Crane observes, "The battle was like the grinding of an immense and terrible machine." And a page later he adds, "The torn bodies expressed the awful machinery in which the men had been entangled." Soldiers were mutilated in the Civil War, Crane implies, like modern industrial workers mangled in their machines.[3]

In fact, Crane's depiction of Civil War soldiers loading their guns reads like a description of busy industrial laborers. There is the noise of clanking steel. There are rows of men bent over their work. There is repetitive, pounding, mechanical motion and an emphasis on speed. "There was a singular absence of heroic poses. The men bending and surging in their haste and rage were in every impossible attitude. The steel ramrods clanked and clanged with incessant din as the men pounded them furiously into the hot rifle barrels." The men might be mistaken for iron mill workers pouring molten metal into molds, rather than soldiers pouring bullets into guns. Indeed, at one point, Crane draws an analogy between his farm boy–soldier and the day laborers of the iron industry. Just after the Union soldiers have repulsed an enemy charge, he writes, Fleming "was grimy and dripping like a laborer in a foundry." In other words, after his initiation into battle, Crane's protagonist looks not so much like a soldier as like a man who has been toiling in a metal mill.[4]

Although he describes the Civil War, Crane projects onto the conflict the concerns of a later day. In fact, Crane's vivid account of a callow youth's introduction to battle often seems to reveal more about the anxieties of the late nineteenth century than it does about the consciousness of the Civil War generation. And the imagery of industry and machinery that so thoroughly pervades Crane's description of the Civil War makes the work seem almost anachronistic. The huge boom in the iron and steel industry, after all, did not occur until after the Civil War. Andrew Carnegie opened his first steel plant in 1875.

As Crane's text demonstrates, the fast and furious pace of industrialization in the late nineteenth century significantly changed the way Americans conceived of, and wrote about, war. Describing the roar of battle, Crane writes, "It was the whirring and thumping of gigantic machinery." War had become a vast machine, and Crane suggests that even the soldiers had become machinelike. Awed by the endurance and skill of the Confederate soldiers charging at him, Fleming marvels, "They must be machines of steel." Elsewhere, the entire Union army, with its soldiers dressed in blue uniforms, is referred to as a "mighty blue machine." The comparison of men to machines inherently suggests that the soldiers have been dehumanized. They have lost their individuality and their free will. Viewing gunners manning a battery, Henry Fleming thinks of them as "methodical idiots! Machine-like fools."[5]

The organization of war and the organization of industry were becoming ever more alike, and American war literature registered the change. War was coming to resemble the operations of a factory or foundry. And the operations of a factory or foundry were coming to resemble war. The author of an 1889 study bearing the ponderous title *Recent Economic Changes and Their Effect on the Production and Distribution of Wealth and the Well-Being of Society* observed that the "modern manufacturing system" had been "brought into a condition analogous to that of a military organization, in which the individual no longer works as independently as formerly, but as a private in the ranks, obeying orders, keeping step, as it were, to the tap of the drum." The result was that the "individualism or independence" of the modern-day worker—like that of the modern-day soldier—had been "in a great degree destroyed."[6]

Another Civil War novel written during the 1890s offers further proof of the era's pervasive preoccupation with modernization and mechanization. *The Captain of Company K*, published in 1891, was written by Joseph Kirkland, a former Union army officer and an established novelist.[7] Though not overtly an antiwar work, *The Captain of Company K* reflects the way in which warfare was being reconceived in the late nineteenth century.

Written in a peculiar blend of romantic and realist styles, *The Captain of Company K* is simultaneously a blandly conventional and radically unconventional work. The basic plot line resembles that of many a Civil War novel. The central protagonist is an upright citizen—"merchant, philanthropist, Sunday-school superintendent, temperance orator . . . with hands white, linen spotless, and well-brushed hair growing thin in front"—who goes off to war, distinguishes himself by performing heroic deeds, and along the way wins the heart of the girl he loves.[8] However, the presence of cowardly soldiers, spiteful officers, wartime profiteers, and other nonheroic figures makes Kirkland's novel stand out from traditional war romances. Also unusual is that Kirkland uses his work to comment on the ways in which warfare was becoming increasingly mechanized and depersonalized.

Long before the soldiers in Kirkland's novel arrive on the battlefield, they are stripped of their independence and made to feel like tiny parts of a huge war machine. At evening dress parade, the soldiers obey a long series of barked commands. Kirkland cynically writes: "While one is learning [the military drill], he is buoyed up with the notion that there is some mighty hidden power and meaning in it, to come out later. Then when it becomes a matter of dull, mechanical routine, behold! there is nothing in it, except a reminder to each of those 3,000 men that he is no longer a human being, but is turned into a mere cog in a machine." A little later in the novel, as the soldiers prepare to head to the battlefront, Kirkland once again contemplates the mechanical qualities of the soldiers' work:

> Handling the musket and bayonet, marching, wheeling, facing, ploying, deploying, loading, firing, charging, halting, dressing, skirmishing, saluting, parading, for days and weeks (not to say years); all for the single purpose of bringing men into a double line, shoulder to shoulder, facing the foe; knowing enough (and not too much) to load and fire until they fall in their tracks or the other fellows run away.
>
> To such simple, mechanical, dull, dogged machine-work has the old art of war come down.

For the rank and file of soldiers, Kirkland makes clear, modern war is "machine-work." Even killing is utterly depersonalized. There is "no more of the exhilarating clash of personal contest. *Nothing* left but stern, defenseless, hopeless 'stand-up-and-take-your-physic'—fortuitous death by an unseen missile from an unknown hand." War lacks the intimacy and thrill of the personal contests of old. Soldiers are drilled in bayonet use, but death, when it comes, is anonymous. It is an "unseen missile" shot by an "unknown" enemy.[9]

Kirkland realized that the norms of warfare had changed with the Civil War. Appropriating the language of the industrial age, he contends that the individual soldier had been turned into "a mere cog in a machine." It is a phrase that would become commonplace in antiwar literature of the World War I era, but it was still new and jarringly discordant in the late nineteenth century.

Kirkland at once describes war as a highly mechanized endeavor in which the soldier is "no longer a human being," and at the same time he allows his fictional fighters to act as stouthearted individuals. Ultimately, it is Kirkland's struggle to reconcile the old and the new, romanticism and realism, conventional and modern war that makes *The Captain of Company K* so interesting—and so revealing of the tensions, literary and otherwise, of his day.

Although Crane and Kirkland rued the mechanization of warfare, other war writers of the late nineteenth century welcomed the application of industrial know-how to combat. Far from bemoaning the convergence of technology and war, Frank Stockton was one novelist of the era who welcomed the trend with enthusiasm. Widely admired in his day, Stockton made a name for himself writing works, including futuristic novels, for both juvenile and adult audiences.

In *The Great Stone of Sardis*, published in 1898 but set in the mid-twentieth century, Stockton presents an inspired inventor named Roland Clewe. Among the magnificent mechanisms that Clewe designs is a submarine that can carry explorers to the North Pole, an Artesian ray that can probe the depths of the earth, and an "extraordinary piece of mechanism, which was called the automatic shell." Stockton prophesies that by the year in which his novel takes place, 1947, the powers of explosives will have reached "so high a point that it [will be] unnecessary to devise any increase in their enormous energy." And he further predicts that progress in this branch of science will have "proceeded so far that an attack upon a fortified port by armored vessels" will be "considered as a thing of the past." Never again will there be "combat between vessels of iron or steel."[10]

In another of his futuristic works, *The Great War Syndicate*, Stockton envisages that technology soon will spell the complete end of war. Published in 1889, *The Great War Syndicate* presents an inspiring tale of unbloody battle in which America prevails and perpetual world peace is guaranteed. The short novel centers on a conflict that arises between the United States and Great Britain (due to a dispute about fisheries). The way that America goes about fighting, however, is thoroughly unprecedented in the annals of warfare. Rather than allowing the president, secretary of war, or a host of three-star generals to coordinate America's war effort, the matter is put entirely in the hands of a handsomely paid alliance of twenty-three powerful businessmen. In turn, this well-heeled cadre—the "great war syndicate" of the book's title—enlists eminent scientists to help devise an efficient war strategy.

The scientists, not the military careerists, are the masterminds behind America's ultimate victory. Entrusted with protecting their nation's sovereignty, the engineers contrive a marvelous new invention: the instantaneous motor-bomb. It is a weapon unlike any previously known, and the magnitude of its force is tremendous. To demonstrate the new bomb's destructive power, the syndicate decides to destroy an unoccupied fort on the Welsh coast. The fort is decimated, and Great Britain realizes that it cannot hope to win. Despite its powerful navy, Britain preemptively admits defeat. In a revealing sentence, Stockton explains, "The [British] Ministry now perceived that the Syndicate had not waged war; it had been simply exhibiting the uselessness of war as at present waged."[11]

Thanks to new weaponry, and the menace of annihilation, actual war is averted. The devastatingly powerful motor-bomb effectively acts as a deterrent. As Stockton elucidates, the war syndicate achieves what all previous generations of generals have not. "The desire to evolve that power which should render opposition useless had long led men from one warlike invention to another. Every one who had constructed a new kind of gun, a new kind of armour, or a new explosive, thought that he had solved the problem, or was on his way to do so. The inventor of the instantaneous motor had done it." America triumphs over Britain, and the war is peacefully concluded with only one life lost. And that single casualty—"one little cloud, one regret"—was purely accidental. "While assisting in the loading of coal," a man named Thomas Hutchins was struck and killed by a falling derrick. Even so, Hutchins is elevated posthumously to heroic stature. The nation mourns his loss, a monument is built in his memory, and his family is handsomely compensated.[12]

Stockton optimistically imagined that new weapons—more specifically, new *American* weapons—would be so destructive that no enemy would ever again dare to challenge the United States with armed force. He rhetorically asks in *The Great War Syndicate*, "Who now could deny that it would be folly to oppose the resources of ordinary warfare to those of what might be called prohibitive warfare?" America, Stockton hoped, would come to play the part of an international peacekeeper. In his story, Great Britain's surrender is followed by the formation of an Anglo-American Syndicate of War that is entrusted with protecting the people of all countries. As long as the members of the syndicate control the "paramount methods of warfare," they will function as the "arbiters of peace."[13]

Whereas Twain—whose *A Connecticut Yankee* was published the same year as the *Great War Syndicate*—and other writers of the era viewed the invention of ever deadlier weaponry with fear, Stockton viewed advances in military technology with optimism. In *A Connecticut Yankee* Twain envisions an apocalyptic scenario in which modern science leads to the complete annihilation of two armies. Stockton, on the other hand, suggests in *The Great War Syndicate* that wars will cease to be fought once a sufficiently destructive weapon is invented. "Hereafter," Stockton explains, "if battles must be fought, they would be battles of annihilation." And Stockton, for one, trusted the nations' leaders to be rational enough to avoid wars of self-destruction.[14]

The Great War Syndicate was a work of fantasy, but Stockton's optimism regarding the potential of technology was real. Nor was Stockton the only one who imagined that the day would dawn when wars would be fought entirely by automatic weapons or, better yet, would not be fought at all. Nikola Tesla, a renowned pioneer in the field of electricity, dreamed of automatic super weapons and death rays. And he predicted that the burden of battle would be entirely displaced onto science: "Machines will meet in a contest without bloodshed, the nations being simply interested, ambitious spectators. When this happy condition is realized, peace will be assured."[15]

Even the pacifist literature of the 1880s and 1890s contains similar expressions of optimism. Peace, certain pacifists believed, would follow after the introduction of modern armaments. Improved weaponry would guarantee the end of war. As one report in the *Peacemaker* asserted in 1894, "Science, [by creating] a frightful force[,] . . . is ready to annihilate war."[16]

The rapid speed with which the technology of industry and warfare was evolving forced American writers of the late nineteenth century to reevaluate war and the role played in it by the individual fighter. But in the relatively peaceful years of the 1880s and early 1890s—during which U.S. forces engaged in the Pine Ridge campaign against the Sioux but no all-out war—the full implications of modern, machine warfare remained largely unknown. Would the pragmatic application of science to the art of killing bring an end to war? Or would it have horrific and unintended consequences? Antiwar writers, as well as mainstream war writers, wrestled with these fundamental and increasingly urgent questions.

AMERICAN WRITERS AT WAR: CUBA AND THE PHILIPPINES

Will not one of these [writers] . . . turn his winged shafts squarely against war and the war-maker?

—Ernest Crosby, "The Absurdities of Militarism," 1901

rriving at the very close of the nineteenth century, the Spanish-American War and the Philippine-American War put to the test traditional notions of warfare in the era of industrialization. Although the conflicts did not evoke the mammoth literary response that the Civil War called forth, they did generate a body of war works. Among the authors who wrote about the short-lived war in Cuba or about the more protracted clash in the Philippines were numerous men and women who staunchly defended America's war aims. But also among them were a noteworthy group of writers who forthrightly challenged America's imperialist ambitions and, more broadly, condemned all wars as morally wrong.

The Spanish-American War was a very different engagement from the Civil War. The contest in Cuba lasted barely one hundred days and lacked the enormous scale of death and destruction, as well as the element of fraternal struggle, that had made the Civil War so extraordinarily traumatic for both soldiers and civilians. Most of the serious combat took place on a single day (July 1, 1898), and fewer than four hundred Americans died in battle. As one historian notes, "Americans took more casualties from camp sewage than from Mausers."[1] All in all, from the American perspective, it was an easy victory. Although the American soldiers suffered terribly from heat, malaria, and yellow fever, the U.S. military action in Cuba was short and successful.

The vicious war in the Philippines that followed was far more painfully protracted. Under the Treaty of Paris, the Spanish government had ceded the Philippines to the United States in 1898 for $20 million, but the Filipinos fiercely resisted annexation by America. Fighting went on for nearly three and a half years, from February 1899 through July 1902, and by 1900 formal combat had devolved into guerilla warfare. Outarmed, the Filipino *insurrectos* aimed not to vanquish the U.S. Army outright but rather to inflict steady losses on its troops. Meanwhile, the Americans were ruthless in their fight against the Filipinos. In mid-1902 America declared the Filipino "insurgency" officially over, but fighting in the Philippines continued until 1913.

These two interconnected, imperialist wars prompted a wide range of reactions from American observers. Whereas almost all writers of the Civil War era drew upon a highly romanticized vocabulary and a familiar set of sentimental and heroic tropes to endorse the war cause, writers at the turn of the century demonstrated no such near unanimity. Instead, authors reacted to the course of events with everything from chauvinistic cocksureness to bitter outrage. Writers such as Charles King and Upton Sinclair (who wrote prolifically under the pseudonyms Ensign Clarke Fitch and Douglas Wells) produced a small library of romantic stories and novels about the wars; others crafted works, both during and soon after the war years, that reflect an explicit anti-imperialist and antiwar agenda.[2]

Among the Americans who wrote about the wars in Cuba and the Philippines were two men who staked out very different positions: Theodore Roosevelt, a devoted war booster, and Ernest Crosby, a devoted war opponent. Respectively jingoistic and antimilitaristic, their writings demonstrate the range of literary responses to the conflicts. Their works also reflect important differences in the two writers' reactions to the mechanical revolution in warfare that was taking place at the turn of the century.

In the United States the Spanish-American War triggered an intense wave of patriotic fervor. War supporters presented the conflict to the reading public as a supreme test of national vigor and virility. Indeed, it is interesting to note how closely the American notion of manhood became intertwined during the war era with the dual concepts of risk and rigor. The foremost proponent of the ideology of martial manliness was Theodore Roosevelt, a patrician turned rugged rancher, who famously embodied, as well as articulated, the philosophy of the "strenuous life."[3] Roosevelt's hearty promotion of war as essential to America's continued well-being dramatically shaped the discourse of the era on the subjects of pacifism and militarism.

Indisputably, Roosevelt played a central role in the Spanish-American War. While serving as assistant secretary of the navy, he had advocated going to war with Spain, and upon America's declaration of war, he helped organize the 1st Volunteer Cavalry Regiment—commingling what he later described as "Easterners and Westerners, Northerners and Southerners, officers and men, cow-boys and college graduates"—and assumed the rank of the contingent's lieutenant colonel.[4] Then, on July 1, 1898, Colonel Roosevelt ascended into history book glory. He led the cavalry regiment—dubbed the "Rough Riders" by contemporary journalists—charging up San Juan Hill and gained both improbable success and immediate fame. Richard Harding Davis, one of a league of roving reporters sent forth to the battlefields by the yellow press, recorded, "Our troops could not retreat, as the trail for two miles behind them was wedged with men. They could not remain where they were, for they were being shot to pieces. There was only one thing they could do—go forward and take the San Juan hills by assault."[5] The dismounted cavalrymen charged up the hill in the tropical heat and conquered the enemy infantry that had been manning the hilltop entrenchment. The Civil War repeatedly demonstrated that such uphill attacks against fortified positions were suicidal, but the Rough Riders had triumphed. Out of a military blunder, Colonel Roosevelt, acting on his own initiative, snatched a military victory. And along the way he also snatched for himself the war-hero status that would eventually propel him into the White House.

Larger than life, Theodore Roosevelt returned home to America at war's end to interpret the meaning of the conflict for the nation's grateful citizens. In a famous speech, "The Strenuous Life," which he delivered at the Hamilton Club in Chicago in April 1899, Roosevelt presented the United States' decision to go to war with Spain as a test of national manhood and might. The options, as put forth by Roosevelt, had been either to "shrink like cowards from the contest, or enter into it as beseemed a brave and high-spirited people." Borrowing the language of the pulpit, Roosevelt extolled the value of active, manly endeavor. He began:

> I wish to preach, not the doctrine of ignoble ease, but the doctrine of the strenuous life, the life of toil and effort, of labor and strife; to preach that highest form of success which comes, not to the man who desires mere easy peace, but to the man who does not shrink from danger, from hardship, or from bitter toil, and who out of these wins the splendid ultimate triumph.

Roosevelt simultaneously applauded the lives of risk-taking men and disparaged all men who would "shrink" from danger.[6]

For Roosevelt, the romance of war lived on, and he insisted that America would be best able to prove itself a leader among nations through future triumphs on the battlefield. "For it is only through strife," he explained, "through hard and dangerous endeavor, that we shall ultimately win the goal of true national greatness." Roosevelt envisioned a future in which American men would rise to protect their nation or risk falling behind bolder men of other nations. Disdaining "the man of timid peace," he preached a gospel of fortitude and fearlessness. He proclaimed:

> The twentieth century looms before us big with the fate of many nations. If we stand idly by, if we seek merely swollen, slothful ease and ignoble peace, if we shrink from the hard contests where men must win at hazard of their lives and at the risk of all they hold dear, then the bolder and stronger peoples will pass us by, and will win for themselves the domination of the world. Let us therefore boldly face the life of strife, resolute to do our duty well and manfully.

Manhood, at least as defined by Roosevelt, entailed a goodly amount of exertion and risk. Strife, he insisted, was essential for both the well-being of the individual and for the well-being of America.[7]

Nonetheless, even Roosevelt could not entirely ignore the fact that machinery challenged the traditional way of warfare that he romanticized and so enthusiastically applauded. He could not remain oblivious to the argument that in modern war the worth of the weaponry mattered more than the worth of the soldiers. In November 1899, a little more than half a year after delivering his speech "The Strenuous Life," Roosevelt published in the *Century* magazine a revealing essay titled "Military Preparedness and Unpreparedness." This and other of Roosevelt's writings of the period reflect his awareness that technology was usurping the role of rough-riding soldiers.

In "Military Preparedness and Unpreparedness" Roosevelt seems to be on the defensive as he justifies his view of heroic warfare. Riled by the claims of a certain French detractor who had suggested that America's decisive victory in the Battle of Manila Bay was due "to a devilish mechanical ingenuity wholly unaccompanied by either humanity or courage," Roosevelt sought to assert the importance of the individual. He protested, "We did not win through any special ingenuity." Instead, he insisted, the Spanish-American

War had been won by dint of the navy's "splendid seamanship" and the "sheer dogged courage" of the army. Courage—individual fortitude—was an essential quotient of war for Roosevelt. Although he acknowledged, "It is . . . sometimes said that . . . mechanical devices will be [invented] of so terrible a character as to nullify the courage which has always in the past been the prime factor in winning battles," he did not concede that such an epoch actually would dawn.[8]

Nonetheless, despite his protestations, Roosevelt knew that warfare was becoming ever more mechanically technical. In fact, he argued that, in order to keep apace, America needed to steer a course of permanent readiness and build an army of mechanically sophisticated soldiers. According to Roosevelt, it was not enough to place trust in Yankee "smartness" and assume that in future conflicts Americans would be "able to win by some novel patent device, some new trick or new invention developed on the spur of the moment by the ingenuity of our people." Instead, he contended, preparedness was essential. Attacking public speakers and newspaper writers opposed to his point of view, Roosevelt wrote: "Whether from sheer ignorance or from demagogy, they frequently assert that, as this is the day of mechanics, even on the sea, and as we have a large mechanical population, we could at once fit out any number of vessels with men who would from the first do their duty thoroughly and well." But the "sea-mechanic," who had "replaced the sailorman," needed "especial training." To forgo preparedness, Roosevelt believed, would be to make America vulnerable to a country that was more mechanically up to date. "In the old days cannon were very simple; sighting was done roughly; and the ordinary merchant seaman speedily grew fit to do his share of work on a frigate. Nowadays men must be carefully trained for a considerable space of time before they can be of any assistance whatever in handling and getting good results from the formidable engines of destruction on battle-ship, cruiser, and torpedo-boat." Evidently, formidable engines, rather than formidable men, would decide the outcome of the wars of the future.[9]

Roosevelt's outlook on war thus rested on a fundamental contradiction. Emotionally, the future president preferred to place his trust in gumption and individual initiative rather than to rely on new-fangled machinery. He recalled with evident nostalgia the days when the tools of warfare had been easier to master. But as even Roosevelt reluctantly realized, war was becoming a skilled trade in which men had to be "carefully trained for a considerable space of time" in the handling of machines. The battles of the future were less likely to be won by men charging valiantly up hills than by men "getting good results from . . . formidable engines of destruction." It was therefore necessary, Roosevelt argued, for men to become adept at handling increasingly complex weaponry. Nonetheless, he insisted that American soldiers and officers were not themselves becoming mechanized. As he wrote in his 1899 memoir *The Rough Riders*, "The battalion chief of a newly raised American regiment . . . is in no danger whatever either of suffering from unhealthy suppression of personal will, or of finding his faculties of self-help numbed by becoming a cog in a gigantic and smooth-running machine."[10]

At the close of the nineteenth century, the machinery of war was becoming more complex, requiring an army of more skilled machinists, but Roosevelt tried to ignore the obvious implications. In chronicling the events of the Spanish-American War, he crafted a war narrative that more nearly resembled the romantic Civil War texts of the 1860s than the realist war texts of the 1890s. Describing the American forces in Cuba, he wrote, "[The troops] were led most gallantly, as American regular officers always lead their men; and the men followed their leaders with the splendid courage always shown by the American regular soldier." His was still a romanticist's war. Indeed, dismissing the new trend in American literature toward psychological, as well as material, realism, he wrote, "I did not see any sign among the fighting men, whether wounded or unwounded, of the very complicated emotions assigned to their kind by some of the realistic modern novelists who have written about battles."[11]

Nonetheless, in Roosevelt's war writings certain lines appear that seem to anticipate the laments of the men who would serve in the trenches during World War I. In *The Rough Riders* Roosevelt recalls with evident frustration that during the Spanish-American War, due to the introduction of smokeless gunpowder, the enemy could remain "entirely invisible." He writes, for example, "It was peculiarly hard to be exposed to the fire of an unseen foe." He also admits that "it was most bewildering to fight an enemy whom one so rarely saw." A generation later, the American poet Alan Seeger, who volunteered in the French Foreign Legion at the start of World War I, would write, "This is what is distressing about the kind of warfare we are up against,— being harried like this by an invisible enemy and standing up against all the dangers of battle without any of its exhilaration or enthusiasm."[12]

* * *

If Roosevelt, who believed in manhood won at a price, epitomized the war supporters' outlook on the Spanish-American War, Ernest Crosby, who believed that no war was worth the price of a man's life, represented the outlook of the war critics. The most prolific writer in the antiwar camp at the turn of the century, and president of the New York Anti-Imperialist League, Crosby insisted that there was nothing glorious about war.[13] In three volumes of poetry and one long novel, all published between 1898 and 1902, he shared his views on the subjects of militarism, imperialism, and technology.[14]

Ernest Crosby came to his radical stance by an unusual route. He was born in 1856 into a long-established family in New York; one of his great-great grandfathers had been a member of the Continental Congress and a signer of the Declaration of Independence. Crosby was educated at the University of the City of New York (now New York University). He went on to earn a law degree from Columbia University and serve a stint in the New York State Legislature (as the successor to Theodore Roosevelt). Later sitting as a judge on the International Court in Alexandria, Egypt, in the early 1890s, he came across a copy in French of Leo Tolstoy's treatise *O Zhizni* (a work known in English as *On Life*).[15] The book immediately changed the trajectory of Crosby's own life. Crosby was powerfully swayed by the Russian writer's spiritual philosophy, including Tolstoy's rejection of all forms of violence and institutions resting on violence, among which Tolstoy counted armies, police, law courts, and prisons. Crosby resigned his post in Egypt, traveled to Russia to meet Count and Countess Tolstoy, and returned home to New York a devoted disciple of Tolstoy's philosophy of love and pacifism. When America went to war with Spain in 1898 and later decided to annex the Philippine Islands, Crosby was at the forefront of the opposition.

In his poetry, Crosby linked his protest against the Spanish-American War and America's incursion in the Philippines with his larger crusade for world peace and social reform. His poem "Enemies," which appeared in a collection titled *War Echoes* that was published in 1898, begins, "Who are you at Washington who presume to declare me the enemy of anybody or to declare any nation my enemy?"[16] Another work, "War and Hell," puts forth Crosby's opinions even more bluntly. The seventeen-part poem begins:

> "War is hell," because it makes men devils.
> You and I, striving for a moment to squeeze or hack

the life out of each other, are we not at once
transformed into demons?
Hell is ever man's handiwork.[17]

Staunchly antiwar and anti-imperialist, Crosby ridiculed those who advanced the argument that the American annexation of the Philippines would redound to the Filipinos' benefit.

Notably, in a poem titled "The Real 'White Man's Burden,'" Crosby offered a stinging parody of Rudyard Kipling's famous poem "The White Man's Burden." Kipling, a British author who, with his American wife, had lived in Vermont for several years in the 1890s, had called on the United States to develop the Philippines in the name of progress. Endorsing the popular notion that America's conquest of the former Spanish territory could be viewed as a philanthropic act, Kipling had entreated Americans to bestow the blessings of civilization on the Filipinos. His poem, published in *McClure's* magazine in February 1899, begins:

> Take up the White Man's burden—
> Send forth the best ye breed—
> Go bind your sons to exile
> To serve your captives' need.

Kipling anticipated that the efforts of the Americans in the Philippines were likely to meet with native resistance. Nonetheless, he righteously insisted that the effort to civilize the Filipinos—whom he described as America's "new-caught, sullen peoples / Half-devil and half-child"—was morally commendable.[18]

Crosby's parody of Kipling's poem—first published in mid-February 1899 in the *New York Times* and later included in his poetry volume *Swords and Ploughshares*—makes quite a different argument. The annexation of the Philippines, according to Crosby, would put the Filipinos at risk of inheriting all of the evils of American civilization. "The Real 'White Man's Burden'" begins:

> Take up the White Man's burden.
> Send forth your sturdy kin,
> And load them down with Bibles
> And cannon-balls and gin.
> Throw in a few diseases

> To spread the tropic climes,
> For there the healthy niggers
> Are quite behind the times.

Throughout the remainder of the poem, Crosby continues to fault Americans for their arrogance and racism as he details the very detrimental impact that imperialism will have upon the natives of the Philippines. Among the gifts of "civilization" that the "uncivilized" Filipinos can look forward to sharing are factories, iron mills, taxes, mortgages, prisons, and electric chairs. Although Crosby expresses his disdain for the falsely "pious words" with which the imperialists "ornament each phrase," he acknowledges the effectiveness of their jingoistic rhetoric. He concludes his poem with the bitter observation that "In a world of canting hypocrites / This kind of business pays."[19]

Crosby's vehement attack on militarism and imperialism finds its fullest expression in his nearly four-hundred-page war novel, *Captain Jinks, Hero.* Published in 1902, the book presents both a merciless mockery of America's role in Cuba and the Philippines and a fascinating consideration of the ever-increasing mechanization of warfare. The book's basic plot tracks an all-American boy named Sam Jinks from his childhood days on his parents' farm playing with metal toy soldiers to his army days in the Cubapine Islands commanding soldiers of flimsy mettle. But the plot is merely a device for airing Crosby's political agenda. As the critic Fred Harvey Harrington aptly notes: "From first to last the book is essentially and obviously propaganda. The events of 1898–1900 are rehearsed in a satiric vein. The Cubans and Filipinos emerge, thinly disguised, as the Cubapinos. Old Glory becomes Old Gory. . . . Nowhere does [Crosby] favor the [American] participants with a word of praise; and throughout, the tale is one of bungling, theft, blood-letting, hypocrisy, and greed."[20] The United States' expansionist ambitions are treated by Crosby as thoroughly crass, calculating, and despicable, and the reader is invited to laugh at the chauvinistic pretensions of the Americans.

In particular, Crosby ridicules the war proponents. Lampooning Roosevelt's doctrine of manly vigor, Crosby depicts American war enthusiasts as uncouth and unfit bigots who compare quite unfavorably to the proud natives of the Cubapines. In a barroom scene that takes place roughly a hundred pages into the novel, a pimple-faced American named Mr. Jackson, a "tall, thin, narrow-chested man with no shoulders, a rounded back, and a gray, tobacco-stained moustache," spouts the Rooseveltian creed. Self-righteously, he proclaims, "Them pore critters need our civilization, that's what they need. . . . We must make real men of 'em. We must give 'em our strength and vigor and intelligence. They're a dirty lot of lazy beggars, that's the long and short of it, and we must turn 'em into gentlemen like us!" Spouted forth by a man who is the very antithesis of the Rough Rider ideal, the self-congratulatory rhetoric is both offensive and utterly absurd.[21]

In *Captain Jinks, Hero*, Crosby not only criticizes America's imperialist ambitions but also condemns the application of modern technology to warfare. Late in the novel, Crosby introduces into the story an inventor named Mr. Cope, who has earned fame for designing powerful rifles and artillery. After hearing Captain Jinks observe that perfect soldiers are ones who "move like clockwork, like marvelous machines," Mr. Cope decides to invent a machine that will take the place of fighting men. "I am at work at a great invention," he proudly announces. Elaborating on his plan, he explains, "Why shouldn't a machine be made to take the place of a soldier? A great idea, isn't it?"[22]

Mr. Cope envisions a future in which machinery will supplant fighting men. The inventor enthusiastically explains to the dubious Captain Jinks: "Now you see we've already done something in that line. A torpedo is simply an iron soldier that swims under water and needs no breath, and does as he is told. Think how absurd it is in battle to have a field-battery come up under fire at a gallop! They swing round, unlimber, load, and fire, then harness again, swing round again, and off they are. Meanwhile perhaps half the men and horses have been killed." There will be no need for such wanton waste of horses, much less of men, in the wars of the future, Mr. Cope insists. Instead of having soldiers risk life and limb in battle, the great inventor proposes: "Wouldn't it be better to have the whole battery a machine, instead of only the guns? The general could stay behind out of range, as he does to-day, and direct the whole thing with an electric battery and a telescope. . . . The principle can be extended to cavalry and infantry just as well. It will be a great thing for the nations that are best at mechanics, and that means you and us." Parodying the optimism of his contemporaries who envisioned technology as holding out promise for a more peaceful future, Crosby makes clear his own dislike not just of militarization but also of mechanization.[23]

Crosby's attack on the romantic conception of warfare, in which valor matters above all else, is ruthless. "I don't see," Captain Jinks says to Mr. Cope, "how you can get on without the courage of brave men." But the inventor reasons, "Courage! Why, what is more courageous than a piece of steel? It wouldn't be easy to frighten it. And it is just so with all soldierly qualities. Do you want obedience? What is more obedient than a machine?" Mystified that Jinks does not understand the immense superiority of machines over mortal men, the old inventor elaborates, "A soldier must be obedient, and he must be without fear, conscience, or a mind of his own. In all these respects a machine can surpass a man." Removing the human element from warfare, Mr. Cope insists, will remove the risks of disobedience and cowardice; it will also reduce war to a cold and carefully calculated science.[24]

Cleverly playing on contemporary concerns about the increasing mechanization of modern warfare, Crosby shows the lie behind the conventional notion of war as a manly crucible. Machine soldiers, Crosby predicts, will be the heroes of the future. The countries with the best machines will be victorious. Tellingly, an illustration accompanying Crosby's text shows a machine soldier. A crank is affixed to his metal rump. A patent number is stamped on his back. And booming from his mouth are the words, "I DO NOT THINK, I OBEY!" The caption underneath the picture reads, "The Perfect Soldier."[25]

Other writers of the period joined Crosby in attacking war and America's imperialist ambitions. For example, the popular author Finley Peter Dunne, in two collections of humorous sketches titled *Mr. Dooley in Peace and War* (1899) and *Mr. Dooley's Opinions* (1901), put a satiric spin on America's acquisition of Spain's former territories. Parodying American smugness, Dunne has the eponymous Mr. Dooley, a garrulous Chicago saloon-keeper, complain that the question of whether to annex the Philippines weighs heavily on his mind. Mr. Dooley—"th' man behind th' guns, four thousan' miles behind thim, an' willin' to be further"—worries about the ramifications of America becoming a colonial empire:

An' what shud I do with the Ph'lippeens? Oh, what shud I do with thim? I can't annex thim because I don't know where they ar-re. I can't let go iv thim because some wan else'll take thim if I do. They are eight thousan' iv thim islands, with a popylation iv wan hundherd millyon naked savages; an' me bedroom's crowded now with me an' th' bed. How can I

take thim in, an' how on earth am I goin' to cover th' nakedness iv thim
savages with me wan shoot iv clothes? An' yet 'twud break me heart to
think iv givin' people I niver see or heerd tell iv back to other people I
don't know.[26]

Still other opponents of the Spanish-American War and America's involve-
ment in the Philippines focused with undisguised and unapologetic directness on the issue of immorality.

Among the most famous of the era's writers to oppose America's actions
was the highly respected literary arbiter and novelist William Dean Howells. Writing to his fellow author and longtime friend Henry James in mid-
April 1898, he described himself as "distracted by the noises of the most
stupid and causeless war that was ever imagined by a kindly and sensible
nation." And in a letter to another correspondent that he posted the same
month, he declared, "I think we are wickedly wrong. We have no right to
interfere in Cuba, and we have no cause of quarrel with Spain. At the very
best we propose to do evil that good may come." Later, upon realizing that
America intended to annex the Philippines, Howells grew even more outraged. Writing again to Henry James, in late July 1898, Howells expounded,
"Our war for humanity has unmasked itself as a war for coaling stations, and
we are going to keep our booty to punish Spain for putting us to the trouble
of using violence in robbing her."[27] Henry James, in turn, wrote to Howells
in August 1898 from the "quaint old garden" of his English estate, "I have
hated, I have almost loathed [the war]."[28]

Howells, who served as a vice president of the New York Anti-Imperialist
League, made no secret of his views either in the private or the public fo-
rum. Nor was it imperialism alone to which he objected. Long before
hostilities broke out with Spain, Howells had used his public pulpit—his
monthly "Editor's Study" column in Harper's New Monthly Magazine—to
air a pacifist agenda. For instance, in May 1890, following his review of a
book concerning the cannibals of Australia, he had observed, "Our race,
in fact, has not been the slowest to murder, at any time, and has gone more
than half-way, usually, to meet the most homicidal savages on their own
ground. Even where its gifts in blood-shedding have not been called out by
contact with an inferior race, it has contrived to kill within its own ethnical
limits in a measure which would not discredit barbarians who hold man-
slaying in honor."[29] Howells objected to war being used to further American
imperialism. More fundamentally, he simply objected to war. In a letter he

wrote during the early summer of 1898, he described himself as someone who thinks "war the most atrocious murder."[30]

Howells's short story "Editha," which first appeared in *Harper's Monthly Magazine* in January 1905, reads as a heavy-handed indictment of not only the Spanish-American War but warfare in general. At the start of the story, a romantically inclined young woman, the Editha of the title, urges her fiancé to volunteer to fight in a war that he abhors. Echoing "the current phrases of the newspapers," she rhapsodizes, "I call it a sacred war. A war for liberty, and humanity, if ever there was one." Her fiancé, George, takes quite a different view of the conflict. "It isn't this war alone," he explains, "though this seems peculiarly wanton and needless; but it's every war—so stupid; it makes me sick." But, yielding to Editha's persistent goading, George finally relents. He volunteers and is killed in the war's first skirmish. After George's death, his mother rails at Editha for her naive bellicosity:

> No, you didn't expect him to get killed. . . . You just expected him to kill some one else, some of those foreigners. . . . You thought it would be all right for my George, *your* George, to kill the sons of those miserable mothers and the husbands of those girls that you would never see the faces of. . . . I thank my God he didn't live to do it! I thank my God they killed him first, and that he ain't livin' with their blood on his hands!

There is no mistaking that George's mother serves as Howell's mouthpiece; her sentiments clearly are his own.[31]

Such a bold condemnation of war by such an extremely influential literary figure—in addition to being a prolific novelist, Howells served as editor of the *Atlantic Monthly* and of *Harper's New Monthly Magazine* and in 1908 would be elected the first president of the American Academy of Arts and Letters—reflects the sea change that took place in American war literature in the decades following the Civil War. By the start of the twentieth century, antiwar writing clearly had become acceptable, if not quite mainstream. Howells, dubbed the "dean of American letters," freely asserted his opposition to war, both in the particular and in the abstract, and he was not penalized in the literary marketplace for so doing.

Nonetheless, many American writers continued to view war as a testing ground for courage, fortitude, and honor. If the popular war literature of the Civil War period is defined by conformity, the war literature of the turn of the century is defined by dissension. But whatever their personal beliefs regarding war's morality, American writers nearly universally recognized that war was fundamentally different from what it had been even a generation earlier.

The Spanish-American War was something of an anomaly. It was a throwback to a less modern era of fighting when a group of volunteers could charge a hill and be crowned with glory. Nevertheless, it is clear that at the turn of the twentieth century both the nature of war and the way that American writers and readers were coming to conceive of war were quickly changing. The individual was being pitted against the machine, and even the most optimistic observers had to concede that the future did not bode well for the glory-seeking soldier.

Theodore Roosevelt's Rough Riders may have represented virile militarism in the popular imagination, but the course of history was veering in a decidedly different direction. The old weapon-maker in Crosby's *Captain Jinks, Hero* boasts, "We inventors are the real military men."[32] That statement eerily echoes the claim of the British journalist Sir Edward Arnold after the grisly Battle of Omdurman in 1898 in which six Maxim machine guns and other modern weapons in the hands of the British resulted in the deaths of eleven thousand Dervishes in the Sudan. (The British forces suffered only forty-eight deaths.) Sir Arnold had proclaimed that the real hero of the contest was not the British soldier on the field but Hiram Maxim, the revered American-born weapons inventor.

Fought two months after Roosevelt triumphed at San Juan Hill, the Battle of Omdurman displayed the immense superiority of machine guns and artillery over older types of weaponry. G. W. Steevens, a British fighter, later described the tremendous onslaught against the Arabs. "The torrent swept into them and hurled them down in whole companies. You saw a rigid line gather itself up and rush on evenly; then before a shrapnel shell or a Maxim the line suddenly quivered and stopped. The line was yet unbroken, but it was quite still. But other lines gathered up again, again, and yet again; they went down, and yet others rushed on."[33] Near battle's end, according to Steevens's account, only three of the Dervishes remained standing to face the three thousand soldiers of the British Third Brigade. These final three were soon killed.

At Omdurman, valor failed in the face of technology. The Dervishes fought with great bravery. Even the victors recognized the courageous performance of the men they defeated. Steevens acknowledges: "The honour of the fight must still go with the men who died. Our men were perfect, but the Dervishes were superb—beyond perfection. . . . Their riflemen, mangled by every kind of death and torment that man can devise, clung round the black flag and the green, emptying their poor, rotten, home-made cartridges dauntlessly. Their spearmen charged death at every minute hopelessly." The army with the better weaponry, not the better fighters, won. And the defeat of the Dervishes was devastating in its comprehensiveness. Steevens remarks, "The dervish army was killed out as hardly an army has been killed out in the history of war."[34]

The impact of machine guns and other innovations vastly transformed warfare, making massed infantry and cavalry charges—the stuff of romantic lore—suicidal. The Dervish army at Omdurman was annihilated. And there was to be no turning back the clock. War was irrevocably changing, but some notions about war died slowly.

Even at the turn of the twentieth century, the romantic conception of combat inspired by Sir Walter Scott was still robust. In May 1897 Ambassador John Hay—poet, novelist, literary critic, politician, and diplomat—delivered a speech glorifying Scott in a commemorative ceremony at Westminster Abbey.[35] Then, a little over a year later, in late July 1898, Hay quoted Sir Walter Scott in a letter to his friend Theodore Roosevelt. Congratulating Roosevelt "on the brilliant campaign which now seems drawing to a close," in which Roosevelt had "gained so much experience and glory," Hay effused:

As Sir Walter wrote:—
   "One crowded hour of glorious life
   Is worth an age without a name."
You have written your name on several pages of your country's history, and they are all honorable to you and comfortable to your friends.
   It has been a splendid little war; begun with the highest motives, carried on with magnificent intelligence and spirit, favored by that Fortune which loves the brave.[36]

In August of that same year, Hay was named secretary of state. In September the Battle of Omdurman was fought. The legacy of Scott might have endured, but splendid little wars were to be no more.

13

THE PACIFIST IDEOLOGY OF WILLIAM JAMES
AND GEORGE KIRKPATRICK

Reflect for a moment on the horrible possibilities of [an] airship carrying a
light machine gun with a good supply of ammunition, or carrying 1,000 or
1,500 pounds of dynamite aloft over an army, a city, or a fleet.
—George R. Kirkpatrick, *War—What For?* 1910

As the twentieth century loomed, Americans were still struggling to interpret the implications of modern, machine warfare. On the first page of the first edition of the *Atlantic Monthly* for 1899 appeared an article by Charles W. Eliot, the president of Harvard University and a chemist by training. The piece, titled "Destructive and Constructive Energies of Our Government Compared," begins:

> We have been witnessing during the past months an extraordinary exhibition of energy on the part of the government of the United States in making sudden preparation for the war with Spain, and in prosecuting that war to a successful issue. Men of science . . . have a special interest in the lessons of the war, because the instruments and means used in modern warfare are comparatively recent results of scientific investigation and of science applied in the useful arts.

Once the new century dawned, the increasing mechanization of battle continued to hold the attention of men of science as well as many other Americans. As Eliot had done, they weighed the effects of "the invention of more and more destructive weapons, like the long-range magazine rifle and the machine gun" and contemplated the future direction of "modern warfare." Amid much debate and dissension, one trend became unmistakably clear. Peace grew ever more popular.[1]

Pacifism as an ideology gained unprecedented support in the decade preceding World War I. Peace societies proliferated, and as the historian

David S. Patterson notes, "Peace work became a popular avocation." The New York Peace Society, the American School Peace League, the Chicago Peace Society, the World Peace Foundation, the Carnegie Foundation for International Peace, and the Church Peace Union were among more than forty-five peace societies and endowed institutions established by Americans in that decade. Indeed, as Patterson archly observes, "The desire for 'peace' became so infectious that even the leading boosters of the Navy League [an organization founded in 1902, with the support of President Theodore Roosevelt, to build up the navy] felt it advisable to proclaim their strong opposition to war."[2]

Once the rocky redoubt of Quakers and other peace sects, pacifism became a mainstream ideology. It was suddenly fashionable in America to stake out a stance against war. College presidents, philanthropists, politicians, clergymen, and jurists joined together in envisioning a day in which war would be fought no more. Through a combination of diplomacy, the institution of world courts, disarmament, and other measures, it was believed that bloody battle could be brought to a permanent halt. The munitions makers, military men, and myriad other war mongers would be overruled by reason and popular consensus—or so the pacifists predicted.

Indeed, even after World War I began, Sidney L. Gulick, the associate secretary of the Commission on Peace and Arbitration and a representative of the Federal Council of the Churches of Christ in America, continued urging his fellow Christians in the still-neutral United States to oppose militarism. Declaring war "an overwhelming anachronism," he wrote, "The method of settling international and interracial difficulties by battle is that of the most primitive barbarism. Vast military preparations signify the survival, in the midst of modern civilization, of ominous features of savagery and indicate how incomplete is our boasted civilization. For civilization is the triumph of reason over force. Militarism makes force triumph regardless of reason." And to make sure that future generations would not be misguided about war, Gulick advocated a rewriting of school textbooks: "Do they glorify wars and military heroes? Is there any corrective exalting the ideals of peace? Do they point out the essential failure of most wars and the inability of war-methods to provide for justice? Do they show that a few heroes gain glory, but that the millions who fight and suffer as a rule gain nothing?" War-making, the pacifists contended, could be replaced by arbitration, goodwill, and new schoolbooks.[3]

The grim reckoning that four years of world war would force upon these Americans still lay in the future. In the relatively pacific years that the United States experienced between the official end of the war in the Philippines and World War I, permanent peace seemed an attainable, if admittedly idealistic, goal. Throughout America, the impulse of reform was powerful, and war—like child labor, vice, and corruption—presented itself as a remediable evil. If sufficient effort was applied by rational and right-minded individuals, so the argument went, belligerence could be eliminated for the good of humankind.

World peace also seemed a particularly urgent goal at the start of the twentieth century. Erupting in early 1904, the Russo-Japanese War offered further proof, as the historian Walter Millis notes, of "the battlefield predominance of the machine gun, the impossibility of the frontal charge, [and] the decisive significance of entrenchment and position warfare."[4] The threat posed by more and more technologically sophisticated and deadly warfare made permanent peace seem essential.

As momentum for world peace and support of the pacifist cause steadily grew in the period preceding World War I, a wide range of American antiwar writers registered their views on the subjects of warfare, nationhood, and modernity. Whether writing from positions of entrenched power or from the margins of power—from the ivy-clad halls of academia or from poster-coated union halls—these writers shared a determination to stop the perpetuation of war. Among those who spoke out about war in the decade preceding World War I were two men of very different backgrounds and political leanings: the retired Harvard professor William James and the staunch socialist George R. Kirkpatrick.

In an essay published in 1910 titled "The Moral Equivalent of War," the prominent physiologist, psychologist, and philosopher William James proposes an alternative to warfare. Although he hails the battlefield as "the supreme theatre of human strenuousness"—as displaying "life *in extremis*"—and acknowledges that war presents an exhilarating experience that revivifies society, James envisions a utopian future free of war. The beneficial qualities of camp life and combat, he contends, can also be found far from actual battle.[5]

James's argument—the central thesis of which he put forth at the Boston Peace Congress of 1904 and later fine-tuned for a speech, "The Psychology of the War Spirit," that he delivered at Stanford University in 1906—at once embraces and rejects the ideals of fortitude and frontiersman bravado put forth by Theodore Roosevelt in "The Strenuous Life." Manly vigor was essential to the well-being of America, James admitted. But war was not.[6]

Proposing a mandatory conscription of young men into an army of workers, James reasons that the energies and passions used to make war could be redirected. Pacifism, he contends, had failed in the past because it failed to offer a sufficiently appealing alternative to the thrill of the fray. But a substitute for war could be found that would instill in Americans "the manly virtues" of hardiness, discipline, and intrepidity. "The martial type of character can be bred without war," or so James insists in "The Moral Equivalent of War."[7]

The battlefield, James argues, could be replaced by coal and iron mines, freight trains, and fishing fleets. To an "army enlisted against *Nature*" the nation's youths could be drafted for a few years "to get the childishness knocked out of them." Framing skyscrapers or constructing tunnels, they could do "their own part in the immemorial human warfare against nature." The well-being of society, according to James, rests upon the cultivation of fortitude and vigor in young men. Yet America's youths need not emulate the rifle-toting Rough Riders.[8]

As a member of the Anti-Imperialist League, James had condemned America's incursions abroad and publicly criticized Roosevelt's enthusiasm for battle.[9] After the publication of Roosevelt's speech "The Strenuous Life," James published a long and scathing response in the *Springfield Republican.* Using the language of the still-nascent field of psychology, James accused Roosevelt, a former Harvard student of his, of being "still mentally in the *Sturm und Drang* period of early adolescence." More pointedly, James wrote, "[He] gushes over war as the ideal condition of human society, for the manly strenuousness which it involves, and treats peace as a condition of blubberlike and swollen ignobility, fit only for huckstering weaklings, dwelling in gray twilight and heedless of the higher life."[10]

Nor was William James the only one in his family to condemn Roosevelt and American imperialism. On these subjects the novelist Henry James was in full agreement with his older brother. In April 1898, as America tensed for war with Spain, Henry James wrote to William, "I confess that the blaze about to come leaves me woefully cold, thrilling with no glorious thrill or holy blood-thirst whatever. I see nothing but the madness, the passion, the hideous clumsiness of rage, of mechanical reverberation." Fourteen months later, in June 1899, with Cuba conquered and America's military energies bent on new conquests, Henry James again shared his thoughts with his older brother. Praising William's letter "The Philippine Tangle," which had appeared in the *Boston Transcript,* Henry wrote: "Your last letter on Roosevelt & the Philippines . . . commands all my admiration & sympathy. I agree with you no end—we have ceased to be, among the big nations, the one great thing that made up for so many crudities, & made us above all superior & unique—the only one with clean hands & no record of across-the-seas murder & theft." Imperialism did not fit with either of the James brothers' vision of America, and in "The Moral Equivalent of War" William James bitterly condemns the war-eager newspaper publishers and pliant politicians who led the nation into "our squalid war with Spain."[11]

In "The Moral Equivalent of War" James also expresses his anxiety about the rapid industrialization of warfare. Comparing the "feeble and irregular" innovations in commercialism to the "steady and rapid development of method and appliances in naval and military affairs," James measures the fast pace with which military science had evolved during his own lifetime:

> Nothing is more striking than to compare the progress of civil conveniences . . . to the progress in military apparatus during the last few decades. The house-appliances of to-day for example, are little better than they were fifty years ago. . . . Houses a couple of hundred years old are still satisfactory places of residence, so little have our standards risen. But the rifle or battleship of fifty years ago was beyond all comparison inferior to those we possess; in power, in speed, in convenience alike. No one has a use now for such superannuated things.

The superannuation of the military innovations of half a century earlier— of the Civil War era, in which James's youngest brothers, Garth "Wilky" Wilkinson James and Robertson James, had fought—presented disturbing evidence of the escalation of war's lethal reach.[12]

James determinedly insisted that war need not play a permanent part in "social evolution," and he challenged those writers who disagreed. "Without any exception known to me," he observed, "militarist authors take a highly mystical view of their subject, and regard war as a biological or sociological necessity, uncontrolled by ordinary psychological checks and motives." James—who in August 1863 had seen his brother "Wilky" return wounded from the 54th Massachusetts Regiment's historic charge on Fort Wagner in

South Carolina, looking more dead than alive—ventured to suggest that war might be a "transitory phenomenon" in the progress of society.[13]

In his rejection of the militaristic status quo, James was joined by many other prominent Americans of his day. His essay "The Moral Equivalent of War" was published by the American Association for International Conciliation, which took as its mission, "to arouse the interest of the American people in the progress of the movement for promoting international peace and relations of comity and good fellowship between nations." The membership of the association's Council of Direction reads like a who's who of prominent Americans of the era. It included the renowned pastor Lyman Abbott; the three-time Democratic Party nominee for president William Jennings Bryan; the U.S. senator, and former secretary of war and secretary of state, Elihu Root; the steel baron turned philanthropist Andrew Carnegie; and even the retired Harvard University president—who only a dozen years earlier had praised the "invention of more and more destructive weapons" as a "wonderful thing" for demonstrating the "immense superiority of the disciplined freeman to the trained automaton"—Charles W. Eliot.[14]

In 1910—the same year that "The Moral Equivalent of War" appeared—the working-class champion George R. Kirkpatrick published a staunchly antiwar book titled *War—What For?*[15] The popular book, of which thirty thousand copies were printed in the first nine months, proved nothing less than a full-length manifesto against war from a socioeconomic perspective. As Kirkpatrick explains on the dedication page, "This book is dedicated to the victims of the civil war in industry; that is, to my brothers and sisters of the working class, the class who furnish the blood and tears and cripples and corpses in all wars—yet win no victories for their own class." Making no secret of his grievance against the moneyed and empowered classes, Kirkpatrick protested the way in which, so he believed, the true interests of the working class are subverted in war.

> So, whenever the capitalists want war and the politicians declare war, the flimflammed, bamboozled, *working* man straps on a knapsack, shoulders a rifle (or takes a policeman's club), kisses his wife and children good-bye, and marches away to fight a war *he* didn't want, a war *he* didn't declare, a war that belittles and wrongs *him* by injuring *his class*,—and marches away to butcher *other* working men whom he *doesn't know* and against whom he *has no quarrel.*

In Kirkpatrick's estimation, the exploitation of labor in industry and the exploitation of labor in warfare were closely linked, and just as industrialization was changing the laborer's workplace, so too was it changing the soldier's battlefield.[16]

Throughout his book, Kirkpatrick repeatedly draws his readers' attention to recent changes in war technology. He writes, for example: "The soldiers of the American Civil War did not use—had not even heard of—the terrible explosives of our day. Melinite, dynamite, cordite, indurite, motorite, ecrasite, peroxilene and other explosive compounds vastly increase the effectiveness of modern arms and in other ways also multiply the dangers of the modern battlefield." War, Kirkpatrick makes clear, had become exponentially more deadly by 1910 than it had been in the 1860s. After reviewing the firepower of such weapons as the Danish "Rexer" rifle (that could fire 300 shots per minute), the updated Maxim gun (that could fire 700 bullets per minute), and the updated Gatling gun (that, "equipped with an electric motor," could discharge 1,800 "death-dealing bullets per minute"), Kirkpatrick concludes that modern war equals suicide for the lowly soldier. "Ordering the working class to go to war with the present fire-arms," he declares, "is like ordering a working man to make a gun, load it, dig his own grave, crawl down into it, and there scream 'Hurrah for death!' and then shoot himself."[17]

Modern warfare, Kirkpatrick contends, spells death by killing machines. And he describes one such machine in detail. "Think of a murdering machine 50 feet long, weighing 260,000 pounds, consuming 612 pounds of smokeless powder per charge, firing a projectile weighing 2,400 pounds through 23½ inches of Krupp steel armor, and having a range of almost nine miles—a monster butchering machine. The United States Government exhibited such a gun at the World's Fair, at St. Louis, in 1904." The individual soldier stands to reap no benefit from war, Kirkpatrick insists. And he indignantly attacks Theodore Roosevelt—whom he labels a self-promoting "mongrel mixture of patrician and brute"—and others who attempt to convince Americans otherwise.[18]

To believe in battlefield glory or patriotic duty, according to Kirkpatrick, is to be duped by corrupt politicians and capitalists, the "flunky-champagne-guzzlers." Commenting on Roosevelt's own war record, Kirkpatrick quotes a passage from *The Rough Riders,* in which Roosevelt recounts, "Two Spaniards leaped from the trenches . . . not ten yards away. As they turned to run I closed in and fired twice, missing the first and killing the second." According to Kirkpatrick, who omitted the fact that the Spaniards fired first, the incident demonstrates not Roosevelt's heroism but his heartlessness. "Surely it requires courage, rare and noble courage, for a wealthy graduate of Harvard University to boast in print that he shot a poor, ignorant fleeing Spanish soldier—very probably a humble working man drafted to war, torn from his weeping wife and children—that he shot such a man, *in the back*." In Kirkpatrick's assessment, Roosevelt and others who are inclined to boast about their bold battlefield deeds are criminals leading others criminally astray. For there should be no exalting of "the vast subject of wholesale murder called war."[19]

Drawing on a stunningly wide variety of sources, Kirkpatrick shapes a refutation of warfare that is at once quite emotional and quite well documented. As the poet Edwin Markham (who in 1910 established the Poetry Society of America) pronounced in a review of *War—What For?* that appeared in the *New York American*, "[Kirkpatrick] tatters all the shibboleths that influence men to go to war. He masses his facts in a cumulative horror." Whether citing the number of cases of venereal diseases among soldiers serving in the British army in India in 1902 or quoting Victor Hugo ("Ah! let us proclaim absolute truths. Let us dishonor war. No; glorious war does not exist. No; it is not good, and it is not useful, to make corpses.") or noting that the U.S. government had a 16-inch cannon that could throw "a shot weighing 2,000 pounds to an extreme range of twenty-one miles," Kirkpatrick doggedly makes his case against the perpetuation of warfare.[20]

Americans in the early twentieth century were increasingly coming to recognize the threat of modern military technology. The concerns raised by contemporary commentators, ranging from working-class radicals to esteemed professors emeritus, both echo and amplify the concerns that had been raised by writers since at least the mid-nineteenth century. Kirkpatrick's condemnation of the "mechanical monster" exhibited at the 1904 World's Fair is reminiscent of Hawthorne's criticism in 1862 of the monstrous *Monitor*. "Human slaughter has become a science," Kirkpatrick feared. "Human strife is to be transferred from the heart and personality of man into cunning contrivances of machinery," Hawthorne worried.[21]

In the interwar lull that followed the official end of the war in the Philippines in 1902, Americans dared to dream of permanent peace and warned one another of the dangers of modern war. The start of World War I brought an end to such abstract speculation. Even as America remained officially neutral, the concrete reality of warfare in Europe—the unprecedented loss of lives on the battlefields of Verdun and the Somme combined with the day-to-day grimness of trench warfare—forced Americans to reassess the meaning of modern war. Then, after Congress declared war on Germany in April 1917, the war took on added immediacy and importance.

The complex role played by war literature during and after World War I belongs to another book. However, as the writings of William James, George R. Kirkpatrick, and the other antiwar writers discussed in this book demonstrate, the genre of modern antiwar literature was solidly established in America by the start of World War I. What is more, it was gaining in popularity.

CONCLUSION

Were men but strong and wise,
Honest as Grant, and calm,
War would be left to the red and black ants,
And the happy world disarm.

—Herman Melville,
"The Armies of the Wilderness," 1866

I n the nearly fifty years that separated the Civil War from World War I, American antiwar writing gradually gained in popularity and public acceptance. During the remainder of the twentieth century, the genre achieved ever greater fame and recognition.

Although American antiwar writing about World War I is now largely thought of as a postwar phenomenon, even as the war was being waged, men and women stepped forward to denounce it. An American journalist named Arthur Sweetser, describing fighting that he witnessed during the opening weeks of the conflict, writes, "Modern battle is the cold, calculating work of science, largely shorn of the human element." The war was still in its infancy, with the introduction of poison gas and other deadly novelties still in the future. Even so, Sweetser deplored the very modern way in which the war was being fought. He describes French soldiers at the First Battle of the Aisne in September 1914, as "poor devils crouching resignedly in the trenches . . . while death flared down on them from above." Those who died were victims of "long-distance slaughter." Those who replaced them were "driven sheep-like to the slaughter." In a succinct summation of what he observed, Sweetser records that there was "no glory, no tremendous action, no wild exultation of battle."[1]

Other American writers joined Sweetser in expressing their disillusionment and dismay. The warfare taking place on the battlefields of Europe was profoundly alienating for both participants and onlookers. The journalist and poet John Reed was among the war's sharpest critics, and in his book

The War in Eastern Europe, published in 1916, he makes clear the dehumanizing effect of modern combat. Describing the scarred landscape that lay between deserted Serbian and Austrian trenches, he writes:

> The ground between was humped into irregular piles of earth. Looking closer, we saw a ghastly thing: from these little mounds protruded pieces of uniform, skulls with draggled hair, upon which shreds of flesh still hung; white bones with rotting hands at the end, bloody bones sticking from boots such as the soldiers wear. An awful smell hung over the place. . . .
>
> We walked on the dead, so thick were they—sometimes our feet sank through into pits of rotting flesh, crunching bones. Little holes opened suddenly, leading deep down and swarming with gray maggots. . . .
>
> For six miles . . . the dead were heaped like that—ten thousand of them.

The nightmarish scene of death that Reed depicts attests to the enormous scale of mass warfare. In "The Armies of the Wilderness" Melville notes that the graves of Civil War soldiers sometimes were too shallow and an occasional "hand reache[d] out of the thin-laid mold." In the World War I wasteland that Reed describes, "most of the bodies were covered only with a film of earth, partly washed away by the rain—many were not buried at all."[2]

The works of Sweetser, Reed, and others evoke the terrible reality of modern battle and make clear their authors' utter rejection of the romantic ideal. After America's declaration of war, Reed contributed an article titled "This Unpopular War" to the short-lived, pacifist magazine *Seven Arts.* In it he wrote, "I'm afraid I never did properly understand the drama and the glory of this war. . . . I tried to see the picturesque, the dramatic, the human; but to me all was drab, and all those millions of men were become cogs in a senseless and uninteresting machine."[3]

One of the most unsettling works of American antiwar literature published during World War I was written by a volunteer war nurse named Ellen La Motte. In her collection of short stories, *The Backwash of War,* La Motte explains, "Well, there are many people to write you of the noble side, the heroic side, the exalted side of war. I must write you of what I have seen, the other side, the backwash." First published in the autumn of 1916, La Motte's work is filled with graphic accounts of futile hospital operations, foul bodies, and prolonged suffering. The men in her stories are often repulsive in their injured state, and they fail to face death bravely. A darkly ironic tale titled "Heroes"—which first appeared in the *Atlantic Monthly* in the summer of 1916—begins, "When he could stand it no longer, he fired a revolver up through the roof of his mouth, but he made a mess of it. The ball tore out his left eye, and then lodged somewhere under his skull, so they bundled him into an ambulance and carried him, cursing and screaming, to the nearest field hospital."[4]

As the works of these and other authors demonstrate, new antiwar literature was circulating, if not always quite freely, even as World War I was being fought. The dehumanizing effects of mass warfare, the absence of the traditional heroic virtues, and the helplessness and horror of war served as the common themes of these texts, as they had served as themes in numerous texts written before the war.

Antiwar literature remained surprisingly consistent in its fundamental points and moral arguments, even as warfare itself was quickly changing in the early twentieth century. As the authors of *Merchants of Death: A Study of the International Armament Industry* would later explain:

Not only were the number of combatants and the financial costs of [World War I] without precedent, but the number and variety of death machines had never been equaled. All the sinister engines of war invented and perfected in the previous half century were used in the fighting, and, naturally enough, there was a further development of these during the war itself. The machine gun was improved, artillery was motorized and its range became longer, sights and fire-control apparatus became more scientific and more accurate.[5]

The modernization of warfare would continue apace throughout the twentieth century. So too would antiwar writers continue to denounce and deplore it.

An explicitly antiwar genre was already well established in American literature by the end of World War I. However, the swift rise in the production of antiwar works in the post–World War I era—and the attendant popularity of the works—was unprecedented in its extent. Indeed, in the 1920s and early 1930s the antiwar perspective came, for the first time, to dominate American war literature. A few profiles of writers and their works will serve to give a sense of the volume and venom of this postwar outpouring of texts.

John Dos Passos, who served as a volunteer ambulance driver during World War I, published three antiwar novels: the autobiographical *One Man's Initiation, 1917* (1920), the lengthy *Three Soldiers* (1921), and the modernist classic *1919* (1932). In each of these works his condemnation of war is unmistakable. Violence is nonsensical and morality is either absent or unrewarded. In *One Man's Initiation* an English soldier shares the following tale, "Before I left the front I saw a man tuck a hand-grenade under the pillow of a poor devil of a German prisoner. The prisoner said, 'Thank you.' The grenade blew him to hell!" Indeed, Dos Passos's first novel is strident and heavy-handed in its antiwar message. At one point, the American protagonist, talking to a group of Frenchmen, comments, "We none of us believe that war is right or useful or anything but a hideous method of mutual suicide." Another American character laments, "Oh, God, it's too damned absurd! An arrangement for mutual suicide and no damned other thing."[6]

Laurence Stallings, who lost a leg in 1922 due to wounds he had sustained in World War I, coauthored the antiwar play *What Price Glory?* (first produced in 1924), wrote an autobiographical novel titled *Plumes* (1924), and composed an introduction and captions for the graphic best seller *The First World War: A Photographic History* (1933). Throughout, he registered his disillusionment with war. As one literary scholar commented in 1935, "Taking his work in all forms as a single whole, Laurence Stallings has done more than any one American author to cut away the romantic glamour of war and to expose its wretchedness."[7] The plot of Stallings's autobiographical novel, for example, follows an American soldier during the four painful years that elapse between when he is shot by a German machine gun and when his mangled leg is finally amputated. The unromantic tone of the work can be judged by considering the following sentence: "The knee was a demon now, and the bone ends gleefully ground the membranes between them." And as if to render his message unmistakable, Stalling has his protagonist admit to a friend, "I grant you that all war is a mistake, a brutal and vicious dance directed by ghastly men. It was the tragedy of our lives that we had to be mutilated at the pleasure of dolts and fools."[8]

Other American postwar writers—including William Faulkner, Thomas Boyd, William March, E. E. Cummings, Elliot H. Paul, and Dalton Trumbo—stepped forward to express their own sense of disillusionment, anger, and frustration.[9] But perhaps no author combined these emotions so effectively or famously as Ernest Hemingway. In his short story collection *In*

Our Time (1925) and in two novels, *The Sun Also Rises* (1926) and *A Farewell to Arms* (1929), Hemingway established his signal, spare style of writing and introduced to his readers an unforgettable rank of physically and emotionally scarred war veterans: Nick Adams, Jake Barnes, and Frederic Henry, respectively.

As a volunteer ambulance driver who received 227 individual wounds from a mortar explosion while being simultaneously hit in the leg by machine-gun fire, Hemingway had experienced the war personally and painfully, and his works register a full awareness of war's absurdities.[10] An exchange in *A Farewell to Arms* between Frederic Henry, an American ambulance driver serving in the Italian army, and a soldier reads:

> "How you like this goddamn war?"
> "Rotten."
> "I say it's rotten. Jesus Christ, I say it's rotten."

And a little later the soldier adds, "Jesus Christ, ain't this a goddamn war?" The same point that Whitman had so tentatively ventured to confide to his diary—"O the hideous damned hell of war"—but did not share with his readers, Hemingway flaunts in his novel. His characters know full well that the war they participate in is ungodly and immoral. As Frederic Henry declares in an oft-quoted passage, "I was always embarrassed by the words sacred, glorious, and sacrifice and the expression in vain. . . . I had seen nothing sacred, and the things that were glorious had no glory and the sacrifices were like the stockyards at Chicago if nothing was done with the meat except to bury it."[11]

Nor was it American writers alone who angrily and publicly denounced the slaughter of World War I. Authors from all the combatant nations, including Siegfried Sassoon and Robert Graves in England, Jaroslav Hašek in Czechoslovakia, and Erich Maria Remarque and Arnold Zweig in Germany, joined together in condemning war in general and the First World War in specific. And their works freely crossed borders.

Indeed, there is no more telling indication of the popular embrace of antiwar literature in America in the post–World War I era than the fact that Erich Maria Remarque's pacifist novel *All Quiet on the Western Front* was designated the Book of the Month Club selection for June 1929. In a review of the work that ran that same month in the *New York Times,* a literary critic praised Remarque's "magnificent physical picture of war." He elaborated,

"In 'All Quiet' we have a picture of that physical horror unsurpassed for vividness, for reality, for convincingness, which lives and spreads and grows until every atom of us is at the Front seeing, mingling, suffering."[12]

The successive decades of the twentieth century brought both new wars and new generations of protest writers, and antiwar literature continued to receive popular and critical acclaim. The floodgates once opened were not to be closed. Notably, in the quarter century following World War II, Norman Mailer, Joseph Heller, and Kurt Vonnegut won tremendous praise for their respective books *The Naked and the Dead* (1948), *Catch-22* (1961), and *Slaughterhouse-Five* (1969).

Full of black humor, arch fatalism, and even outright absurdity, these books shredded any remnant notion of war's grandeur. The memorable conclusion of Heller's *Catch-22*, for example, finds the protagonist—an American bombardier named Yossarian who is in the process of deserting the Air Force to escape to Sweden—jumping to escape the knife of a vindictive whore. Even more outlandish, in Vonnegut's work the protagonist, Billy Pilgrim, visits a far-off planet named Tralfamadore. There he is astounded to realize that the inhabitants of that whole planet live in peace. "As you know," he tells a crowd of onlookers, "I am from a planet that has been engaged in senseless slaughter since the beginning of time."[13]

Other antiwar writers of the era—including William Styron, James Jones, Randall Jarrell, and John Hersey—also wrote well-received works of fiction and poetry about World War II and the Korean War. And like so many authors before them, they pointed to the impossibility of achieving heroism in modern battle. The new weaponry had become far too dehumanizing. On the first page of William Styron's novella *The Long March* (1952), faulty ammunition left over from World War II explodes at a boot camp in North Carolina, killing eight marines in training for Korea. Styron writes, "It was not so much as if they had departed this life but as if, sprayed from a hose, they were only shreds of bone, gut, and dangling tissue to which it would have been impossible ever to impute the quality of life." Theirs is an utterly pointless and horrific death.[14]

Writers in the aftermath of World War II also weighed the morality of the atomic attacks on Hiroshima and Nagasaki and worried about a future apocalyptic showdown. In *Hiroshima* (1946), a highly acclaimed work of nonfiction, the journalist and novelist John Hersey traces the first atom bomb's immediate impact on the lives of six survivors. Quoting a German Jesuit priest on the work's final page, Hersey writes, "The crux of the matter is whether total war in its present form is justifiable, even when it serves a just purpose. Does it have material and spiritual evil as its consequences which far exceed whatever good might result?"[15] A dozen years later, the popular novelist and former World War II correspondent John Steinbeck was even blunter, "The next war, if we are so stupid as to let it happen, will be the last of any kind. There will be no one left to remember anything."[16]

The numerous antiwar works written after World War II were powerful and pointed. But the decades following the Vietnam War marked the true apotheosis of American antiwar literature. Whereas the works of dissenters had been shunned and censored during the Civil War era, those of writers of the post–Vietnam War era were promptly praised and canonized. Full of cynicism, dark irony, and bitter disillusionment, these works appealed to their readers' own sense that the lengthy war, the longest in U.S. history, had been a costly and immoral mistake.

The flourishing of antiwar literature in this postwar period, and the critical embrace of its style and sensibility, is reflected in the number of prestigious literary awards, which antiwar works were nominated for—and often won—between the mid-1970s and the mid-1990s. Robert Stone's *Dog Soldiers* (1974), Tim O'Brien's *Going After Cacciato* (1978), and Larry Heinemann's *Paco's Story* (1986) all won the National Book Award. Thom Jones's *The Pugilist at Rest* (1993) and Tobias Wolff's *In Pharaoh's Army: Memories of a Lost War* (1994) were National Book Award finalists. Tim O'Brien's *The Things They Carried* (1990) was a finalist for both the Pulitzer Prize and the National Book Critics Circle Award. And Robert Olen Butler's *A Good Scent from a Strange Mountain* (1992) was awarded the Pulitzer Prize for Fiction.

Equally indicative, if not more so, of the broad cultural appeal of antiwar works in the late twentieth century is the fact that so many movies critical of the Vietnam War were hugely successful both at the box office and with film critics. Among these movies were *Coming Home* (1978), *The Deer Hunter* (1978), *Apocalypse Now* (1979), *Platoon* (1986), *Full Metal Jacket* (1987), *Casualties of War* (1989), and *Born on the Fourth of July* (1989). In a review of *Casualties of War* the esteemed film critic Pauline Kael wrote,

"This movie about war and rape—[director Brian] De Palma's nineteenth film—is the culmination of his best work."[17]

The antiwar upstarts were upstarts no more. The insurgents had stormed the gates of literary (and cinematic) respectability and gained control.

What is the significance when a body of protest literature becomes a majority literature? What happens when a literature that challenged the norm becomes the norm? The most obvious casualty of the rise in popularity of antiwar literature has been the conventionally romantic and idealized way of thinking and writing about war. Most soldiers and civilians entered the Civil War believing that individual fulfillment was still attainable on the battlefield. Valor, glory, loyalty, and self-sacrifice were noble qualities that were widely believed to flourish during wartime. A strong faith in war's redeeming aspects, and in the soundness of the cause, helped to sustain war supporters and to mitigate war's hardships.

Irrecoverable, in the wake of two world wars and the conflicts of the late twentieth and early twenty-first centuries, is the idealistic romanticism of the Civil War era. Yet a new type of romanticism has emerged and taken hold of our shared imagination. It is the romanticism of the lone man who must struggle to survive the absurdities and the horrors of modern war. He is at the center of Joseph Heller's *Catch-22*. He is at the center of Kurt Vonnegut's *Slaughterhouse-Five*. He is at the center of such seminal works of Vietnam literature as Philip Caputo's *A Rumor of War*, Larry Heinemann's *Paco's Story*, Tim O'Brien's *Going After Cacciato*, and Michael Herr's *Dispatches*. Whether soldier, officer, or journalist, he is a man who has become disillusioned. He has lost faith in his cause. He has lost faith in his country. He has lost faith in his God. Neither saint nor martyr, he is a man whose greatest accomplishment is simply to endure the unendurable: to survive modern war. The epigraph that appears at the beginning of *A Rumor of War*, Philip Caputo's account of his experiences as an infantry officer in Vietnam, is from Matthew 24:6–13 and concludes, "But he that shall endure unto the end, he shall be saved." And Caputo concludes his own narrative with these lines: "We had done nothing more than endure. We had survived, and that was our only victory."[18]

As a nation of readers, we have gone from idolizing the valiant hero to idolizing the alienated antihero. We have gone from being a nation of romantics to a nation of skeptics. Even so, wars continue to be fought.

One thing the proliferation of antiwar works has not accomplished is putting an end to war. The antiwar writers who wrote in the decades following the Civil War did not prevent the Spanish-American War or the Philippine-American War. The antiwar writers who wrote in the years following those conflicts did not prevent World War I. The antiwar writers who wrote after World War I did not prevent World War II. And so on. To the present day, Americans continue, all too frequently, to engage in war.

As we proceed into the twenty-first century and await the literature that will be written about the Iraq War, it is useful to reflect on the war writing that has taken place since the Civil War. What has been its impact? Generations of American readers now have read and embraced antiwar books. To what effect? Has a cataclysmic World War III been avoided? Has a nuclear showdown been prevented because someone somewhere read Hawthorne, Hemingway, or Heller? It is gratifying to think so but impossible to know.

On the other hand, should we conclude that antiwar writers have failed? Is antiwar literature, perhaps, inherently futile? At the start of *Slaughterhouse-Five,* Kurt Vonnegut admits that writing an antiwar book is about as pointless as writing an antiglacier book. According to Vonnegut, there will always be wars and will always be glaciers, and it is as impossible to stop the one as the other. Similarly, at the start of *A Rumor of War,* Philip Caputo writes, "This book ought not to be regarded as a protest. Protest arises from a belief that one can change things or influence events. I am not egotistical enough to believe I can."[19] Even Mark Twain mused about the inefficacy of writing against war. Nevertheless, despite authors' periodic pronouncements of powerlessness, the existence of so much antiwar literature evinces an underlying faith that words can bring about change.

Will America ever cease to engage in war? "War shall yet be, and to the end," predicts Herman Melville in "A Utilitarian View of the *Monitor's* Fight."[20] His prophecy, borne out by the course of history, seems all too depressingly likely. But the future cannot be read. Possibly, the day will yet dawn when the nations will war no more. Until then, it remains to be seen how Americans will continue to write about, and rail against, war.

NOTES

INTRODUCTION

1. Henry D. Thoreau, *Walden: A Fully Annotated Edition*, ed. Jeffrey S. Cramer (New Haven: Yale University Press, 2004), 219, 222.

2. Ibid., 274–276.

3. Only in certain battlefield photographs of the era was the war starkly presented without the usual romantic gloss. Matthew Brady, a prominent photographer of the era, displayed in his New York gallery in October 1862 a selection of graphic images taken by two of his employees shortly after the Battle of Antietam. As the *New York Times* reported, "Mr. Brady has done something to bring home to us the terrible reality and earnestness of war. If he has not brought bodies and laid them in our dooryards and along the streets, he has done something very like it." The reality depicted in these photographs from Antietam is, as Alan Trachtenberg notes in *Reading American Photographs*, "the reality of violence, the effects of shells and bullets on human flesh and bone." Most writers of the era, however, offered no such boldly graphic depictions of war's carnage. *New York Times* quoted in Susan Sontag, *Regarding the Pain of Others* (New York: Farrar, Straus, and Giroux, 2003), 62–63; Alan Trachtenberg, *Reading American Photographs* (New York: Hill and Wang, 1989), 74.

4. These wars with Native American tribes did not result in the publication of antiwar literature as such and fall beyond the scope of this study.

5. John Underhill, *Newes from America; or, A New and Experimentall Discoverie of New England; Containing, a True Relation of Their War-like Proceedings These Two Yeares Last Past* (London: J. D[awson] for Peter Cole, 1638), 2.

6. John Limon, *Writing after War: American War Fiction from Realism to Postmodernism* (New York: Oxford University Press, 1994), 7; Walt Whitman, *Specimen Days* (1882; Boston: David R. Godine, 1971), 60.

7. Underhill, 39, 32.

8. The full title of the essay is "A Narrative of the Late Massacres, in Lancaster County, of a Number of Indians, Friends of This Province, By Persons Unknown. With Some Observations on the Same." Benjamin Franklin, *The Works of Benjamin Franklin*, ed. John Bigelow, vol. 4 (New York: Putnam, 1904), 25, 28, 45.

9. Underhill, 2.

10. The works that have come closest to focusing on the subject are Thomas C. Leonard, *Above the Battle: War-Making in America from Appomattox to Versailles* (1978); Wayne Charles Miller, *An Armed America, Its Face in Fiction: A History of the American Military Novel* (1970); Peter Aichinger, *The American Soldier in Fiction, 1880–1963: A History of Attitudes toward*

Warfare and the Military Establishment (1975); and Rebecca W. Smith, *The Civil War and Its Aftermath in American Fiction, 1861–1899* (1937). A broad study of the subsequent period is provided in Jeffrey Walsh, *American War Literature, 1914 to Vietnam* (1982).

11. The literary critic Leslie Fiedler once commented, "The chief lasting accomplishment of World War I was the invention of the antiwar novel. . . . It is certainly true that before the 1920's that genre did not exist, though it had been prophesied in . . . *The Red Badge of Courage;* and that since the 1920's, it has become a standard form: both a standard way of responding to combat experience and a standard way of starting a literary career." Fiedler's observation reflects the neglect that scholars continue to pay to American antiwar writers—including novelists such as Ernest Crosby, Harold Frederic, Mark Twain, and Joseph Kirkland—who expressed their criticism of war during the nearly fifty years that separated the Civil War from World War I. Leslie Fielder, foreword to *The Good Soldier Schweik,* by Jaroslav Hasek (1930; New York: New American Library, 1963), vi.

Similarly, Peter Aichinger asserts, "It seems possible to show that in the period before the nation actually went to war against a major external enemy the novels were objective and idealistic; after World War I the novels reflected the horror and chagrin of a people who had tasted combat for the first time." Peter Aichinger, *The American Soldier in Fiction, 1880–1963: A History of Attitudes toward Warfare and the Military Establishment* (Ames: Iowa State University Press, 1975), x.

12. For example, Bernard Bergonzi contends, "The dominant movement in the literature of the Great War was . . . from a myth-dominated to a demythologized world. Violent action could be regarded as meaningful, even sacred, when it was sanctified by the traditional canons of heroic behavior; when these canons came to seem no longer acceptable, then killing or being killed in war appeared meaningless and horrible." And Samuel Hynes argues that the war "altered the ways in which men and women thought not only about war but about the world, and about culture and its expressions." The change caused by World War I, he claims, "was so vast and so abrupt as to make the years after the war seem discontinuous from the years before." Bernard Bergonzi, *Heroes' Twilight: A Study of the Literature of the Great War,* 2nd ed. (London: Macmillan, 1980), 198; and Samuel Hynes, *A War Imagined: The First World War and English Culture* (London: Bodley Head, 1990), ix.

13. Paul Fussell, *The Great War and Modern Memory* (New York: Oxford University Press, 1975), 21. Writing fifteen years later, after Fussell's work had come to influence a generation of scholars, Samuel Hynes explained, "This sense of radical discontinuity of present from past is an essential element in what eventually took form as the Myth of the War." Hynes, ix.

14. Fussell, 24.

15. Jennifer C. James, *A Freedom Bought with Blood: African American War Literature from the Civil War to World War II* (Chapel Hill: University of North Carolina Press, 2007), 27, 128.

16. Faith Barrett and Cristanne Miller, eds., *"Words for the Hour": A New Anthology of American Civil War Poetry* (Amherst: University of Massachusetts Press, 2005), 75.

17. Laura E. Richards and Maude Howe Elliott, *Julia Ward Howe, 1819–1910,* vol. 1 (Boston: Houghton Mifflin, 1916), 302; and Julia Ward Howe, *Reminiscences, 1819–1899* (Boston: Houghton, Mifflin, 1899), 341. Howe's change of outlook generally has been attributed to her realization of the social and economic devastation caused by the Civil War and her opposition to the Franco-Prussian War. Franny Nudelman suggests that the cause for Howe's ideo-

logical reversal lay nearer to home. Nudelman hypothesizes that Howe's embrace of pacifism was linked to the death of her young son Sammy in May 1863. "As long as Howe viewed war in heroic terms, women were exemplary in their devout response to the spectacle of male violence. When she decided that war was an abomination, however, maternal grief served to legitimate organized, political action." Franny Nudelman, *John Brown's Body: Slavery, Violence, and the Culture of War* (Chapel Hill: University of North Carolina Press, 2004), 170.

18. The social reformer Jane Addams, among other women pacifists, was prominent in opposing World War I. Notably, the *Four Lights,* a short-lived, biweekly literary publication of the Woman's Peace Party of New York, was dedicated to expressing the views of the peace movement in America. Additionally, American women writers wrote a wide range of short stories, novels, and poems critical of the war. See, for example, Ellen La Motte, *The Backwash of War* (1916) and Madeleine Z. Doty, *Behind the Battle Line* (1918). Addams's account of her manifold efforts in the cause of peace during and after World War I appears in Jane Addams, *Peace and Bread in Time of War* (1922; New York: King's Crown Press, 1945).

19. L. H. Butterfield, Marc Friedlaender, and Mary-Jo Kline, eds., *The Book of Abigail and John: Selected Letters of the Adams Family, 1762–1784* (Cambridge: Harvard University Press, 1975), 188.

20. His translation of *The Iliad* was completed in 1870, and his translation of *The Odyssey* was finished in 1872.

21. Edmund Wilson writes, "Stephen Crane, in *The Red Badge of Courage,* was influenced by Tolstoy's *Sevastopol,* though he had apparently not yet read *War and Peace.*" R. W. Stallman notes that Barbusse's famous novel *Under Fire* was "influenced by Crane." Paul Fussell reports that Sassoon and Owen read Barbusse's novel with enthusiasm in the late fall of 1917. Sassoon even used a passage from Barbusse's novel as an epigraph to his own volumes of poetry *Counter-Attack.* Philip Caputo uses passages from five of Sassoon's poems and two of Owen's poems to head various chapters and sections of his war memoir, and Caputo forthrightly states in the fifth chapter of his work, "I had read all the serious books to come out of the World Wars, and Wilfred Owen's poetry about the Western Front." Edmund Wilson, *Patriotic Gore: Studies in the Literature of the American Civil* War (1962; New York: Norton, 1994), 684; R. W. Stallman, *Stephen Crane: A Biography* (New York: George Braziller, 1968), 180; Fussell, 232, 289; Philip Caputo, *A Rumor of War* (New York: Ballantine, 1978), 76.

CHAPTER 1

1. The two-day encounter, the biggest and bloodiest battle fought in the western theater of the Civil War, ended when Confederate forces exploited a gap in the Union lines and forced Rosecrans's army into retreat, but it was a hollow victory. The Confederate Army of Tennessee sustained greater losses (18,454) than the Union Army of the Cumberland (16,170) and would be defeated two months later at the Battle of Chattanooga.

2. See, for example, Peter Cozzens, *This Terrible Sound: The Battle of Chickamauga* (Urbana: University of Illinois Press, 1992).

3. Byron Farwell, *The Encyclopedia of Nineteenth-Century Land Warfare: An Illustrated World View* (New York: Norton, 2001), 190.

4. At the time of the battle Fahnestock held the rank of captain; before he was mustered out of service in June 1865, he would rise to the rank of colonel. For a biographical sketch of

his life, see, James M. Rice, *Peoria City and County, Illinois: A Record of Settlement, Organization, Progress and Achievement,* vol. 2 (Chicago: S. J. Clarke, 1912), 745–746. As that work notes, "While in the army [Fahnestock] kept a diary of each day's work, the battles in which he was engaged, and a complete record of the life of the camps."

5. Allen L. Fahnestock, "Journal of Colonel Allen L. Fahnestock, 86th Illinois Volunteer Infantry," the Fahnestock Collection, Peoria Public Library, Peoria, Illinois, 51. The spelling, punctuation, and capitalization of Fahnestock's handwritten journal have been standardized here.

6. Ibid., 51–52.

7. Ibid., 52.

8. Ibid.

9. The letter is housed with Allen L. Fahnestock's diary in the Peoria Public Library. Fahnestock actually gave the library a neatly rewritten, presentation copy of the diary that had been copied from the original. It is impossible to know what, if any, changes were made.

10. Moore was born in 1844, but many reference works inaccurately list her date of birth as April 12, 1852, which would mean that by the time Moore entered her teenage years, the Confederacy would already have been defeated. (Her thirteenth birthday would have arrived three days after Lee surrendered to Grant at Appomattox.) See, for example, Linda Mainiero, ed., *American Women Writers,* vol. 1 (New York: Frederick Ungar, 1979), 472; Janet Gray, ed., *She Wields a Pen: American Women Poets of the Nineteenth Century* (London: J. M. Dent, 1997), 232; and Sid S. Johnson, *Some Biographies of Old Settlers: Historical, Personal and Reminiscent,* vol. 1 (Tyler, Texas: Sid S. Johnson, 1900), 328–331. For an early biographical sketch of Moore, that accurately reflects that she was in her late teens during the early years of the war, see Ida Raymond, *Southland Writers: Biographical and Critical Sketches of the Living Female Writers of the South,* vol. 2 (Philadelphia: Claxton, Remsen, and Haffelfinger, 1870), 962–963. For a more detailed and comprehensive biography of Moore's life, see Patricia Brady, "Mollie Moore Davis: A Literary Life," in *Louisiana Women Writers: New Essays and a Comprehensive Biography,* ed. Dorothy H. Brown and Barbara C. Ewell (Baton Rouge: Louisiana State University Press, 1992), 99–118.

Moore, who married in 1874, is also known by her married name, Mary (or Mollie) Evelyn Moore Davis. By the time of her death in 1909, she had written more than two dozen books of poetry, fiction, and history.

11. Mollie E. Moore, *Minding the Gap and Other Poems* (Houston: Cushing and Cave, 1867), 221–222.

12. Ibid., 223–224.

13. James Wood Davidson, *The Living Writers of the South* (New York: Carlton, 1869), 396. The following year, another critic praised Moore's work as follows, "Taking Miss Moore's poems all in all, they indicate a wide range of excellence, a lofty sweep of thought, a subtle gift in allegory and personification, and richness in exquisite fancies." Raymond, 968.

14. Ambrose Bierce, *The Complete Short Stories of Ambrose Bierce,* ed. Ernest Jerome Hopkins (Lincoln: University of Nebraska Press, 1984), 314.

15. Ibid., 315–316.

16. Ibid., 316, 318.

17. Vincent Starrett, *Buried Caesars: Essays in Literary Appreciation* (Chicago: Covici-McGee, 1923), 54.

18. The line was subsequently quoted when Moore's poem "Minding the Gap" appeared in the *Southern Literary Messenger* in early 1864 and also when the poem appeared in *The Southern Amaranth,* an anthology of war poems published in 1869. Mollie E. Moore, "Minding the Gap," *Southern Literary Messenger* 38, no. 1 (January 1864): 29n; Sallie A. Brock, *The Southern Amaranth* (New York: Wilcox and Rockwell, 1869), 178n.

19. Ambrose Bierce, *The Enlarged Devil's Dictionary,* ed. Ernest Jerome Hopkins (New York: Doubleday, 1967), 95.

20. Bierce, *The Complete Short Stories of Ambrose Bierce,* 318.

21. Moore, 222, 224.

CHAPTER 2

1. William Peterfield Trent et al., eds., *Cambridge History of American Literature,* vol. 2 (New York: Macmillan, 1918), 287. The quotation is from a chapter by Will D. Howe titled "Poets of the Civil War I: The North."

2. Edmund Wilson, *Patriotic Gore,* 466.

3. Quoted in Trent, 287.

4. Barrett and Miller, 47.

5. Ibid., 49.

6. Howe, 275.

7. Barrett and Miller, 75.

8. One of the citizens killed in Baltimore in the clash with the Massachusetts soldiers had been a friend and college classmate of Randall's. Walter Burgwyn Jones, ed., *Confederate War Poems* (1959; Nashville: Bill Coats, 1990), 74n.

9. Quoted in Trent, 295.

10. Jones, 75n.

11. Ibid., 74n, 50–51.

12. Ibid., 24, 69n.

13. Drew Gilpin Faust notes, "Most Civil War wounds were inflicted by minié balls shot from rifles: 94 percent of Union injuries were caused by bullets; 5.5 percent by artillery; and less than 0.4 percent by saber or bayonet." Drew Gilpin Faust, *This Republic of Suffering: Death and the American Civil War* (New York: Knopf, 2008), 41. George Worthington Adams confirms, "Bullets . . . were the overwhelming cause of Civil War battle wounds." George Worthington Adams, *Doctors in Blue* (New York: Henry Schuman, 1952), 114.

14. Jones, 22.

15. Ibid., 51.

16. Barrett and Miller, 183.

17. Ibid., 184.

18. Alice Fahs, *The Imagined Civil War: Popular Literature of the North and South, 1861–1865* (Chapel Hill: University of North Carolina Press, 2001), 4.

19. Trent, 307. Alice Fahs notes, "Every Southern popular publication produced numerous poems to commemorate Jackson's death." Fahs, 334n. See, too, the chapter "The Death of Stonewall," in Charles Royster, *The Destructive War: William Tecumseh Sherman, Stonewall Jackson, and the Americans* (1991; New York: Vintage Books, 1993).

20. Brock, v.

21. Frank Moore, ed., *Rebel Rhymes and Rhapsodies* (New York: Putnam, 1864), 245.

22. Trent, 296.

23. Drew Gilpin Faust, *The Creation of Confederate Nationalism* (Baton Rouge: Louisiana State University Press, 1988), 8.

24. "The Latest Rebel Poetry," *Harper's Weekly* 8, no. 396 (July 30, 1864): 483.

25. [Daniel McCook,] "The Second Division at Shiloh," *Harper's New Monthly Magazine* 28, no. 168 (May 1864): 831, 828. The article originally appeared with the byline "By a Staff Officer." McCook is identified as the author in the index to *Harper's New Monthly Magazine* for the period.

CHAPTER 3

1. Mark Twain, *Life on the Mississippi* (1883; New York: Harper and Bros., 1904), 347–348.

2. Walter Scott, *Ivanhoe* (1819; New York: Longmans, Green, 1908), 360.

3. Fred Lewis Pattee, *First Century of American Literature, 1770–1870* (New York: D. Appleton-Century, 1935), 287–288; S. G. Goodrich, *Recollections of a Lifetime*, vol. 2 (New York: Miller, Orton, and Mulligan, 1856), 107–108.

4. Henry Adams, *The Education of Henry Adams*, ed. Ernest Samuels (1918; Boston: Houghton Mifflin, 1973), 39.

5. Virginia Ingraham Burr, ed., *The Secret Eye: The Journal of Ella Gertrude Clanton Thomas, 1848–1889* (Chapel Hill: University of North Carolina Press, 1990), 134.

6. Also, to a different "fancy ball" one of Mrs. Thomas's female acquaintances "wore the very becoming costume of Diana Vernon," the heroine from *Rob Roy*. Ibid., 166, 113.

7. Grace Warren Landrum, "Sir Walter Scott and His Literary Rivals in the Old South," *American Literature* 2 (1930): 262.

8. From the address Hay delivered in May 1897 at the unveiling of the bust of Sir Walter Scott in the Poets' Corner of Westminster Abbey; the address was published as "An Appreciation" in Richard Holt Hutton, *The Life of Sir Walter Scott* (Philadelphia: J. D. Morris, 1905), vi–viii.

9. G. Harrison Orians, "The Romance Ferment after *Waverley*," *American Literature* 3, no. 4 (January 1932): 409, 430.

10. S.L.C., "Thoughts upon English Poetry," *Southern Literary Messenger* 16 (August 1850): 510.

11. David Kaser, *Books and Libraries in Camp and Battle: The Civil War Experience* (Westport, Conn.: Greenwood Press, 1984), 18.

12. Faust, *The Creation of Confederate Nationalism*, 10.

13. Mary Boykin Miller Chesnut, *The Private Mary Chesnut: The Unpublished Civil War Diaries*, ed. C. Vann Woodward and Elisabeth Muhlenfeld (New York: Oxford University Press, 1984), 192, 262.

14. Charles Bohun, "Immortal Fictions," *DeBow's Review* 2, no. 5 (November 1866): 457.

15. In May 1889 the prominent literary critic and author William Dean Howells, a staunch advocate for realism over romanticism, still felt it necessary to rail against the "purblind worshippers of Scott." Earlier that year, Andrew D. White, the first president of Cornell, had written in *Scribner's:* "Never was there a more healthful and health-ministering literature than that which [Scott] gave to the world." See Howells's "Editor's Study" column for *Harper's Monthly* in May 1889 in William Dean Howells, *Editor's Study*, ed. James W. Simpson (Troy,

N.Y.: Whiston, 1983), 19; Andrew D. White, "Walter Scott at Work: Introduction," *Scribner's Magazine* 5, no. 2 (February 1889): 132.

16. Twain, *Life on the Mississippi,* 348.

17. Bergonzi, 13.

18. "The Virginians of the Valley" appeared in the wartime collection *Rebel Rhymes and Rhapsodies* and in many later anthologies, including *War Lyrics and Songs of the South* (1866) and *Bugle Echoes* (1882). Cited in Frank Moore, *Rebel Rhymes and Rhapsodies,* 284–285.

19. For a full-length study of Ashby, see Paul Christopher Anderson, *Blood Image: Turner Ashby in the Civil War and the Southern Mind* (Baton Rouge: Louisiana State University Press, 2002).

20. Jones, 16.

21. Ibid. In *Blood Image* Anderson describes General Ashby as "a man who claimed family origins at Ashby de La Zouche, scene of the famous inspriational tournament in Walter Scott's *Ivanhoe.*" Anderson, 123.

22. Burton Egbert Stevenson, *Poems of American History* (Boston: Houghton Mifflin, 1936), 439.

23. Bayard entered into history as a fearless knight, and Preston was not the only Civil War poet to invoke his name. In a work titled "Ashes of Glory," Augustus Julian Requier refers to "Arthur's knights," "Gallic Henry," and "peerless-born Bayard." Barrett and Miller, 171.

24. Stevenson, 439.

25. Bierce, *Devil's Dictionary,* 70.

CHAPTER 4

1. Herman Melville, *Battle-Pieces and Aspects of the War* (1866; New York: De Capo Press, 1995), 14.

2. "Reviews and Literary Notices," rev. of *Battle-Pieces and Aspects of the War,* by Herman Melville, *Atlantic Monthly* 19 (February 1867): 252.

3. "Literary Notices," rev. of *Battle-Pieces and Aspects of the War,* by Herman Melville, and rev. of *An Introductory Latin Book,* by Albert Herkness, both in *Ladies' Repository* 26 (November 1866): 699.

4. Jay Leyda, *The Melville Log,* vol. 1 (New York: Gordian, 1951), 460, 444, 443.

5. Ibid., 463–464; from the entry on *Pierre* written by Russell J. Reising in George Perkins, Barbara Perkins, and Phillip Leininger, eds., *Benet's Reader's Encyclopedia of American Literature* (New York: Harper Collins, 1991), 847; and Robert Penn Warren, "Melville's Poems," *Southern Review* 3 (1967): 799.

6. Leyda, 1:446.

7. Even before the war, Melville cited his poor health as grounds for not allowing his name to be listed in the annual Pittsfield, Massachusetts, militia census, which tracked the men of fighting age who were fit to defend the Berkshires. The accident occurred on November 7, 1862. An account of it, from the *Berkshire County Eagle,* appears in *The Melville Log.* Stanton Garner, *The Civil War World of Herman Melville* (Lawrence: University Press of Kansas, 1993), 37, 204–205, 321; Leyda, vol. 2, 655. Regarding Melville's mental state in the 1860s, see ed. Donald Yannella and Hershel Parker's *The Endless Winding Way in Melville: New Charts by Kring and Carey* (Glassboro, N.J.: Melville Society, 1981).

8. Garner, 299–329.

9. Herman Melville, *Typee, Omoo, Mardi* (New York: Library of America, 1982), 150.

10. From a letter dated May 29, 1846, to his brother Gansevoort in London (who had died, unbeknownst to Melville, on May 12). Leyda, v ol. 1, 215. Leyda reads Melville's handwriting as "military order," but "military ardor" seems the more convincing reading. Other writers, including such New Englanders as John Greenleaf Whittier, Henry David Thoreau, and James Russell Lowell, were publicly opposed to the Mexican War. The best work on the literature of the war remains Robert W. Johannsen's *To the Halls of the Montezumas: The Mexican War in the American Imagination* (New York: Oxford University Press, 1985).

11. Also, beginning in the summer of 1847, Melville anonymously published a series of comic sketches about the war titled "Authentic Anecdotes of Old Zack" in the humor magazine *Yankee Doodle*. See Luther Stearns Mansfield, "Melville's Comic Articles on Zachary Taylor," *American Literature* 9 (January 1938): 411–418.

12. Melville, *Typee, Omoo, Mardi*, 1105.

13. Ibid., 1102.

14. Ibid., 1186.

15. Richard D. Sharp, "War and Pacifism in the Novels of Herman Melville," *College Language Association Journal* 29, no. 1 (1985): 71. Sharp's essay offers a good analysis of Melville's outlook on war; Joyce Sparer Adler's longer study *War in Melville's Imagination* (New York: New York University Press, 1981) also makes a valuable contribution to the subject.

16. Herman Melville, *White-Jacket* (1850; London: Oxford University Press, 1966), 71.

17. Ibid., 330.

18. Ibid., 332.

19. H. Judge Moore, *Scott's Campaign in Mexico* (Charleston, S.C.: J. B. Nixon, 1849), 61–62.

20. Ibid., 62–63.

21. Henri Barbusse, *Under Fire*, trans. Fitzwater Wray (New York: Dutton, 1917), 297–298.

22. Elsewhere in his memoir, Caputo recalls, "Once I had seen pigs eating napalm-charred corpses—a memorable sight, pigs eating roast people." Caputo, 295, 4; Bierce's story was first published in June 1889. Bierce, *The Complete Short Stories of Ambrose Bierce*, 322.

23. Melville, *White-Jacket*, 331.

24. The quotation is from the dedication page of Herman Melville, *Battle-Pieces*, iii.

25. Melville, *Battle-Pieces*, "The Armies of the Wilderness," 93.

26. Ibid., "Inscription for Graves at Pea Ridge, Arkansas," 166.

27. Ibid., "The Armies of the Wilderness," 93.

28. Ibid., "The Fall of Richmond," 135.

29. Ibid., "Look-out Mountain," 88.

30. Ibid., "The Fall of Richmond," 136.

31. The same phrase appears in both "The Armies of the Wilderness" and "The Fortitude of the North under the Disaster of the Second Manassas." Melville, *Battle-Pieces*, 94, 167.

32. Melville, *Battle-Pieces*, "A Meditation," 241.

33. Ibid., 242.

34. Melville, *Battle-Pieces*, v. Union troops entered Richmond on April 3, 1865.

35. Melville's letter apparently arrived too late. The poem was published as it appeared in the "uncorrected draught," although the title listed in the table of contents read, "Inscrip-

tion to the Dead at Fredericksburg." Herman Melville, *The Writings of Herman Melville*, ed. Harrison Hayford, Hershel Parker, and G. Thomas Tanselle, vol. 14 (Chicago: Northwestern University Press, 1993), 389–390.

36. Ibid., 390–391.

37. Ibid.

38. Ibid.

39. It is not known precisely when the bonfire occurred. Robert Penn Warren notes, "It is assumed that the burning of the poems took place when Melville left Arrowhead [his house in Massachusetts], in October 1863." Stanton Garner places the event in the spring of 1862; Jay Leyda guesses that the bonfire took place during the summer of 1862. Warren, 835n; Garner, 164; Leyda, vol. 2, 653.

40. The poem appears in Leyda, vol. 2, 653.

41. Ibid.

42. Leon Howard, *Herman Melville: A Biography* (Berkeley: University of California Press, 1951), 278–279.

43. Warren, 806n.

44. Melville, *Battle-Pieces*, 96.

45. Ibid., 101.

46. Ibid., 43.

47. Wilfred Owen, *Poems by Wilfred Owen* (London: Chatto and Windus, 1921), 18–19.

48. Born in 1828, Winthrop hailed from an eminent New England family and could count among his ancestors John Winthrop and Jonathan Edwards. His novels, as well as some of his poetry, were published after his death and won him a measure of posthumous fame. Parsons, in addition to writing poetry, was a diligent translator of Dante.

49. The poem appeared in two different volumes of Parsons's works in the decade following the war. Thomas William Parsons, *The Magnolia* (Cambridge, Mass.: John Wilson and Son, 1866), and Thomas William Parsons, *The Shadow of the Obelisk and Other Poems* (London: Hatchards, 1872), 94.

50. Melville, *Battle-Pieces*, "The Stone Fleet," 32.

51. Ibid., "Malvern Hill," 68.

52. Ibid., "The Armies of the Wilderness," 97.

53. Ibid., 97, 103.

54. George H. Boker, *Poems of the War* (Boston: Ticknor and Fields, 1864), 117.

55. Melville, *Battle-Pieces*, "The Armies of the Wilderness," 101.

56. Ibid., "Donelson," 43.

57. The line, quoting the medieval French historian Froissart, appears in an endnote Melville included in *Battle-Pieces* about his poem "The House-top (July, 1863)," 249.

58. Melville, *Battle-Pieces*, v.

59. These lines appear entirely in capital letters, of larger and smaller font sizes. Ibid., "The Conflict of Convictions," 18.

60. Ibid., 183, 165, 190, 166, 135, 84.

61. Reviewed September 6, 1866. Quoted in Leyda, vol. 2, 683.

62. "Book Notices," *Massachusetts Teacher: A Journal of Home and School Education* 19, no. 10 (October 1866): 362.

63. Leyda, vol. 2, 683.

64. Ibid., vol. 2, 682.

65. There is some debate among Melville scholars as to the precise number of books sold. Lee Rust Brown claims that fewer than 500 copies of the original edition were ever sold. Timothy Sweet maintains that 535 copies sold in the decade following the war. Stanton Garner notes that in the book's first year and a half in print, "fewer than 500 copies were sold, some to his own friends and relatives." Whatever the exact number, sales of the book clearly were weak. A letter sent from Harper and Bros. to Melville in early December 1866 informs the author that of 1,260 copies printed, there were currently "sold, or in the hands of book-sellers" 551 copies. Lee Rust Brown, introduction to Melville, *Battle-Pieces*, xv; Timothy Sweet, *Traces of War: Poetry, Photography, and the Crisis of the Union* (Baltimore: Johns Hopkins University Press, 1990), 5; Garner, 37; Leyda, vol. 2, 684.

66. Daniel Aaron, *The Unwritten War: American Writers and the Civil War* (New York: Oxford University Press, 1973), 90.

CHAPTER 5

1. The article, titled "Port Hudson," appeared in *Harper's New Monthly Magazine* in August 1867. John William De Forest, *A Volunteer's Adventures: A Union Captain's Record of the Civil War*, ed. James H. Croushore (New Haven: Yale University Press, 1946), 116–117.

2. Ibid., 144.

3. John William De Forest, *Poems: Medley and Palestina* (New Haven: Tuttle, Morehouse, and Taylor, 1902), ix.

4. Quoted in Wilson, *Patriotic Gore*, 673.

5. James F. Light, *John William De Forest* (New York: Twayne, 1965), 75; De Forest, *A Volunteer's Adventures*, xvii–xviii.

6. Light, 64.

7. Wilson, 675, 672. In the introduction to *A Volunteer's Adventures*, Stanley T. Williams refers to him during this prewar period as the "somewhat dilettantish De Forest." De Forest, *A Volunteer's Adventures*, vii.

8. De Forest would later combine his wartime letters and articles into a manuscript for what he intended to be the first of two volumes titled *Military Life*. However, the work was not published until 1946, as *A Volunteer's Adventures*. Also, in a collection of verse, *Poems: Medley and Palestina*, De Forest dealt with certain war topics in a section titled "Under the Colors," but this volume was not published until 1902.

9. From a letter dated September, 2, 1862, De Forest, *A Volunteer's Adventures*, 41.

10. From a letter dated August 6, 1862, ibid., 35.

11. The article, which appeared in the *Galaxy* in June 1868, was reprinted in De Forest, *A Volunteer's Adventures*, 92.

12. Ibid., 102.

13. Ibid., 123.

14. Ibid.

15. Ibid., 123–124.

16. Ibid., 123.

17. Edmund Clarence Stedman, ed., *An American Anthology, 1787–1900* (Boston: Houghton Mifflin, 1900), 53–54.

18. Edgar Allan Poe, *Great Short Works of Edgar Allan Poe* (New York: Harper and Row, 1970), 68. There are multiple versions of this poem, all bearing the same title, "Lenore." The 1843 version is quoted here.

19. Harriet Beecher Stowe, *Uncle Tom's Cabin* (1852; Oxford: Oxford University Press, 1998), 296, 303, 294.

20. Ibid., 301.

21. In *John Brown's Body,* Franny Nudelman considers how nineteenth-century mourners treated the dead and the challenges posed to customary death rituals by the Civil War.

22. Faust, 6, 10.

23. Ibid., 11.

24. Fahs, 100–101, 96.

25. Charles W. Kent, *Southern Poems* (Boston: Houghton Mifflin, 1913), 72–73. Various versions of the poem exist with slightly different wording. "Curls of gold" might appear in a different version as "tresses of gold" and "smiling, child-like lips" might appear as "purple child-like lips," but the general meaning remains very much the same.

26. Ibid.

27. Ibid., 72.

28. Emily V. Mason, *The Southern Poems of the War* (Baltimore: John Murphy, 1867), 192.

29. Barrett and Miller, 163–164.

30. John William De Forest, *Miss Ravenel's Conversion from Secession to Loyalty* (1867; New York: Harper and Bros., 1939), 267.

31. De Forest, *A Volunteer's Adventures,* 117.

32. Adams notes, "One investigation showed that 82 per cent of the corpses on a portion of a battlefield showed wounds of the head, chest or neck." Adams, 115.

33. Sheeran continues, "But what was most shocking of all: the underbrush on one part of the battefield took fire and for nearly a mile burned the dead bodies and many of the wounded to a crisp." Quoted in John Wesley Brinsfield Jr., ed., *The Spirit Divided: Memoirs of Civil War Chaplains, the Confederacy* (Macon, Ga.: Mercer University Press, 2005), 159.

34. Lee Steinmetz, ed., *The Poetry of the American Civil War* (1960; East Lansing: Michigan State University Press, 1991), 228.

35. Stowe, 303.

36. Bierce, *The Complete Short Stories of Ambrose Bierce,* 318.

37. "The Long March" appeared in *Discovery* magazine in 1952 and in book form in 1956. William Styron, *The Long March and In the Clap Shack* (New York: Vintage Books, 1993), 63.

38. De Forest, *A Volunteer's Adventures,* 109.

39. De Forest, *Miss Ravenel's Conversion,* 249.

40. Ibid., 258.

41. Ibid., 257, 261–262.

42. From a letter dated June 29, 1862, De Forest, *A Volunteer's Adventures,* 29.

43. From a letter dated September 2, 1862, ibid., 41.

44. From letters dated July 13, 1862, and February 25, 1863, ibid., 30, 80.

45. From a letter dated February 25, 1863, ibid., 80. Thomas De Quincey, a well-known English author and intellectual, wrote, "For, if once a man indulges himself in murder, very soon he comes to think little of robbing, and from robbing he comes next to drinking and Sabbath-breaking, and from that to incivility and procrastination." Thomas De Quincey, *The*

Collected Writings of Thomas De Quincey, ed. David Masson, vol. 13 (London: A. and C. Black, 1897), 56.

46. Interestingly, the character in the novel that De Forest most nearly resembles is the upright, if rather dull, Captain Colbourne, whom Miss Ravenel marries at story's end.

47. Light, 87.

48. "Literary Notices," *Harper's New Monthly Magazine* 35 (August 1867): 401.

49. Light, 88. James A. Hijiya adds, "The novel did not sell; hundreds of copies remained in a warehouse for decades." James A. Hijiya, *J. W. De Forest and the Rise of American Gentility* (Hanover, N.H.: University Press of New England, 1988), 69.

50. "Literary Notices," rev. of *Miss Ravenel's Conversion, Ladies' Repository* 27 (August 1867): 508.

51. Thomas Myers, *Walking Point: American Narratives of Vietnam* (New York: Oxford University Press, 1988), 15.

52. Amanda Claybaugh, "The Autobiography of a Substitute: Trauma, History, Howells," *Yale Journal of Criticism* 18, no. 1 (Spring 2005): 45.

53. "Rebel Romance," rev. of *Miss Ravenel's Conversion from Secession to Loyalty,* by John William De Forest, *Time,* August 21, 1939, 57.

54. Ibid., 59, Professor Gordon S. Haight, quoted in the *Time* book review.

55. Writing in 1887, Howells described De Forest as "a novelist whose work has in some respects not only not been surpassed, but not approached, among us." Howells, *Editor's Study,* 66.

56. Ibid., 81.

CHAPTER 6

1. From a letter to Louisa Van Velsor Whitman. Walt Whitman, *Walt Whitman: The Correspondence,* ed. Edwin Haviland Miller, vol. 1 (New York: New York University Press, 2007), 114–115.

2. Walt Whitman, *Complete Poetry and Selected Prose,* ed. James E. Miller Jr. (Boston: Houghton Mifflin, 1959), 41.

3. Ibid., 221. The lines originally appeared as an epigraph to the "Drum-Taps" section of poems in the 1871 edition of *Leaves of Grass* and later were incorporated into "The Wound-Dresser."

4. Ibid., 204.

5. Ibid., 201–202.

6. From a letter to his mother, December 29, 1862. Whitman, *Correspondence,* 58.

7. From a letter to Nathaniel Bloom and John Frederick Schiller Gray, March 19, 1863. Ibid., 80.

8. Diary entry of December 22, 1862; reprinted in Charles I. Glicksberg, *Walt Whitman and the Civil War: A Collection of Original Articles and Manuscripts* (Philadelphia: University of Pennsylvania Press, 1933), 69–70.

9. From a letter to his mother dated December 29, 1862, Whitman, *Correspondence,* 59.

10. Although there exists an official form (reproduced in the 1971 edition of *Specimen Days*) indicating that Whitman was appointed a "delegate" by the Christian Commission in early 1863, it is not an affiliation that Whitman ever refers to in his letters, and historians have

tended to discount the idea that Whitman was serving in the hospitals on behalf of the Christian Commission. Indeed, in an account of his volunteer work published in the *New York Times* in December 1864, Whitman wrote, "The reader has doubtless inferred the fact that my visits among the wounded and sick have been as an Independent Missionary, in my own style, and not as agent of any commission." See Whitman, *Specimen Days*, 15, and Walt Whitman, "Visits among Army Hospitals," *New York Times*, December 11, 1864, 2. Whitman would title a poem about his war work "The Wound-Dresser."

11. Whitman, "Visits among Army Hospitals," 2.

12. From a letter to Nicholas Wyckoff or Daniel L. Northrup, May 14, 1863, Whitman, *Correspondence*, 101–102.

13. Whitman, "Visits among Army Hospitals," 2.

14. Whitman, *Complete Poetry and Selected Prose*, 25.

15. Walt Whitman, "Some War Memoranda—Jotted Down at the Time," *North American Review* 144, no. 362 (January 1887): 55–61; Walt Whitman, "Army Hospitals and Cases: Memoranda at the Time, 1863–66." *Century* 36, no. 6 (October 1888): 825–830.

16. Anthony Szczesiul, "The Maturing Vision of Walt Whitman's 1871 Version of Drum-Taps," *Walt Whitman Quarterly Review* 10 (Winter 1993): 130.

17. "The Good Gray Poet," *Boston Daily Globe*, August 24, 1881. A copy of the article can be found in Whitman's personal papers in the Charles E. Feinberg Collection of the Papers of Walt Whitman. Manuscript Division, Library of Congress.

18. From "A Backward Glance o'er Travel'd Roads," Whitman, *Complete Poetry and Selected Prose*, 450.

19. Walt Whitman, *Specimen Days*, 11.

20. Letter to Charles W. Eldridge, the publisher of the third edition of *Leaves of Grass*, November 17, 1863. Whitman, *Correspondence*, 185.

21. From "A Backward Glance o'er Travel'd Roads," Whitman, *Complete Poetry and Selected Prose*, 450.

22. Whitman, *Specimen Days*, 12.

23. Ibid.

24. Walt Whitman, *The Collected Writings of Walt Whitman: Prose Works, 1892*, ed. Floyd Stovall, vol.2 (New York: New York University Press, 1964), 706.

25. Whitman, *Specimen Days*, 12.

26. Ibid., 60.

27. Ibid., 20–21.

28. Ibid., 60.

29. Ibid.

30. The poem "A Battle" appears in Whitman's journal after his entry for December 26, 1862. Walt Whitman Papers, Thomas Biggs Harned Collection of the Papers of Walt Whitman, Manuscript Division, Library of Congress. A published copy of the poem can be found in Glicksberg, 121–123. The order in which Whitman intended the lines to appear is not always clear. I present the lines in the order that my own study of the handwritten journal entry leads me to believe is most accurate. Likewise, I present the text according to my reading of the handwritten version.

31. Whitman Papers, Harned Collection.

32. Ibid.

33. Ibid.

34. Ibid.

35. In a speech believed to have been delivered at the Michigan Military Academy in June 1879, Sherman stated, "War is at best barbarism. . . . Its glory is all moonshine. It is only those who have neither fired a shot nor heard the shrieks and groans of the wounded who cry aloud for blood, more vengeance, more desolation. War is hell." In 1880 he told an audience of veterans in Columbus, Ohio, "There is many a boy here to-day who looks on war as all glory, but, boys, it is all hell. You can bear this warning voice to generations yet to come." Emily Morison Beck, ed., *Familiar Quotations,* 15th ed. (Boston: Little, Brown , 1980), 579; Royster, 253.

36. Whitman, *Complete Poetry and Selected Prose,* 29.

37. Whitman Papers, Harned Collection.

38. In Whitman's journal the line "the dead lying thick!" is clearly legible but is crossed out and replaced by "how the dead lie." Ibid.

39. Ibid.

40. Carl Schurz, *The Reminiscences of Carl Schurz,* vol. 3 (New York: McClure, 1908), 37. The passage first appeared in Carl Schurz, "The Battle of Gettysburg," *McClure's Magazine,* 29, no. 3 (July 1907): 272-283.

41. Schurz died in 1906. The publication of his multivolume memoirs clearly did not hurt his posthumous fame. A park in New York City, now the site of Gracie Mansion, the official residence of the mayor, was named for him in 1910.

42. Whitman Papers, Harned Collection.

43. Whitman, *Complete Poetry and Selected Prose,* 226.

44. Ibid., 227.

45. In December 1864, Whitman recorded, "My note books are full of memoranda of the cases of this Summer, and the wounded from Chancellorsville." Whitman, "Visits among Army Hospitals," 2.

46. Whitman, *Specimen Days,* 20. The passages first appeared in *Memoranda during the War.*

47. From letters dated July 7, 1863, and March 22, 1864, Whitman, *Correspondence,* 114, 204.

48. Most famously, Kurt Vonnegut, who survived the firebombing of Dresden in an actual slaughterhouse, titled his antiwar satire about World War II *Slaughterhouse-Five.*

49. Whitman, *Specimen Days,* 20.

50. The poem was originally titled "The Dresser." Whitman, *Complete Poetry and Selected Prose,* 221.

51. Ibid., 222, 228, 217.

52. Of his collection of war poems, Whitman further explained, "It also has the blast of the trumpet, & the drum pounds & whirrs in it, & then an undertone of sweetest comradeship & human love, threading its steady thread inside the chaos, & heard at every lull & interstice thereof." Letter to William O'Connor dated January 6, 1865, Whitman, *Correspondence,* 246–247.

53. Letter to Thomas P. Sawyer, April 21, 1863. Ibid., 92.

54. This description appears in one of Whitman's wartime journals, in the draft of a poem titled "Finale," which follows an entry for December 17, 1863. Whitman Papers, Harned Collection.

55. Redpath, who earlier in the year had published Louisa May Alcott's *Hospital Sketches,* replied in late October, "I could easily publish a small Book, but the one you propose . . .

implies an expenditure that may be beyond my means." Letter to James Redpath dated October 21, 1863, and corresponding footnote, and a letter to Louisa Van Velsor Whitman dated April 12, 1864, Whitman, *Correspondence*, 170-172, 210.

56. George Rice Carpenter, *Walt Whitman* (New York: Macmillan, 1909), 99.

57. The reviews from the *Boston Commonwealth* (February 24, 1866), the *Nation* (November 16, 1865), the *New York Times* (November 22, 1865), and *Radical* (March 1866) are reprinted in Kenneth M. Price, ed., *Walt Whitman: The Contemporary Reviews* (Cambridge: Cambridge University Press, 1996), 120, 115, 118, 121. *Independent*, December 7, 1865, 2.

58. Whitman, *Specimen Days*, 20.

59. George M. Fredrickson, *The Inner Civil War: Northern Intellectuals and the Crisis of the Union* (New York: Harper and Row, 1965), 95.

60. Whitman, *Complete Poetry and Selected Prose*, 461.

CHAPTER 7

1. From "A Backward Glance o'er Travel'd Roads," Whitman, *Complete Poetry and Selected Prose*, 443.

2. The peace organizations in existence before the war were all based in the North, and many of their members supported the antislavery cause. In *Pacifism in the United States* Peter Brock notes that members of the established peace organizations were "drawn toward a full or at least qualified endorsement of the Unionist war effort." Brock further adds, "The coming of war . . . witnessed a flight from the peace camp of a large number of the stalwarts of the old peace movement." Peter Brock, *Pacifism in the United States: From the Colonial Era to the First World War* (Princeton, N.J.: Princeton University Press, 1968), 689, 691.

3. As Merle Curti records, the unresponsiveness of the American Peace Society led one veteran of the peace movement, Joshua P. Blanchard, to rebuke the society for its "bewildering infidelity to its principles." Blanchard went so far as to take the society to task in print for refusing to make use of its influence to end the war. Merle Curti, *Peace or War: The American Struggle, 1636-1936* (New York: Norton, 1936), 59.

4. Charles Chatfield, ed., *Peace Movements in America* (New York: Shocken Books, 1973), xi.

5. For more on the subject of political dissenters, see Thomas J. Pressly, *Americans Interpret Their Civil War* (New York: Free Press, 1962), 129-144. For more on the peace sects, see Edward Needles Wright, *Conscientious Objectors in the Civil War* (1931; New York: A. S. Barnes, 1961), 6-38.

6. Privately published by John W. Foster, a Quaker from Rhode Island, the pamphlet "War and Christianity Irreconcilable: An Address to Christians" is largely composed of extracts from earlier works by pacifist writers. Another wartime pamphlet by a Quaker author was titled "A Brief Exposition of the Testimony of Peace, as Exemplified by the Life and Early Precepts of Jesus Christ, and the Early Christians, and Held by the Religious Society of Friends." Brock, 719-721.

7. "Ein Feste Burg Ist Unser Gott," John Greenleaf Whittier, *In War Time, and Other Poems* (Boston: Ticknor and Fields, 1863), 18.

8. Brock, 722.

9. From an unsigned review of Henry Howard Brownell's poetry volume *Lyrics of a Day; or, Newspaper-Poetry*, *North American Review* 99 (July 1864): 320.

10. Brock, 725.

11. For example, from 1869 to 1876 the *North American Review* included only one article on the war, and from 1869 to 1873 *Harper's* ran only two. Gerald F. Linderman, *Embattled Courage: The Experience of Combat in the American Civil War* (New York: Free Press, 1987), 271.

12. Albion W. Tourgée, "The Renaissance of Nationalism," *North American Review* 144, no. 362 (January 1887): 1.

13. Harold Frederic, *The Copperhead* (New York: Scribner's, 1893), 112.

14. Edmund Wilson, *The Devils and Canon Barham: Ten Essays on Poets, Novelists, and Monsters* (New York: Farrar, Straus, and Giroux, 1973), 61.

15. Ibid., 56.

16. Wayne Charles Miller notes in *An Armed America*, "Scholars and critics are divided over the character of [Henry] Fleming [the novel's protagonist]. . . . From [an] admiration of Henry there are shades of descending opinion through various greys to black." At the darkest extreme, the book is read as presenting what the scholar Ihab Habib Hassan describes as "the subtleties of self-deception, and the vast, brutal anonymity of war, in which the private response and the public demand are so fiercely, so hopelessly, at odds." Miller himself concludes, "Stephen Crane, in *The Red Badge of Courage,* is the first American novelist to present war as chaotic and absurd, an experience without meaning; he is the first to present the plight of the average man amidst such circumstances; and he is the first to debunk the conception of traditional heroism." Miller, *An Armed America*, 71–72, 81. Frederick J. Hoffman asserts in *The Twenties: American Writing in the Postwar Decade*, "Crane was the only genuine predecessor of the 1920s generation of writers." Similarly, in his study *The American Soldier in Fiction*, Peter Aichinger describes Crane's "depiction of battle" as "a forecast of the formless, incomprehensible, dehumanized slaughter that was to characterize the protest of the World War I novelists." Frederick J. Hoffman, *The Twenties: American Writing in the Postwar Decade* (New York: Viking Press, 1955), 55; Aichinger, xxi.

17. Stephen Crane, *Great Short Works of Stephen Crane* (New York: Harper and Row, 1968), 6, 5, 56.

18. Ibid., 44–45.

19. Harold Frederic, "Stephen Crane's Triumph," *New York Times,* January 26, 1896, 22.

20. John Dos Passos, *The Fourteenth Chronicle: Letters and Diaries of John Dos Passos,* ed. Townsend Ludington (Boston: Gambit, 1973), 212.

21. Perkins, *Benet's Reader's Encyclopedia of American Literature,* 227.

22. Stallman, 177.

23. Ambrose Bierce, *Phantoms of a Blood-Stained Period: The Complete Civil War Writings of Ambrose Bierce,* ed. Russell Duncan and David. J. Klooster (Amherst: University of Massachusetts Press, 2002), 183.

24. Ibid., 181–182, 184.

25. F. Foster, "Some Aspects of Courage," *North American Review* 166, no. 499 (June 1898): 679–680.

26. Bierce, *The Complete Short Stories,* 267.

27. The essay was published in the December 25, 1881, issue of *Wasp.* Bierce, *Phantoms of a Blood-Stained Period,* 106.

28. Whitman, *Specimen Days,* 20.

29. Bierce, *Phantoms of a Blood-Stained Period,* 107.

30. From an advertisement, placed by G. P. Putnam's Sons, in the *Century.* "Books," *Century* 55, no. 6 (April 1898): 10 of advertisement pages.

31. Richard Saunders, *Ambrose Bierce: The Making of a Misanthrope* (San Francisco: Chronicle Books, 1985), 61.

32. James R. Mock, *Censorship 1917* (Princeton: Princeton University Press, 1941), 159–160, 162, 167.

33. Leo Tolstoy, *The Sebastopol Sketches,* trans. David McDuff (1855; Middlesex, Eng.: Penguin Books, 1986), 108.

CHAPTER 8

1. Walter Millis, *Arms and Men: A Study in American Military History* (New York: Putnam, 1956), 20.

2. Quoted in Edward Hagerman, *The American Civil War and the Origins of Modern Warfare: Ideas, Organization, and Field Command* (Bloomington: Indiana University Press, 1988), 25.

3. Linderman, 160.

4. Joseph Kirkland, *The Captain of Company K* (Chicago: Dibble, 1891), 264–265.

5. John Limon, *Writing after War,* 28.

6. Ambrose Bierce, *Phantoms of a Blood-Stained Period,* 106.

7. Jean de Bloch, *The Future of War,* trans. R. C. Long (1899; New York: Garland, 1971), xviii–xix.

8. Jack London, "The Impossibility of War," *Overland Monthly* 35 (March 19, 1900): 279.

9. Roosevelt's memoir was serialized in *Scribner's Magazine* in the first half of 1899 and then was published as a book. Theodore Roosevelt, *The Rough Riders* (New York: Scribner's, 1899), 9, 89. Stephen Crane, *The War Dispatches of Stephen Crane,* ed. R. W. Stallman and E. R. Hagemann (New York: New York University Press, 1964), 186.

10. London, 278–280; Bloch, xxxviii. *San Francisco Town Talk* also prophesied that London could "safely count upon being 'discovered'" by the literary world, once *The Son of the Wolf* was published. "Chit-Chat," *Overland Monthly* 35, no. 210 (June 1900): 568.

11. H. C. Engelbrecht and F. C. Hanighen, *Merchants of Death: A Study of the International Armament Industry* (New York: Dodd, Mead, 1934), 87.

12. Hiram Maxim, *My Life* (London: Methuen, 1915), 258.

13. Ibid., 264–266.

14. The "distinguished general" is quoted but not identified in an article by Lieutenant William R. Hamilton that appeared in the *Century* in late 1888. William R. Hamilton, "American Machine Cannon and Dynamite Guns," *Century Illustrated Monthly Magazine* 36, no. 6 (October 1888): 885.

15. From "Liebestod," Alan Seeger, *Poems* (New York: Scribner's, 1916), 160. From a letter dated December 8, 1914, Alan Seeger, *Letters and Diary of Alan Seeger* (New York: Scribner's, 1917), 29.

CHAPTER 9

1. Nathaniel Hawthorne, *The Complete Writings of Nathaniel Hawthorne,* vol. 17 (Boston: Houghton Mifflin, 1918), 382n.

2. Nathaniel Hawthorne, *The Centenary Edition of the Works of Nathaniel Hawthorne: The Letters, 1857–1864,* ed. Thomas Woodson et al., vol. 18 (Columbus: Ohio State University Press, 1987), 382, 380.

3. In "Chiefly about War Matters" Hawthorne describes rebel prisoners as "simple, bumpkin-like fellows . . . peasants, and of a very low order: a class of people with whom our Northern rural population has not a single trait in common" and finds other faults with the South and its inhabitants. Hawthorne, *Complete Writings,* 400.

4. Ibid., 398.

5. From a letter dated May 26, 1861, Hawthorne, *Centenary Edition,* 381.

6. From a letter dated February 13, 1862, ibid., 428.

7. From letters dated February 13, 1862, and May 26, 1861, ibid., 428, 381.

8. From a letter dated February 13, 1862, ibid., 427.

9. Hawthorne, *Complete Writings,* 407–408.

10. Ibid., 409.

11. Ibid., 404, 408–413.

12. Ibid., 411–413.

13. Epes Sargent. "Ericsson and His Inventions," *Atlantic Monthly* 10, no. 57 (July 1862): 80.

14. Hawthorne, *Complete Writings,* 402.

15. Ibid., 388–389.

16. From a letter to William D. Ticknor, May 17, 1862, Hawthorne, *Centenary Edition,* 457.

17. Hawthorne, *Complete Writings,* 391.

18. Nathaniel Hawthorne, *The Complete Works of Nathaniel Hawthorne,* vol. 11 (Boston: Houghton, Mifflin, 1883), 254.

19. Ibid.

20. Ibid., 255.

21. Ibid., 255, 259.

22. Ibid., 256.

23. Ibid., 259–260.

24. Melville, *Battle-Pieces,* 61–62.

25. Ibid., 55–57.

26. Ibid., 58, 60, 248n.

27. The poem, written in early 1862, appeared in Longfellow's *Songs of War* (1863); Barrett and Miller, 80–81.

28. Ibid., 81.

29. From George H. Boker, "The Cruise of the Monitor," in Stevenson, 468.

30. Letter from Henry Adams to Charles Francis Adams Jr., April 11, 1862. Worthington Chauncey Ford, ed., *A Cycle of Adams Letters, 1861–1865,* vol. 1 (Boston: Houghton Mifflin, 1920), 135.

CHAPTER 10

1. Mark Twain, *A Pen Warmed-Up in Hell: Mark Twain in Protest,* ed. Frederick Anderson (New York: Harper and Row, 1972), 18, 23, 36–37.

2. Ibid., 38.

3. Ibid., 39–40.

4. Ibid., 39.

5. Ibid., 35.

6. Mark Twain, *A Connecticut Yankee in King Arthur's Court* (1889; New York: Oxford University Press, 1996), 20, 36.

7. Ibid., 355.

8. Ibid., 321, 513.

9. Ibid., 556, 542, 565.

10. Ibid., 563–564.

11. Ibid., 570.

12. Ibid., 168.

13. Hamilton, "American Machine Cannon and Dynamite Guns," 885.

14. Bierce, *Phantoms of a Blood-Stained Period*, 313, 311.

15. John Millis, "Electricity in War, II. In Land Warfare," *Scribner's Magazine* 6, no. 4 (October 1889): 424–425.

16. From a letter dated January 9, 1899. Twain, *A Pen Warmed-Up in Hell*, 72–73.

17. Twain even held the patents for a couple of gadgets and gizmos, including a pregummed scrapbook. John F. Kasson, *Civilizing the Machine: Technology and Republican Values in America, 1776–1900* (New York: Grossman, 1976), 203. For more information on the subject, see George Hiram Brownell, "Mark Twain's Inventions," *Twainian* 3 (January 1944): 1–5.

18. Albert Bigelow Paine, *Mark Twain: A Biography*, vol. 3 (New York: Harper and Bros., 1912), 904.

19. Albert Bigelow Paine, ed., *Mark Twain's Letters*, vol. 2 (New York: Harper and Bros., 1917), 534.

20. Kasson, 203.

21. Paine, *Mark Twain: A Biography*, 909–910.

22. Ibid., 914.

23. Indeed, progress on the typesetter came to be linked, in Twain's mind, to progress on *A Connecticut Yankee*. He hoped that both projects—machine and manuscript—would be completed on the same day. Kasson, 205.

24. From 1897 to 1908 Twain worked on various drafts of a work known as *The Mysterious Stranger*, setting it alternately in Austria, in Hannibal, Missouri, and in a print shop. A heavily edited version of the work was published in 1916, six years after Twain's death, by his literary executor, Albert Bigelow Paine. "The Chronicle of Young Satan" is the first of Twain's three attempts to write the tale. The sections quoted here are believed to have been written in 1900.

25. Twain, *A Pen Warmed-Up in Hell*, 55.

26. Ibid., 55–56, 60.

27. Ibid., 94.

28. Ibid., 107. The story was deemed by the editors of *Harper's Bazaar* "not quite suited to a woman's magazine." It was not published until 1923. Shelley Fisher Fishkin, ed., *A Historical Guide to Mark Twain* (New York: Oxford University Press, 2002), 246.

29. Ibid., 108–111.

30. Ibid., 60–61.

31. Ibid., 56.

CHAPTER 11

1. Wayne Charles Miller argues in *An Armed America*, "Crane manages, for the first time in the history of the American military novel, to depict the utter helplessness of the individual within the impersonal framework of a social unit engaged in a massive and mechanized war." Miller, 75.

2. Stephen Crane, *Great Short Works of Stephen Crane*, 60, 90.

3. Ibid., 48–49. Amy Kaplan notes the prevalence of machine imagery in her essay "The Spectacle of War in Crane's Revision of History." She writes, "Although Henry resents the machinery of war and the powerlessness it entails and envisions himself as a primitive warrior to escape from this machine, his atavistic fantasies, rather than offering him an escape, entrench him more solidly in the machinery of the army." Amy Kaplan, "The Spectacle of War in Crane's Revision of History," in *New Essays on* The Red Badge of Courage, ed. Lee Clark Mitchell (Cambridge: Cambridge University Press, 1986), 90.

4. Crane, *Great Short Works of Stephen Crane*, 34, 36.

5. Ibid., 114, 39, 64, 41.

6. David A. Wells, *Recent Economic Changes and Their Effect on the Production and Distribution of Wealth and the Well-Being of Society* (New York: D. Appleton, 1889), 93.

7. Joseph Kirkland, the son of the writer Caroline Kirkland, had previously published two realist novels about the West, *Zury: The Meanest Man in Spring County* (1887) and *The McVeys* (1888).

8. Kirkland, 11.

9. Ibid., 37, 82–83.

10. Frank R. Stockton, *The Great Stone of Sardis* (New York: Harper and Bros., 1898), 123–124.

11. The work was first serialized in Collier's *Once a Week* and then published in book form. Frank R. Stockton, *Great War Syndicate* (New York: P. F. Collier, 1889), 104.

12. Ibid., 107, 109.

13. Ibid., 104, 107.

14. Ibid., 111.

15. Nikola Tesla, "The Problem of Increasing Human Energy," *Century Illustrated Monthly Magazine* 60 (June 1900): 183.

16. From the *Peacemaker* 12 (1894): 118; quoted in Thomas C. Leonard, *Above the Battle: War-Making in America from Appomattox to Versailles* (New York: Oxford University Press, 1978), 223 n11.

CHAPTER 12

1. The Mauser rifle, which used a smokeless powder, was the standard weapon of the Spanish forces during the Spanish-American War. Leonard, 63.

2. King wrote *Ray's Daughter: A Story of Manila* (1901), *Found in the Philippines* (1901), *A Conquering Corps Badge and Other Stories of the Philippines* (1901), and *Comrades in Arms: A Tale of Two Hemispheres* (1904). In addition, King published numerous Civil War romances during the 1880s and 1890s. Upton Sinclair and other authors produced dime novels celebrating various aspects of the wars for the True Blue, Starry Flag, and Columbia Library

series. Other romantic war stories were published in popular magazines of the era, including *Scribner's Magazine, Harper's Round Table* (a boys' magazine), and *Cosmopolitan*. See Perry E. Gianakos, "Ernest Howard Crosby: A Forgotten Tolstoyan Antimilitarist and Anti-imperialist," in Chatfield, *Peace Movements in America*. Chatfield, 17n.

3. Theodore Roosevelt, *The Strenuous Life and Other Essays* (New York: Review of Reviews, 1910).

4. He later was promoted to colonel of the regiment. Quotation from Roosevelt, *The Rough Riders*, 19.

5. Richard Harding Davis, *The Notes of a War Correspondent* (New York: Scribner's, 1911), 94–95.

6. Roosevelt, *The Strenuous Life and Other Essays*, 8, 3.

7. Ibid., 22, 4, 21.

8. Ibid., 138–140.

9. Ibid., 139, 143–144.

10. Roosevelt, *The Rough Riders*, 47.

11. Ibid., 84, 107.

12. Ibid., 88–90, 94; Seeger, *Letters and Diary*, 20–21. From a letter Seeger wrote to his father on November 12, 1914.

13. Crosby served for five years, 1900 to 1905, as president of the New York Anti-Imperialist League.

14. The works of poetry are *War Echoes* (1898), *Plain Talk in Psalm and Parable* (1899), and *Swords and Ploughshares* (1902). The novel is *Captain Jinks, Hero* (1902).

15. Crosby would pay special tribute to Tolstoy in *Tolstoy and His Message* (1903), in which he would also record his first encounter with Tolstoy's pacifist writings.

16. Ernest Crosby, *War Echoes* (Philadelphia: Innes and Sons, 1898), 4.

17. Ernest Crosby, *Swords and Plowshares* (New York: Funk and Wagnalls, 1902), 11.

18. Rudyard Kipling, *Rudyard Kipling's Verse* (London: Hodder and Stoughton, 1949), 323.

19. Crosby, *Swords and Plowshares*, 33–35. The poem appeared in the *New York Times*, February 15, 1899.

20. Fred Harvey Harrington, "Literary Aspects of American Anti-Imperialism, 1898–1902," *New England Quarterly* 10 (December 1937): 665.

21. Ernest Crosby, *Captain Jinks, Hero* (New York: Funk and Wagnalls, 1902), 108, 111.

22. Ibid., 331, 339–340.

23. Ibid., 340–341.

24. Ibid., 341–342.

25. The illustration appears between pages 324 and 325.

26. Finley Peter Dunne, *Mr. Dooley in Peace and War* (Boston: Small, Maynard, 1899), 53, 44–45.

27. From letters to Henry James dated April 17, 1898, and July 31 1898, and from a letter to his sister Aurelia dated April 3, 1898, William Dean Howells, *Life in Letters of William Dean Howells*, ed. Mildred Howells, vol. 2 (New York: Doubleday, Doran , 1928), 89–90, 95.

28. From a letter dated August 19, 1898, Henry James, *The Letters of Henry James*, ed. Percy Lubbock, vol. 1 (New York: Scribner's, 1920), 291–292.

29. Howells, *Editor's Study*, 254.

30. From a letter to Henry D. Lloyd. Howells, *Life in Letters*, 92.

31. William Dean Howells, "Editha," in William Dean Howells and Henry Mills Alden, eds., *Different Girls* (New York: Harper and Bros., 1906), 134–135, 138, 156–157.

32. Crosby, 342.

33. G. W. Steevens, *With Kitchener to Khartum* (New York: Dodd, Mead, 1898), 264.

34. Ibid., 282, 285.

35. The occasion of Hay's speech was the unveiling of a bust of Sir Walter Scott in the Poets' Corner of Westminster Abbey. Hay proclaimed, "His spirit is everywhere; he is revered wherever the English speech has travelled." John Hay, "An Appreciation," in Hutton, vi.

36. From a letter dated July 27, 1898, John Hay, *The Life and Letters of John Hay*, ed. William Roscoe Thayer, vol. 2 (1915; Boston: Houghton Mifflin, 1929), 337.

CHAPTER 13

1. The long and scholarly essay first appeared as Charles W. Eliot, "Destructive and Constructive Energies of Our Government Compared," *Proceedings of the American Association for the Advancement of Science*, 47 (Salem, Mass: Salem Press, 1898). The essay was subsequently published in the *Atlantic Monthly*. Charles W. Eliot, "Destructive and Constructive Energies of Our Government Compared," *Atlantic Monthly* 83, no. 495 (January 1899): 1, 5.

2. David S. Patterson, "An Interpretation of the American Peace Movement, 1898–1914," in Chatfield, *Peace Movements in America*, 20–21, 31.

3. Sidney L. Gulick, *The Fight for Peace* (New York: Fleming H. Revell, 1915), 20–21, 76. Writing again after World War I, Gulick would grimly reflect, "We have elaborated new means of destruction of unimaginable power, the further development of which staggers our minds as we try to think of what may overtake us all should another war break out among the civilized nations." Sidney L. Gulick, *The Christian Crusade for a Warless World* (New York: Macmillan, 1922), ix–x.

4. W. Millis, *Arms and Men*, 187.

5. William James, "The Moral Equivalent of War" (New York: American Association for International Conciliation, 1910), 12, 4.

6. James first delivered the speech on October 7, 1904, the final day of the World Peace Congress. It was published as "Remnants of the Peace Banquet" in the *Atlantic Monthly* 94 (December 1904): 845–847.

7. James, "The Moral Equivalent of War," 18.

8. Ibid., 17.

9. In a letter dated September 18, 1900, to Henry Lee Higginson, a prominent Bostonian, James lamented, "Our conduct [in the Philippines] has been one protracted infamy towards the Islanders, and one protracted lie towards ourselves." Quoted in Bliss Perry, *Life and Letters of Henry Lee Higginson*, vol. 2 (Boston: Atlantic Monthly Press, 1921), 429.

10. From the *Springfield Republican*, June 4, 1900. Quoted in Ralph Barton Perry, *The Thoughts and Character of William James* (New York: George Braziller, 1954), 246.

11. Letters by Henry James of April 20, 1898, and June 3, 1899. Ignas K. Skrupskelis and Elizabeth M. Berkeley, eds., *The Correspondence of William James: William and Henry 1897–1910*, vol. 3 (Charlottesville: University Press of Virginia, 1994), 28, 62–63; James, "The Moral Equivalent of War," 6.

12. James, "The Moral Equivalent of War," 19–20.

13. Ibid., 8–9.

14. Ibid., 2; Eliot, 5–6. The list of members of the Council of Direction of the American Association for International Conciliation appears on an unnumbered page following James's essay.

15. Kirkpatrick would run for vice president on the Socialist ticket in 1916.

16. George R. Kirkpatrick, *War—What For?* (West La Fayette, Ohio: George R. Kirkpatrick, 1910), 3, 45.

17. Ibid., 88, 81–82.

18. Ibid., 92, 179.

19. Ibid., 259, 179, 13. Ironically, a copy of *War—What For?* was eventually purchased by the Roosevelt Memorial Association for Harvard College Library and became part of the Theodore Roosevelt Collection.

20. Ibid., 352, 223, 240, 91. Brief excerpts from Markham's review, as well as many other reviews, appear in a two-page section titled "Comment" at the back of the fifth edition of *War—What For?*

21. Ibid., 92.

CONCLUSION

1. Arthur Sweetser, *Roadside Glimpses of the Great War* (New York: Macmillan, 1916), 197, 199.

2. During the first year and half of the war, Reed spent many months touring the contending countries as a correspondent for *Metropolitan Magazine*. He visited the belligerent capitals in Europe and witnessed action on five fronts. After he returned to the United States from the war arena, Reed frequently spoke at antiwar meetings and was eventually indicted under the Espionage Act for a piece he contributed to the socialist publication the *Masses*. John Reed, *The War in Eastern Europe* (New York: Scribner's, 1916), 97–98.

3. John Reed, "This Unpopular War," *Seven Arts* 2 (August 1917): 399–400.

4. Ellen La Motte, *The Backwash of War* (New York: Putnam, 1916), 105, 3. The book was kept out of France and England from the time of its publication. In the United States it went through several printings but was suppressed in mid-1918.

5. Engelbrecht and Hanighen, 155.

6. John Dos Passos, *One Man's Initiation, 1917* (1920; New York: Cornell Press, 1969), 92, 164, 72.

7. The literary scholar was Harlan Hatcher, who would later become president of University of Michigan. Harlan Hatcher, *Creating the Modern American Novel* (1935; New York, Russell and Russell, 1965), 227.

8. Laurence Stallings, *Plumes* (New York: Harcourt, Brace, 1924), 237, 126.

9. See, for example, William Faulkner, *Soldier's Pay* (1926); Thomas Boyd *Through the Wheat* (1923); William March, *Company K* (1933); E. E. Cummings, *The Enormous Room* (1922); Elliot H. Paul, *Impromptu* (1923); and Dalton Trumbo, *Johnny Got His Gun* (1939).

10. Charles A. Fenton, *The Apprenticeship of Ernest Hemingway: The Early Years* (1954; New York: Viking Press, 1968), 68.

11. Ernest Hemingway, *A Farewell to Arms* (1929; New York: Scribner's, 1969), 35, 184–185.

12. Louis Kronenberger, "War's Horror as a German Private Saw It," *New York Times,* June 2, 1929, 5.

13. Kurt Vonnegut, *Slaughterhouse-Five* (1969; New York: Random House, 1999), 148.

14. Styron, 3.

15. John Hersey, *Hiroshima* (1946; New York: Vintage Books, 1989), 90.

16. John Steinbeck, *Once There Was a War* (New York: Viking Press, 1958), x.

17. Pauline Kael, "A Wounded Apparition," rev. of *Casualties of War, New Yorker,* August 21, 1989, 79.

18. Caputo, ix, 320.

19. Ibid., xxi.

20. Melville, *Battle-Pieces,* 62.

Aaron, Daniel. *The Unwritten War: American Writers and the Civil War.* New York: Oxford University Press, 1973.

Adams, George Worthington. *Doctors in Blue.* New York: Henry Schuman, 1952.

Adams, Henry. *The Education of Henry Adams.* Ed. Ernest Samuels. 1918; Boston: Houghton Mifflin, 1973.

Addams, Jane. *Peace and Bread in Time of War.* 1922; New York: King's Crown Press, 1945.

Adler, Joyce Sparer. *War in Melville's Imagination.* New York: New York University Press, 1981.

Aichinger, Peter. *The American Soldier in Fiction, 1880–1963: A History of Attitudes toward Warfare and the Military Establishment.* Ames: Iowa State University Press, 1975.

Anderson, Paul Christopher. *Blood Image: Turner Ashby in the Civil War and the Southern Mind.* Baton Rouge: Louisiana State University Press, 2002.

Barbusse, Henri. *Under Fire.* Trans. Fitzwater Wray. New York: Dutton, 1917.

Barrett, Faith, and Cristanne Miller, eds. *"Words for the Hour": A New Anthology of American Civil War Poetry.* Amherst: University of Massachusetts Press, 2005.

Beck, Emily Morison, ed. *Familiar Quotations.* 15th ed. Boston: Little, Brown, 1980.

Bergonzi, Bernard. *Heroes' Twilight: A Study of the Literature of the Great War.* 2nd ed. London: Macmillan, 1980.

Bierce, Ambrose. *The Complete Short Stories of Ambrose Bierce.* Ed. Ernest Jerome Hopkins. Lincoln: University of Nebraska Press, 1984.

———. *The Enlarged Devil's Dictionary.* Ed. Ernest Jerome Hopkins. New York: Doubleday, 1967.

———. *Phantoms of a Blood-Stained Period: The Complete Civil War Writings of Ambrose Bierce.* Ed. Russell Duncan and David J. Klooster. Amherst: University of Massachusetts Press, 2002.

Bloch, Jean de. *The Future of War.* Trans. R. C. Long. 1899; New York: Garland, 1971.

Bohun, Charles. "Immortal Fictions." *DeBow's Review* 2, no. 5 (November 1866): 455–461.

Boker, George H. *Poems of the War.* Boston: Ticknor and Fields, 1864.

"Book Notices." *Massachusetts Teacher: A Journal of Home and School Education* 19, no. 10 (October 1866): 362.

"Books." Advertisement for *In the Midst of Life,* by Ambrose Bierce. *Century* 55, no. 6 (April 1898): 10 of advertisement pages.

Brady, Patricia. "Mollie Moore Davis: A Literary Life." In *Louisiana Women Writers: New Essays and a Comprehensive Biography,* ed. Dorothy H. Brown and Barbara C. Ewell, 99–118. Baton Rouge: Louisiana State University Press, 1992.

Brinsfield, John Wesley, Jr., ed. *The Spirit Divided: Memoirs of Civil War Chaplains— The Confederacy.* Macon, Ga.: Mercer University Press, 2005.

Brock, Peter. *Pacifism in the United States: From the Colonial Era to the First World War.* Princeton, N.J.: Princeton University Press, 1968.

Brock, Sallie A. *The Southern Amaranth.* New York: Wilcox and Rockwell, 1869.

Brownell, George Hiram. "Mark Twain's Inventions." *Twainian* 3 (January 1944): 1–5.

Brownell, Henry Howard. *Lyrics of a Day; or, Newspaper-Poetry, by a Volunteer in the United States Service.* New York: Carleton, 1864.

———. *War-lyrics and Other Poems.* Boston: Ticknor and Fields, 1866.

Burr, Virginia Ingraham, ed. *The Secret Eye: The Journal of Ella Gertrude Clanton Thomas, 1848–1889.* Chapel Hill: University of North Carolina Press, 1990.

Butterfield, L. H., Marc Friedlaender, and Mary-Jo Kline, eds. *The Book of Abigail and John: Selected Letters of the Adams Family, 1762–1784.* Cambridge: Harvard University Press, 1975.

Caputo, Philip. *A Rumor of War.* New York: Ballantine, 1978.

Carpenter, George Rice. *Walt Whitman.* New York: Macmillan, 1909.

Chatfield, Charles, ed. *Peace Movements in America.* New York: Shocken Books, 1973.

Chesnut, Mary Boykin Miller. *The Private Mary Chesnut: The Unpublished Civil War Diaries.* Ed. C. Vann Woodward and Elisabeth Muhlenfeld. New York: Oxford University Press, 1984.

"Chit-Chat." *Overland Monthly* 35, no. 210 (June 1900): 567–568.

Claybaugh, Amanda. "The Autobiography of a Substitute: Trauma, History, Howells." *Yale Journal of Criticism* 18, no. 1 (Spring 2005): 45–65.

Collins, Francis A. *The Fighting Engineers: The Minute Men of Our Industrial Army.* New York: Century, 1918.

Cozzens, Peter. *This Terrible Sound: The Battle of Chickamauga.* Urbana: University of Illinois Press, 1992.

Crane, Stephen. *Great Short Works of Stephen Crane.* New York: Harper and Row, 1968.

———. *The War Dispatches of Stephen Crane.* Ed. R. W. Stallman and E. R. Hagemann. New York: New York University Press, 1964.

Crosby, Ernest. *The Absurdities of Militarism.* Boston: American Peace Society, 1901.

———. *Captain Jinks, Hero.* New York: Funk and Wagnalls, 1902.

———. *Swords and Plowshares.* New York: Funk and Wagnalls, 1902.

———. *War Echoes.* Philadelphia: Innes and Sons, 1898.

Curti, Merle. *Peace or War: The American Struggle, 1636–1936.* New York: Norton, 1936.

Davidson, James Wood. *The Living Writers of the South.* New York: Carlton, 1869.

Davis, Richard Harding. *The Notes of a War Correspondent.* New York: Scribner's, 1911.

Dawes, James. *The Language of War: Literature and Culture in the U.S. from the Civil War through World War II.* Cambridge: Harvard University Press, 2002.

De Forest, John William. *Miss Ravenel's Conversion from Secession to Loyalty.* 1867; New York: Harper and Bros., 1939.

———. *Poems: Medley and Palestina.* New Haven: Tuttle, Morehouse, and Taylor, 1902.

———. *A Volunteer's Adventures: A Union Captain's Record of the Civil War.* Ed. James H. Croushore. New Haven: Yale University Press, 1946.

De Quincey, Thomas. *The Collected Writings of Thomas De Quincey.* Ed. David Masson. Vol. 13. London: A. and C. Black, 1897.

Dos Passos, John. *The Fourteenth Chronicle: Letters and Diaries of John Dos Passos.* Ed. Townsend Ludington. Boston: Gambit, 1973.

———. *One Man's Initiation, 1917.* 1920; New York: Cornell Press, 1969.

Doty, Madeleine Z. *Behind the Battle Line.* New York: Macmillan, 1918.

Dunne, Finley Peter. *Mr. Dooley in Peace and War.* Boston: Small, Maynard, 1899.

Eliot, Charles W. "Destructive and Constructive Energies of Our Government Compared." *Atlantic Monthly* 83, no. 495 (January 1899): 1–19.

Engelbrecht, H. C., and F. C. Hanighen. *Merchants of Death: A Study of the International Armament Industry.* New York: Dodd, Mead, 1934.

Fahnestock, Allen L. "Journal of Colonel Allen L. Fahnestock, 86th Illinois Volunteer Infantry." Fahnestock Collection. Peoria Public Library, Peoria, Illinois.

Fahs, Alice. *The Imagined Civil War: Popular Literature of the North and South, 1861–1865.* Chapel Hill: University of North Carolina Press, 2001.

Farwell, Byron. *The Encyclopedia of Nineteenth-Century Land Warfare: An Illustrated World View.* New York: Norton, 2001.

Faust, Drew Gilpin. *The Creation of Confederate Nationalism.* Baton Rouge: Louisiana State University Press, 1988.

———. *This Republic of Suffering: Death and the American Civil War.* New York: Knopf, 2008.

Fenton, Charles A. *The Apprenticeship of Ernest Hemingway: The Early Years.* 1954; New York: Viking Press, 1968.

Fielder, Leslie. Foreword to *The Good Soldier Schweik,* by Jaroslav Hasek. 1930; New York: New American Library, 1963.

Fishkin, Shelley Fisher, ed. *A Historical Guide to Mark Twain.* New York: Oxford University Press, 2002.

Ford, Worthington Chauncey, ed. *A Cycle of Adams Letters, 1861–1865*. Vol. 1. Boston: Houghton Mifflin, 1920.

Foster, F. "Some Aspects of Courage." *North American Review* 166, no. 499 (June 1898): 678–686.

Franklin, Benjamin. *The Works of Benjamin Franklin*. Ed. John Bigelow. Vol. 4. New York: Putnam, 1904.

Frederic, Harold. *The Copperhead*. New York: Scribner's, 1893.

———. "Stephen Crane's Triumph." *New York Times,* January 26, 1896, 22.

Fredrickson, George M. *The Inner Civil War: Northern Intellectuals and the Crisis of the Union*. New York: Harper and Row, 1965.

Fussell, Paul. *The Great War and Modern Memory*. New York: Oxford University Press, 1975.

Garner, Stanton. *The Civil War World of Herman Melville*. Lawrence: University Press of Kansas, 1993.

Glicksberg, Charles I. *Walt Whitman and the Civil War: A Collection of Original Articles and Manuscripts*. Philadelphia: University of Pennsylvania Press, 1933.

Goodrich, S. G. *Recollections of a Lifetime*. Vol. 2. New York: Miller, Orton, and Mulligan, 1856.

Gray, Janet, ed. *She Wields a Pen: American Women Poets of the Nineteenth Century*. London: J. M. Dent, 1997.

Gulick, Sidney L. *The Christian Crusade for a Warless World*. New York: Macmillan, 1922.

———. *The Fight for Peace*. New York: Fleming H. Revell, 1915.

Hagerman, Edward. *The American Civil War and the Origins of Modern Warfare: Ideas, Organization, and Field Command*. Bloomington: Indiana University Press, 1988.

Hamilton, William R. "American Machine Cannon and Dynamite Guns." *Century Illustrated Monthly Magazine* 36, no. 6 (October 1888): 885–893.

Harrington, Fred Harvey. "Literary Aspects of American Anti-Imperialism, 1898–1902." *New England Quarterly* 10 (December 1937): 650–667.

Hatcher, Harlan. *Creating the Modern American Novel*. 1935; New York, Russell and Russell, 1965.

Hawthorne, Nathaniel. *The Centenary Edition of the Works of Nathaniel Hawthorne: The Letters, 1857–1864*. Ed. Thomas Woodson et al. Vol. 18. Columbus: Ohio State University Press, 1987.

———. *The Complete Works of Nathaniel Hawthorne*. Vol. 11. Boston: Houghton, Mifflin, 1883.

———. *The Complete Writings of Nathaniel Hawthorne*. Vol. 17. Boston: Houghton Mifflin, 1918.

Hay, John. *The Life and Letters of John Hay*. Ed. William Roscoe Thayer. Vol. 2. 1915; Boston: Houghton Mifflin, 1929.

Hemingway, Ernest. *A Farewell to Arms*. 1929; New York: Scribner's, 1969.

Hersey, John. *Hiroshima*. 1946; New York: Vintage Books, 1989.

Hijiya, James A. *J. W. De Forest and the Rise of American Gentility*. Hanover, N.H.: Published for Brown University Press by University Press of New England, 1988.

Hoffman, Frederick J. *The Twenties: American Writing in the Postwar Decade*. New York: Viking Press, 1955.

Howard, Leon. *Herman Melville: A Biography*. Berkeley: University of California Press, 1951.

Howe, Julia Ward. *Reminiscences, 1819–1899*. Boston: Houghton, Mifflin, 1899.

Howells, William Dean. *Editor's Study*. Ed. James W. Simpson. Troy, N.Y.: Whiston, 1983.

———. *Life in Letters of William Dean Howells*. Ed. Mildred Howells. Vol. 2. New York: Doubleday, Doran, 1928.

Howells, William Dean, and Henry Mills Alden, eds. *Different Girls*. New York: Harper and Bros., 1906.

Hughes, W. S. "Modern Aggressive Torpedoes." *Scribner's Magazine* 1, no. 4 (April 1887): 427–437.

Hutton, Richard Holt. *The Life of Sir Walter Scott*. Philadelphia: J. D. Morris, 1905.

Hynes, Samuel. *A War Imagined: The First World War and English Culture*. London: Bodley Head, 1990.

James, Henry. *The Letters of Henry James*. Ed. Percy Lubbock. Vol. 1. New York: Scribner's, 1920.

James, Jennifer C. *A Freedom Bought with Blood: African American War Literature from the Civil War to World War II*. Chapel Hill: University of North Carolina Press, 2007.

James, William. "The Moral Equivalent of War." New York: American Association for International Conciliation, 1910.

———. "Remnants of the Peace Banquet." *Atlantic Monthly* 94 (December 1904): 845–847.

Johannsen, Robert W. *To the Halls of the Montezumas: The Mexican War in the American Imagination*. New York: Oxford University Press, 1985.

Johnson, Sid S. *Some Biographies of Old Settlers: Historical, Personal, and Reminiscent*. Vol. 1. Tyler, Texas: Sid S. Johnson, 1900.

Jones, Walter Burgwyn, ed. *Confederate War Poems*. 1959; Nashville: Bill Coats, 1990.

Kael, Pauline. "A Wounded Apparition." Rev. of *Casualties of War*. *New Yorker*, August 21, 1989, 76–79.

Kaplan, Amy. "The Spectacle of War in Crane's Revision of History." In *New Essays on The Red Badge of Courage*, ed. Lee Clark Mitchell, 77–108. Cambridge: Cambridge University Press, 1986.

Kaser, David. *Books and Libraries in Camp and Battle: The Civil War Experience.* Westport, Conn.: Greenwood Press, 1984.

Kasson, John F. *Civilizing the Machine: Technology and Republican Values in America, 1776–1900.* New York: Grossman, 1976.

Kent, Charles W. *Southern Poems.* Boston: Houghton Mifflin, 1913.

Kipling, Rudyard. *Rudyard Kipling's Verse.* London: Hodder and Stoughton, 1949.

Kirkland, Joseph. *The Captain of Company K.* Chicago: Dibble, 1891.

Kirkpatrick, George R. *War—What For?* West La Fayette, Ohio: George R. Kirkpatrick, 1910.

Kronenberger, Louis. "War's Horror as a German Private Saw It." *New York Times,* June 2, 1929, 5.

La Motte, Ellen. *The Backwash of War: The Human Wreckage of the Battlefield as Witnessed by an American Hospital Nurse.* New York: Putnam, 1916.

Landrum, Grace Warren. "Sir Walter Scott and His Literary Rivals in the Old South." *American Literature* 2 (1930): 256–276.

"The Latest Rebel Poetry." *Harper's Weekly* 8, no. 396 (July 30, 1864): 483.

Leonard, Thomas C. *Above the Battle: War-Making in America from Appomattox to Versailles.* New York: Oxford University Press: 1978.

Leyda, Jay. *The Melville Log.* Vols. 1 and 2. New York: Gordian, 1951.

Light, James F. *John William De Forest.* New York: Twayne, 1965.

Limon, John. *Writing after War: American War Fiction from Realism to Postmodernism.* New York: Oxford University Press, 1994.

Linderman, Gerald F. *Embattled Courage: The Experience of Combat in the American Civil War.* New York: Free Press, 1987.

"Literary Notices." Rev. of *Battle-Pieces and Aspects of the War,* by Herman Melville. *Ladies' Repository* 26 (November 1866): 699.

———. Rev. of *An Introductory Latin Book,* by Albert Herkness. *Ladies' Repository* 26 (November 1866): 699.

———. Rev. of *Miss Ravenel's Conversion from Secession to Loyalty,* by John William De Forest. *Ladies' Repository* 27 (August 1867): 508.

Lively, Richard A. *Fiction Fights the Civil War.* Chapel Hill: University of North Carolina Press, 1957.

London, Jack. "The Impossibility of War." *Overland Monthly* 35 (March 19, 1900): 278–282.

Mainiero, Linda, ed. *American Women Writers.* Vol. 1. New York: Frederick Ungar, 1979.

Mansfield, Luther Stearns. "Melville's Comic Articles on Zachary Taylor." *American Literature* 9 (January 1938): 411–418.

Mason, Emily V. *The Southern Poems of the War.* Baltimore: John Murphy, 1867.

Maxim, Hiram. *My Life.* London: Methuen, 1915.

[McCook, Daniel.] "The Second Division at Shiloh." *Harper's New Monthly Magazine* 28, no. 168 (May 1864): 828–833.

Melville, Herman. *Battle-Pieces and Aspects of the War.* 1866; New York: De Capo Press, 1995.

———. *Typee, Omoo, Mardi.* New York: Library of America, 1982.

———. *White-Jacket.* 1850; London: Oxford University Press, 1966.

———. *The Writings of Herman Melville.* Ed. Harrison Hayford, Hershel Parker, and G. Thomas Tanselle. Vol. 14. Chicago: Northwestern University Press, 1993.

Miller, Wayne Charles. *An Armed America, Its Face in Fiction: A History of the American Military Novel.* New York: New York University Press, 1970.

Millis, John. "Electricity in War, II. In Land Warfare." *Scribner's Magazine* 6, no. 4 (October 1889): 424–435.

Millis, Walter. *Arms and Men: A Study in American Military History.* New York: Putnam, 1956.

Mock, James R. *Censorship, 1917.* Princeton: Princeton University Press, 1941.

Moore, Frank, ed. *Rebel Rhymes and Rhapsodies.* New York: Putnam, 1864.

Moore, H. Judge. *Scott's Campaign in Mexico.* Charleston, S.C.: J. B. Nixon, 1849.

Moore, Mollie E. "Minding the Gap." *Southern Literary Messenger* 38, no. 1 (January 1864): 28–29.

———. *Minding the Gap and Other Poems.* Houston: Cushing and Cave, 1867.

Myers, Thomas. *Walking Point: American Narratives of Vietnam.* New York: Oxford University Press, 1988.

Nudelman, Franny. *John Brown's Body: Slavery, Violence, and the Culture of War.* Chapel Hill: University of North Carolina Press, 2004.

Orians, Harrison. "The Romance Ferment after *Waverley*." *American Literature* 3, no. 4 (January 1932): 408–431.

Owen, Wilfred. *Poems by Wilfred Owen.* London: Chatto and Windus, 1921.

Paine, Albert Bigelow. *Mark Twain: A Biography.* Vol. 3. New York: Harper and Bros., 1912.

———, ed. *Mark Twain's Letters.* Vol. 2. New York: Harper and Bros., 1917.

Parsons, Thomas William. *The Magnolia.* Cambridge, Mass.: John Wilson and Son, 1866.

———. *The Shadow of the Obelisk and Other Poems.* London: Hatchards, 1872.

Pattee, Fred Lewis. *First Century of American Literature, 1770–1870.* New York: D. Appleton-Century, 1935.

Perkins, George, Barbara Perkins, and Phillip Leininger, eds. *Benet's Reader's Encyclopedia of American Literature.* New York: Harper Collins, 1991.

Perry, Bliss. *Life and Letters of Henry Lee Higginson.* Vol. 2. Boston: Atlantic Monthly Press, 1921.

Perry, Ralph Barton. *The Thoughts and Character of William James.* New York: George Braziller, 1954.

Poe, Edgar Allan. *Great Short Works of Edgar Allan Poe.* New York: Harper and Row, 1970.

Pressly, Thomas J. *Americans Interpret Their Civil War.* New York: Free Press, 1962.

Price, Kenneth M., ed. *Walt Whitman: The Contemporary Reviews.* Cambridge: Cambridge University Press, 1996.

Raymond, Ida. *Southland Writers.* Vol. 2. Philadelphia: Claxton, Remsen, and Haffelfinger, 1870.

"Rebel Romance." Rev. of *Miss Ravenel's Conversion from Secession to Loyalty,* by John William De Forest. *Time,* August 21, 1939, 57–59.

Reed, John. "This Unpopular War." *Seven Arts* 2 (August 1917): 397–408.

———. *The War in Eastern Europe.* New York: Scribner's, 1916.

Rev. of *Drum-Taps,* by Walt Whitman. *Independent,* December 7, 1865, 2.

Rev. of *Lyrics of a Day: or, Newspaper-Poetry,* by Howard Henry Brownell. *North American Review* 99 (July 1864): 320.

"Reviews and Literary Notices." Rev. of *Battle-Pieces and Aspects of the War,* by Herman Melville. *Atlantic Monthly* 19 (February 1867): 252–253.

Rice, James M. *Peoria City and County, Illinois: A Record of Settlement, Organization, Progress and Achievement.* Vol. 2. Chicago: S. J. Clarke, 1912.

Richards, Laura E., and Maude Howe Elliott. *Julia Ward Howe, 1819–1910.* Vol. 1. Boston: Houghton Mifflin, 1916.

Roosevelt, Theodore. *The Rough Riders.* New York: Scribner's, 1899.

———. *The Strenuous Life and Other Essays.* New York: Review of Reviews, 1910.

Royster, Charles. *The Destructive War: William Tecumseh Sherman, Stonewall Jackson, and the Americans.* 1991; New York: Vintage Books, 1993.

Sargent, Epes. "Ericsson and His Inventions." *Atlantic Monthly* 10, no. 57 (July 1862): 68–81.

Saunders, Richard. *Ambrose Bierce: The Making of a Misanthrope.* San Francisco: Chronicle Books, 1985.

Scarry, Elaine. *The Body in Pain.* New York: Oxford University Press, 1985.

Schurz, Carl. *The Reminiscences of Carl Schurz.* Vol. 3. New York: McClure, 1908.

Scott, Walter. *Ivanhoe.* 1819; New York: Longmans, Green, 1908.

Seeger, Alan. *Letters and Diary of Alan Seeger.* New York: Scribner's, 1917.

———. *Poems.* New York: Scribner's, 1916.

Sharp, Richard D. "War and Pacifism in the Novels of Herman Melville." *College Language Association Journal* 29, no. 1 (1985): 57–81.

Skrupskelis, Ignas K., and Elizabeth M. Berkeley, eds. *The Correspondence of William James: William and Henry, 1897–1910.* Vol. 3. Charlottesville: University Press of Virginia, 1994.

S.L.C. "Thoughts upon English Poetry." *Southern Literary Messenger* 16 (August 1850): 509–512.

Smith, Rebecca W. "The Civil War and Its Aftermath in American Fiction, 1861–1899." Chicago: University of Chicago Libraries, 1937.

Sontag, Susan. *Regarding the Pain of Others.* New York: Farrar, Straus, and Giroux, 2003.

Stallings, Laurence. *Plumes.* New York: Harcourt, Brace, 1924.

Stallman, R. W. *Stephen Crane: A Biography.* New York: George Braziller, 1968.

Starrett, Vincent. *Buried Caesars: Essays in Literary Appreciation.* Chicago: Covici-McGee, 1923.

Stedman, Edmund Clarence, ed. *An American Anthology, 1787–1900.* Boston: Houghton Mifflin, 1900.

Steevens, G. W. *With Kitchener to Khartum.* New York: Dodd, Mead, 1898.

Steinbeck, John. *Once There Was a War.* New York: Viking Press, 1958.

Steinmetz, Lee, ed. *The Poetry of the American Civil War.* 1960; East Lansing: Michigan State University Press, 1991.

Stevenson, Burton Egbert, ed. *Poems of American History.* Boston: Houghton Mifflin, 1936.

Stockton, Frank R. *The Great Stone of Sardis.* New York: Harper and Bros., 1898.

———. *Great War Syndicate.* New York: P. F. Collier, 1889.

Stowe, Harriet Beecher. *Uncle Tom's Cabin.* 1852; Oxford: Oxford University Press, 1998.

Styron, William. *The Long March and In the Clap Shack.* New York: Vintage Books, 1993.

Sweet, Timothy. *Traces of War: Poetry, Photography, and the Crisis of the Union.* Baltimore: Johns Hopkins University Press, 1990.

Sweetser, Arthur. *Roadside Glimpses of the Great War.* New York: Macmillan, 1916.

Szczesiul, Anthony. "The Maturing Vision of Walt Whitman's 1871 Version of Drum-Taps." *Walt Whitman Quarterly Review* 10 (Winter 1993): 127–141.

Tesla, Nikola. "The Problem of Increasing Human Energy." *Century Illustrated Monthly Magazine* 60 (June 1900): 175–211.

Thoreau, Henry D. *Walden: A Fully Annotated Edition.* Ed. Jeffrey S. Cramer. New Haven: Yale University Press, 2004.

Tolstoy, Leo. *The Sebastopol Sketches.* Trans. David McDuff. 1855; Middlesex, Eng.: Penguin, 1986.

Tourgée, Albion W. "The Renaissance of Nationalism." *North American Review* 144, no. 362 (January 1887): 1–11.

Trachtenberg, Alan. *Reading American Photographs.* New York: Hill and Wang, 1989.

Trent, William Peterfield, et al., eds. *Cambridge History of American Literature.* Vol. 2. New York: Macmillan, 1918.

Twain, Mark. *A Connecticut Yankee in King Arthur's Court.* 1889; New York: Oxford University Press, 1996.

———. *Life on the Mississippi.* 1883; New York: Harper and Bros., 1904.

——. *A Pen Warmed-Up in Hell: Mark Twain in Protest.* Ed. Frederick Anderson. New York: Harper and Row, 1972.

Underhill, John. *Newes from America; or, A New and Experimentall Discoverie of New England; Containing, a True Relation of their War-like Proceedings These Two Yeares Last Past.* London: J. D[awson] for Peter Cole, 1638.

Vonnegut, Kurt. *Slaughterhouse-Five.* 1969; New York: Random House, 1999.

Walsh, Jeffrey. *American War Literature, 1914 to Vietnam.* New York: St. Martin's, 1982.

Warren, Robert Penn. "Melville's Poems." *Southern Review* 3 (1967): 799–855.

Wells, David A. *Recent Economic Changes and Their Effect on the Production and Distribution of Wealth and the Well-Being of Society.* New York: D. Appleton, 1889.

White, Andrew D. "Walter Scott at Work: Introduction." *Scribner's Magazine* 5, no. 2 (February 1889): 131–132.

Whitman, Walt. "Army Hospitals and Cases: Memoranda at the Time, 1863–66." *Century* 36, no. 6 (October 1888): 825–830.

——. *The Collected Writings of Walt Whitman: Prose Works, 1892.* Ed. Floyd Stovall. New York: New York University Press, 1964.

——. *Complete Poetry and Selected Prose.* Ed. James E. Miller Jr. Vol. 2. Boston: Houghton Mifflin, 1959.

——. Papers. Charles E. Feinberg Collection of the Papers of Walt Whitman. Manuscript Division, Library of Congress.

——. Papers. Thomas Biggs Harned Collection of the Papers of Walt Whitman. Manuscript Division, Library of Congress.

——. "Some War Memoranda—Jotted Down at the Time." *North American Review* 144, no. 362 (January 1887): 55–61.

——. *Specimen Days.* 1882; Boston: David R. Godine, 1971.

——. "Visits among Army Hospitals." *New York Times,* December 11, 1864, 1–2.

——. *Walt Whitman: The Correspondence.* Ed. Edwin Haviland Miller. Vol. 1. New York: New York University Press, 2007.

Whittier, John Greenleaf. *In War Time, and Other Poems.* Boston: Ticknor and Fields, 1863.

Wilson, Edmund. *The Devils and Canon Barham: Ten Essays on Poets, Novelists, and Monsters.* New York: Farrar, Straus, and Giroux, 1973.

——. *Patriotic Gore: Studies in the Literature of the American Civil War.* 1962; New York: Norton, 1994.

Wright, Edward Needles. *Conscientious Objectors in the Civil War.* 1931; New York: A. S. Barnes, 1961.

Yannella, Donald, and Hershel Parker, eds. *The Endless Winding Way in Melville: New Charts by Kring and Carey.* Glassboro, N.J.: Melville Society, 1981.

INDEX